M. BOTVINNIK

KINGS OF CHESS

CHESS CHAMPIONS OF THE
TWENTIETH CENTURY:
LASKER, CAPABLANCA, ALEKHINE, EUWE
AND BOTVINNIK

by

WILLIAM WINTER

NEW YORK
DOVER PUBLICATIONS, INC.

Published in Canada by General Publishing Company, Ltd., 30 Lesmill Road, Don Mills, Toronto, Ontario.

Published in the United Kingdom by Constable and Company, Ltd., 10 Orange Street, London, W.C.2.

This Dover edition, first published in 1966, is an unabridged and corrected republication of the work originally published by Carroll and Nicholson, Ltd. in 1954.

This edition is published by special arrangement with Sir Isaac Pitman and Sons, Ltd.

International Standard Book Number: 0-486-21556-3
Library of Congress Catalog Card Number: 66-15934

Manufactured in the United States of America

Dover Publications, Inc.
180 Varick Street
New York, N. Y. 10014

CONTENTS

CONTENTS

LIST OF ILLUSTRATIONS

THE CHESS CHAMPIONSHIP OF THE WORLD IN THE TWENTIETH CENTURY

INTRODUCTION

IN bringing before the chess-playing public this account of the matches contested for the highest crown of chess ability, the title of Champion of the World, I am actuated by the desire to give present-day players some idea of the colourful personalities who strove for it, their general concepts of play and the conditions under which they fought. I have limited the work to the matches played in the present century, not only because it seems a convenient time to begin, but because the earlier encounters between the world's greatest players were conducted under such irregular conditions that it is hard to say which can really be considered as genuine world championship matches. The general consensus of chess opinion proclaims Staunton, Anderssen, Morphy and Steinitz as the world champions of the nineteenth century, but of these Staunton played only one big match, Anderssen was acclaimed as champion after his tournament victory in 1851 while the great American, Morphy, who stood head and shoulders above all the players of his time, never actually called himself champion of the world. On Morphy's retirement Anderssen quietly slipped into the vacant place but his successes were gained in tournaments rather than in matches and, like Morphy, he never used the title. Steinitz, after his victory over Anderssen in 1866, was the first to acclaim himself world champion, and his right to the title was generally recognized by the chess world until his defeat by Lasker in 1894. From then onwards the title was held in unbroken and undisputed succession by Lasker, Capablanca, Alekhine, Euwe and then Alekhine again until it was left vacant by the death of the last named in 1946.

By this time the International Chess Federation had come into being as the governing body of world chess, and it was decided to arrange a five-round tournament between the six most prominent players of the world, the winner to be proclaimed official world champion. At the same time it was decided that future contests should be by match against a challenger chosen as a result of a series of candidates' tournaments, open to the whole world. Championship matches in future will take place every three years. This is a great improvement upon the old system in which the only control exercised over the choice of contestants had been the unofficial consensus of opinion among players and organizers. While this generally worked out fairly well it was open to abuses, not the least of which was the fact that occasionally the logical contender had to be passed over owing to the inability of his supporters to raise the necessary funds. Nevertheless, all the challengers were great players and the matches described in this book have produced the finest possible examples of contemporary chess art. Many of the games are, of course, fairly well known, but others have been almost completely forgotten and no apology is necessary for presenting them together, in such a fashion as will enable the chess student to trace, through their medium, the processes by which the game has developed in the last fifty years.

Thus, in the earlier matches we have the supreme tactician Lasker, triumphing over the orthodox Tarrasch and the romantic Marshall and Janovsky, only to succumb in the end to the new and highly improved strategical accuracy of Capablanca.

The later matches show that this in itself is not sufficient when faced by a combination of sound strategy plus imaginative tactics while the last contests of all, the

World Championship tournament and the Botvinnik *v.* Bronstein match, tend to bring the imaginative qualities once more to the forefront and show that principles once deemed to be fundamental can be broken with impunity by the greatest masters of the game, however necessary they may be to lesser mortals.

On the theoretical side also there have been many changes and the openings chosen in these matches give a clear picture of the progressive development of chess thought in this field. In the earlier matches the Ruy Lopez and its prototype, the Four Knights' game, predominated, with the Queen's Gambit declined, in what is called the normal fashion, in second place. There were also a few scattered examples of the French and Sicilian Defences and that was all. The one example of the King's Gambit in the Lasker *v.* Janovsky match occurred when the contest was practically decided and the solitary Slav Defence played by Schlechter against Lasker's Queen's Gambit caused a buzz of astonishment throughout the chess world. One English commentator went so far as to place a note against Black's second move: "To this weak move may be attributed the loss of the game." He quite ignored the fact that, at one period, Black held a winning position but the remark is interesting as indicative of the narrow outlook on the openings during the first decade of the century.

In what may be termed the middle series of matches, from Capablanca *v.* Lasker to the second world war, the Queen's Gambit was by far the most popular method of opening the game. In Alekhine *v.* Capablanca the King's pawn was only played once and was rarely seen in the next four encounters.

These later matches, however, did show changes in the defence. The normal line was replaced in popularity by the Slav, the revolutionary of the Schlechter match, and occasional Indian Defences made their appearance, but it

11

was not until the emergence of the new Soviet school that the enormous versatility possible in opening the game was given free rein in championship encounters. The first six games of the Botvinnik–Bronstein match all had different openings. All this, of course, has had its inevitable reflection in general chess play, and we have reached a position where, so far from chess being played out as was alleged by the pessimists in the early twenties, we are far from discovering the possibilities inherent in the first few moves. So far from being exhausted, our knowledge of the chess openings is only just beginning.

A word about the notes. In annotating the games I have consulted all the available authorities in so far as this is possible under present-day conditions, and have naturally, whenever I could, quoted the players' own remarks. Occasional long variations have been attributed to the annotators who, to the best of my knowledge and belief, first discovered them, but the majority must be considered as a synthesis of general published remarks and my own researches. I believe that I have discovered one or two variations previously unknown. As this book is not intended to be a treatise on the openings, I have curtailed the analysis of that part of the game to indicating the changes which modern ideas have brought about in each particular case and have designed the notes as a whole so as to give a general picture of the struggle and explain the ideas governing the minds of the players.

As regards the biographies, I am in the happy position of having known personally all the masters concerned, with the exception of Schlechter, and hope in the brief space available to bring them before my readers, not only as chess players, but also as human beings. Each in his way is a unique personality and I have tried my best to give a picture of them as they appeared to me.

I account it a privilege to have known them.

CHAPTER I

DR. EMMANUEL LASKER

IN some ways Lasker must be considered the greatest of all the champions. He retained his title for twenty-seven years, during which period he proved himself both in matches and tournaments as the greatest chess fighter that the world has ever seen. In some ways he was unique among chess players. Unlike his rivals, Steinitz, who founded the modern school of scientific chess, and Tarrasch, who perfected it, he contributed little or nothing to the theory of the game.

He wrote one fine book, the *Chess Manual*, in which he expounded lucidly the theories of others but offers no fresh concepts of his own, beyond his insistence that chess is primarily neither a science nor an art, but a struggle in which the object is to defeat the man sitting opposite, no matter what theoretical rules are broken in the process. As Réti says: "Lasker was a philosopher who played chess." Quite early in his life he wrote a philosophical treatise *Der Kampf* (The Struggle), in which he tried to discover general laws for overcoming the difficulties of life. In this work he adduced chess as the highest example of a purely intellectual and straightforward struggle, in which his task was to beat the particular opponent by any means permitted by the laws of the game. Consequently his play was governed by considerations quite apart from those present to the minds of most masters, i.e. the necessity of finding the best lines of play.

It is well known that he deliberately made bad moves in order to prevent players of lesser ability reaching balanced positions by orthodox correct play. His object was to set his opponents continual problems, often running grave risks himself in the process. In the great New York tournament of 1924, in which he won first prize, he was strategically lost at some period or other in at least half of his games, but only actually lost one. In the others his ingenuity in contriving tactical combinations and, if all else failed, his almost uncanny endgame play, saved him from disaster. In other words, the problems he set were too difficult for his opponents, although they comprised all the leading players of the world. He was greatly assisted by his careful study of the characteristics of each particular adversary, so that he knew the type of risk he could safely take against each one of them. Unlike Capablanca, who always played the board, Lasker definitely played the man. "This," he said himself, "is entirely in line with my theoretical conception of the fight. A game of chess is a fight in which all possible factors must be made use of and in which a knowledge of the opponent's good and bad qualities is of the greatest importance." He then proceeded to analyse the strength and weakness of all the tournament competitors in a manner which certainly makes his own play more intelligible. (This was during the New York Tournament, 1924, before mentioned.) His attitude to chess is well exemplified by a game which I played against him in the Nottingham International Tournament of 1936. After over half an hour's thought I placed a Knight on a square on which it could be taken by a pawn. Lasker replied instantaneously with a quiet defensive move and I soon found that all I had gained by my "brilliancy" was the loss of valuable thinking time.

After the game was over a spectator asked him what would have happened had he taken the Knight. "I do not know," he replied. "I was playing a strong master and if a strong master thinks for half an hour and then plays a piece where I can take it, I think that it will not be healthy for me to take it, and I let it alone." This simple attitude was typical of Lasker. Other masters, always concerned to make the objectively best move, would have examined every variation of the sacrifice before rejecting it. All Lasker considered was that he had gained valuable time on the clock.

In his early days he was inclined to carry his theories of the fight into his relations with his fellow masters, and there was bitter hostility between him and Dr. Tarrasch who were not on speaking terms during the progress of their match, but when I met him he was an urbane old gentleman, quiet and courteous, with a kind word for everyone. He even took with a smile the onslaught of a coffee-house player whose egregious blunders he had mildly criticized after a skittle game. "What do you know about it you silly old man?" raved the irate duffer. "Very little," replied the ex-champion of the world. As an opponent he was the soul of courtesy, sitting at the board with scarcely a movement except to light one cigar from the butt of another, and he was quite without those irritating mannerisms with which so many players unconsciously disturb their adversary's train of thought. The secret of his success lay in his marvellous powers of analysis far in excess of that possessed by any of his rivals, and a positional sense amounting to genius. At the critical stage of a game his pieces always seemed to be on the right squares and he was a master of the art of unmasking hidden batteries, usually by the sacrifice of a pawn, in positions where his opponent had every right to think that, by all the canons of the game, the old master was completely lost. In the end he had to succumb to Capablanca, who had no weaknesses, and proved that even the greatest individual talent could not prevail against an equal talent plus a perfect technique, but it is certain that no champion has ever stood so high above his contemporaries as Dr. Emmanuel Lasker.

Lasker's best tournament performances were: Nuremberg

1896, London 1899, Paris 1900, Mährisch-Ostrau 1923, New York 1924, 1st. St. Petersburg 1909, equal 1st with Rubinstein. Moscow 1935, 3rd. All these were first-rate tournaments, with the world's best players among the opposition. In addition, he won many smaller events. In world championship matches he beat Steinitz by 20 games to 7, Marshall by 8–0, Tarrasch by 8–3, and Janovsky by 7–1, a record which speaks for itself. Lasker was born in 1868 and died in New York during the second world war.

THE LASKER v. MARSHALL MATCH

F. J. MARSHALL

Lasker's first challenger, Frank J. Marshall, of New York, was one of the outstanding figures of the early twentieth century. In his later days he was described in the magazine *Life* as "a pre-occupied old gentleman who looks like a Shakespearian actor, smokes strong cigars, and always takes a pocket board to bed with him." In his charming and racy autobiography, Marshall admits the truth of this description but says in excuse that the board was only a little one. Certainly his life was bound up in chess. Born in New York in 1877, he began to play at the age of ten and from then onwards his career was one continual round of tournament after tournament, broken only by chess organizational work and the management of the famous Marshall Chess Club of New York, founded by himself and his devoted wife, "my Carrie."

More, perhaps, than any other master, Marshall really loved chess for its own sake rather than for the fame and prestige it brought him. Paradoxically his actual results might have been better had he loved the game less for in his everlasting search for the beautiful he was sometimes inclined to ignore the prosaic business of collecting points.

In contradiction to Lasker, who set out with the sole idea of beating his opponent, Marshall cared little for results but devoted his life to the creation of works of art on the chess board. In this he was brilliantly successful and his best games have left an indelible impression on the game. He was particularly dangerous in difficult positions and the term "Marshall swindle" has become synonymous with a profound and brilliant combination which snatches victory from the jaws of defeat. Apart from other claims to fame, Marshall must rank as the most travelled master. There is no quarter of the civilized globe into which he did not penetrate at one time or another, and the charm of his genial personality—no less than the brilliance of his play— won him golden opinions wherever he went. He was the perfect chess ambassador.

I first met him in the Masters' Tournament at the St. James's Club, London, in 1927, where I was instrumental in helping him to win third prize by defeating Dr. Vidmar in the last round. To show his gratitude Marshall and an American friend, who had come over with him, invited me to a champagne supper of which my recollections are somewhat hazy. Later I was with him at the International Team Tournaments in Prague and Warsaw, where he led the American team to success. Into these national battles he threw himself with a fervour quite foreign to the phlegmatic temperament which he displayed in his own individual tournaments, and, on the first occasion, when he was asked to make a speech at the concluding banquet, he was so overcome by emotion that he could only wave the Stars and Stripes and shout "Hip-Hip-Hurrah."

Marshall's influence on American chess was incalculable and it is largely due to his efforts that the United States became, in the 1930's, the strongest chess-playing country in the world. He was in the logical line of succession to Morphy and Pillsbury and played chess in the same grand style.

17

Marshall's career in international tournaments began in 1899 when he attended the great London Congress. Probably on account of his youth he was not admitted to the principal event, but he brilliantly won the minor tournament, which included several masters of great experience and high repute.

In 1900 he played in his first really big contest, at Paris, where he electrified the chess world by winning third prize behind Lasker and Pillsbury, both of whom he defeated in their individual games. From this point he was established as one of the world's leading players. His greatest triumph was Cambridge Springs, 1904, in which he won first prize ahead of Lasker, Schlechter, and Janovsky.

Other notable first prizes were Nuremberg 1906, in which he did not lose a game, Scheveningen 1905, and Düsseldorf 1908, and he also won innumerable lesser prizes all over the world. He won the U.S.A. Championship in 1909 by defeating Showalter and held it until 1936 when he voluntarily resigned, devoting the rest of his life to fostering and encouraging the development of the game among the younger generation.

In matches he was less successful than in tournaments, losing heavily to Tarrasch and Capablanca as well as to Lasker. This type of chess, in which caution must always be the predominant factor, did not suit him, although he did win two matches out of three played against Janovsky. Of the latter he remarked: "Janovsky is tremendously stubborn. He follows the wrong path with more determination than any man I ever met." Nevertheless, the meeting of two such incurable romantics produced some highly attractive specimens of the chess art.

Essentially human and filled with the zest for life, Marshall belonged to a race of chess masters now unfortunately becoming extinct, but he leaves an imperishable mark on the minds of all who knew him. A great player and a charming man. Who could want a better epitaph?

DR. EMMANUEL LASKER

THE MATCH

The match between Dr. Emmanuel Lasker and Frank J. Marshall was played in New York in 1907 for a purse subscribed by the chess lovers of the United States. The conditions were that the first to win eight games should be the victor. Although the result was naturally very disappointing to the American champion and his supporters, it was by no means so one-sided as appears from the score, and in several of the games the champion had to fight very hard to avert defeat. With his usual acute psychological insight into his opponent's characteristics Lasker realized that Marshall's great strength lay in attack and he strained every nerve to maintain the initiative in his own hands or alternatively to simplify into an endgame. Here Lasker was undoubtedly superior and this factor contributed largely to the one-sidedness of the result. With the exception of the first, which is a superb example of the champion's technical skill, none of the games was outstanding.

Final score: Lasker 8; Marshall 0; Drawn 8.

FIRST MATCH GAME

White: F. J. Marshall. Black: Dr. E. Lasker.

1 P—K4

Unusual for Marshall, who nearly invariably opened with the Queen's Gambit. In later games in the match he reverted to his favourite.

1 ...	P—K4
2 Kt—KB3	Kt—QB3
3 B—Kt5	Kt—B3
4 P—Q4	

The open Ruy Lopez, played universally in the early stages

of the opening but later considered rightly to be inferior to
4 Castles.

4	...	P×P
5	Castles	B—K2
6	P—K5	

Dr. Tarrasch recommends 6 R—K1, Castles; 7 Kt×P,
but the text was almost routine at the time when the match
was played.

6	...	Kt—K5
7	Kt×P	Castles
8	Kt—B5	

With this attack, favoured by Dr. Zukertort, White could
obtain the advantage of two Bishops, but it involves considerable loss of time.

8	...	P—Q4
9	B×Kt	

But this cannot be right and merely leaves himself with
the inferior development without compensating advantage.
Correct was 9 Kt×B ch, Kt×Kt; 10 P—KB3, Kt—B4;
11 P—QKt4, Kt—K3; 12 P—KB4, with considerable
attacking chances.

9	...	P×B
10	Kt×B ch	Q×Kt
11	R—K1	Q—R5

The commencement of one of Lasker's fine sacrificial
combinations, but since White can obtain equality with the
best defence, it is possible that the simple 11 ... P—B3
was objectively stronger. Psychology probably played a
part in Lasker's choice here: Marshall liked to attack, not
to be attacked.

12	B—K3	P—B3
13	P—KB3	P×P
14	P×Kt	P—Q5

BLACK

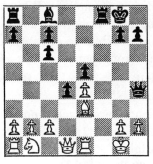

WHITE

In this position White cannot save the Bishop. If 15 B—Q2, B—Kt5; 16 Q—B1, R—B7 (threatening 17 ... B—B6); 17 B—Kt5, R×P ch; 18 K×R, Q—R6 ch; 19 K—Kt1, B—B6; 20 Q—Q2, Q—Kt5 ch; 21 K—B1, R—KB1; 22 Q—B2, B—Kt7 ch; 23 K—Kt1, R×Q; 24 K×R, Q—B6 ch; 25 K—Kt1, B—R6; forcing mate. A beautiful combination.

> 15 P—KKt3

But this is not the best. The simple answer 15 Q—Q2, P×B; 16 Q×P gives approximately an equal game.

> 15 ...   Q—B3
> 16 B×P

Again he cannot save the Bishop. If 16 B—Q2, Q—B7 ch; 17 K—R1, B—R6; 18 R—KKt1, P—KR4; 19 P—KKt4, B×P; 20 R×B, P×R and White has no defence against the threat of P—Kt6.

> 16 ...   P×B
> 17 R—B1   Q×R ch
> 18 Q×Q   R×Q ch
> 19 K×R   R—QKt1

From now on Lasker's endgame skill is shown in its highest form. Most players would have checked with the

21

Bishop either at R3 or R6, but Lasker realizes that the best diagonal for the Bishop depends on White's play and therefore retains the option. One great advantage of the text move is that it forces White to advance his QKtP, and so deprives him of the strong manœuvre Kt—Q2 and Kt—Kt3.

	20 P—Kt3	R—Kt4
	21 P—B4	

This move, which allows Black a powerful passed pawn, seems forced. If 21 Kt—R3, R—QR4; 22 Kt—B4, B—R3 would win comfortably, and if 21 K—K2, Black can play 21 ... R—KR4; 22 P—KR4, P—Kt4, followed if 23 P×P by R—R8.

	21 ...	R—KR4
	22 K—Kt1	P—B4
	23 Kt—Q2	K—B2
	24 R—B1 ch	

Dr. Tarrasch rightly condemns this move which drives the King to a better square and brings the Rook from an effective post to an ineffective one. Probably Marshall was anxious to gain time on the clock.

	24 ...	K—K2
	25 P—QR3	R—R3

So as to bring the Rook to attack the new weakness, the QRP. Had White refrained from the check on the 24th move, he could have answered this move by P—QKt4. Now 26 P—QKt4 would be met by 26 ... R—R3; 27 P×P, R×P, or if 27 R—B3, B—Kt5; 28 R—Q3, B—K7; 29 R—Kt3, P×P; 30 P×P, R—R7, winning quickly in either case.

	26 P—KR4	R—R3
	27 R—R1	

It makes little difference whether this or 27 P—R4 is played, e.g. 27 P—R4, B—Kt5; 28 K—B2, R—B3 ch; 29 K—K1, K—K3, with positions analogous to the game.

27 ...	B—Kt5
28 K—B2	K—K3
29 P—R4	K—K4
30 K—Kt2	R—KB3
31 R—K1	P—Q6

Decisive. The Black King now enters the White entrenchments with fatal effect.

32 R—KB1	K—Q5
33 R×R	P×R
34 K—B2	P—B3

Winning the KP by "zugzwang." He could also win by 34 ... K—B6; 35 K—K3, B—Q8, or 35 K—K1, P—QR4.

35 P—QR5	P—QR3
36 Kt—B1	K×P
37 K—K1	B—K7
38 Kt—Q2 ch	K—K6
39 Kt—Kt1	P—B4
40 Kt—Q2	P—R4
41 Kt—Kt1	K—B6

White could resign now, but the finish is amusing.

42 Kt—B3	K×P
43 Kt—R4	P—B5
44 Kt×P	P—B6
45 Kt—K4 ch	K—B5
46 Kt—Q6	P—B4

If White now moves his Knight he is mated after K—K6.

47 P—Kt4	P×P
48 P—B5	P—Kt6
49 Kt—B4	K—Kt6
50 Kt—K3	P—Kt7
Resigns	

A fine game by Lasker, who was just a little better than his opponent in all departments.

THIRD MATCH GAME

White: F. J. Marshall. Black: Dr. E. Lasker.

1 P—Q4	P—Q4
2 P—QB4	P—K3
3 Kt—QB3	Kt—KB3
4 B—Kt5	B—K2
5 P—K3	Kt—K5

Lasker's own system of defence to which he has given his name. It is one of the soundest methods of defending the Queen's Gambit provided Black does not mind a rather cramped position in the early stages. Usually this move is preceded by 5 ... Castles, but it does not make much difference.

6 B×B	Q×B
7 B—Q3	

This is an ineffective move against Lasker's defence. Better is 7 Q—B2, Kt×Kt; 8 Q×Kt, or 7 P×P, Kt×Kt; 8 P×Kt, P×P; 9 Q—Kt3 followed by P—QB4.

7 ...	Kt×Kt
8 P×Kt	Kt—Q2
9 Kt—B3	Castles
10 Castles	

Slightly better is 10 Q—B2, Kt—B3; 11 Castles and 12 Kt—K5. The Knight is not quite so well placed for defensive purposes at KB3 as he is in the game.

10 ...	R—Q1
11 Q—B2	Kt—B1
12 Kt—K5	P—QB4
13 QR—Kt1	Q—B2
14 Q—Kt3	

This and the following Queen moves indicate that Marshall was unable to find a plan. Whatever the risks, he should continue with 14 P—KB4, and if 14 ... P—QKt3; 15

BP×P, KP×P; 16 P—B5, P—B3; 17 Kt—Kt4, followed
by an attack with the heavy pieces on the King's side,
R—B3, R—Kt3, etc.

14 ...		P—QKt3
15	BP×P	KP×P
16	Q—R4	B—Kt2
17	Q—Q1	R—Q3
18	Q—Kt4	R—K1

Preventing 19 P—KB4 because of P—B3; Black's
strategy is clear. If he can build up an adequate defence
on the King's wing he must obtain an advantage on the
other side by exchanging pawns at the right moment, either
saddling White with a weak backward QBP, or securing a
two-to-one pawn majority for the ending.

19	Q—Kt3	R(Q3)—K3
20	B—B5	R(K3)—K2
21	P—KB4	B—B1

Forcing the exchange of Bishops and so making the defence
easier. White cannot reply 22 B—B2 because of 22 ...
P—B3, winning the KP.

22	B×B	R×B
23	Q—B3	Q—Q3
24	KR—B1	

He must prevent 24 ... P×P; 25 BP×P, R—B7.

24	...	R(K2)—B2
25	P—KR3	P—KR3

Preparing the powerful Knight march Kt—R2, B3, and
K5.

26	K—R2

A poor move which puts the King on the same diagonal as
the Black Queen. It is, however, very difficult to find a
continuation for White whose King's side initiative has
disappeared while his Queen's side weakness remains.

Comparatively best seems pure defence by 26 Q—B2, Kt—R2; 27 Q—Kt2.

26 ...		Kt—R2
27	Q—R5	Kt—B3
28	Q—B5	P × P
29	KP × P	

BLACK

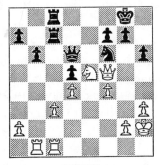

WHITE

At last Marshall is able to lay a trap for his opponent. If Black plays 29 ... R × P; then 30 Q × R ch, R × Q; 31 R × R ch, K—R2; 32 R—R8 ch, K × R; 33 Kt × P ch, and wins, but Lasker is not to be caught by such snares.

29 ...	Kt—K5

In his turn Lasker makes a sacrificial combination which White is almost compelled to accept as his position on the Queen's wing is no longer defensible. The ensuing play is very fine.

30	Kt × P	R × Kt
31	Q × R(B8) ch	R—B1
32	Q—Kt7	

If 32 Q—Kt4, 32 R × P wins at once, a sad consequence of his unfortunate 26th move.

32 ...	Q × P ch
33	K—Kt1

If 33 K—R1, Kt—B7 ch; 34 K—Kt1, Kt×P ch; 35 P×Kt (if 35 K—R1, Kt—B7 ch; 36 K—Kt1, R—B4; 37 R—KB1, Q—R5 and wins); 35 ... Q—Kt6 ch; 36 K—R1, Q×P ch; 37 K—Kt1, Q—Kt5 ch; 38 K—R1, R—B4 and wins.

33 ...	Q—K6 ch
34 K—R2	

If 34 K—R1, Kt—B7 ch; 35 K—R2, Q—B5 ch, as in previous note, as 36 P—Kt3 is met by Q—B4.

34 ...	Q—Kt6 ch
35 K—Kt1	Kt—Q7

A beautiful waiting move, which must have been seen by Lasker when he sacrificed the exchange on move 29. Although White is able to bring his Queen back into play with a check he cannot save the game.

36 Q×QP ch	K—R1
37 K—R1	

If 37 R—KB1, Kt×R; 38 R×Kt, Q—K6 ch and wins.

37 ...	Kt—B6
38 P×Kt	

38 Q×Kt, R×Q; 39 P×R, Q×RP ch, etc., would prolong but not save the game.

38 ...	Q×RP ch
39 K—Kt1	Q—Kt6 ch
40 K—R1	R—B5
41 Q—Q8 ch	K—R2
42 R—KB1	R—B4
Resigns	

A beautiful finish. Had he played 42 ... R—R5 ch; 43 Q×R, White could still have shown plenty of fight, but as played he cannot avoid mate for if 43 Q—K8, Q—R5 ch, and mates next move.

TENTH MATCH GAME

White: Dr. E. Lasker. Black: F. J. Marshall.

1	P—K4		P—K3
2	P—Q4		P—Q4
3	Kt—QB3		Kt—KB3
4	B—Kt5		B—Kt5

The MacCutcheon variation, almost in its infancy in 1907. The modern continuation for White is 5 P—K5, P—KR3; 6 B—Q2, B×Kt; 7 P×B, Kt—K5, a very complicated game on which the analysts have not yet reached a conclusion. Lasker chooses a simpler line, leading to equality, a wise choice as Marshall was a personal acquaintance of the inventor of the opening and no doubt knew all its tricks.

5	P×P		Q×P

Best. After 5 ... P×P the Black Bishop is out of place at QKt5, and will probably have to retreat, with loss of valuable time.

6	B×Kt		P×B
7	Q—Q2		B×Kt
8	Q×B		Kt—B3
9	Kt—B3		Q—K5 ch
10	K—Q2		

Better than 10 B—K2 to which Black can play 10 ... R—KKt1; 11 R—KKt1, P—K4, with an excellent game.

10	...		B—Q2
11	R—Q1		

In the eighth match game, Lasker played 11 R—K1, Q—B5 ch; 12 Q—K3, Q—Q3; 13 K—B1, Castles QR, with an equal game. This seems rather better than the line chosen here as it delays the advance of Black's KP.

11	...		Castles QR
12	K—B1		P—K4

With this excellent move Black obtains the initiative.

BLACK

WHITE

13 B—QKt5

After this Black is able to win a pawn by a complicated series of exchanges. 13 P—Q5 would be a mistake on account of 13 ... Kt—Kt5; 14 B—B4, B—Kt4; 15 Q×Kt, Q×B, winning the QP, but 13 P×P, P×P; 14 B—Kt5 is safe enough.

13 ...	Kt×P
14 Kt×Kt	P×Kt
15 R×P	Q×P
16 B×B ch	R×B
17 R×R	

Rather stronger may be 17 KR—Q1 to which Black appears to have nothing better than 17 ... R×R; 18 Q×R (threatening mate in two); 18 ... Q—Kt4 ch; 19 P—B4, Q—KB4; 19 Q×RP, Q×KBP ch; 20 R—Q2 best, P—B3; 21 Q—R8 ch, Q—Kt1; 22 Q×Q ch, K×Q; 23 R—Q7 and Black could hardly hope to win.

17 ...	Q×R ch
18 R—Q1	Q×P
19 Q×P	R—KB1
20 P—R4	

29

This advance causes him some trouble later on. If he wished to make a loophole for his King, 20 P—R3 was natural and good.

20 ...		P—QR3
21	K—Kt1	Q—R4
22	R—Q3	R—K1
23	Q—Q4	K—Kt1
24	Q—Q7	Q—R8 ch
25	K—R2	Q—K5
26	Q×P	Q×P ch
27	R—QR3	Q—B3

If 27 ... Q—K5; 28 R—K3 and Black is compelled to repeat moves.

28	Q×P	Q—Q4 ch
29	P—Kt3	

If 29 R—Kt3, R—K5 wins for Black.

29 ...		R—K7
30	R—R4	

The White position looks dangerous, but this move enables him to get his Rook back into play just in time.

30 ...		R×P

Black maintains his pawn ahead, but with all the pawns on the same side of the board his chances of success are minute. Here he has many attacking moves but White can always defend himself. If, for instance, 30 ... Q—K4, threatening R—K8; 31 P—B4 or if 30 Q—Q8, R—QB4.

31	Q—R8 ch	K—R2
32	K—Kt2	

Threatening 32 Q—Q4 ch with an easy draw.

32 ...		P—B4
33	R—QB4	R—B8
34	K—R2	

So as to answer 34 ... Q—Q8 by 35 Q—K5, Q—Kt8 ch; 36 K—R3 with a forced draw.

34 ...	R—B2
35 Q—QB8	P—Kt3
36 R—KKt4	Q—Q2

The threat of R—Kt8 compels Black to offer the exchange of Queens, after which there are no winning chances left. A very good game, particularly by Marshall, who would probably have won against any lesser antagonist. The remaining moves were: 37 Q×Q, R×Q; 38 R—KB4, P—Kt4; 39 R—B6, R—Q4; 40 K—Kt2, K—Kt2; 41 R—R6, P—Kt5; 42 R—R7 ch, K—B3; 43 R—R6 ch, R—Q3; 44 R—R8, K—Kt4; 45 R—Kt8 ch, R—Kt3; 46 R—QB8, P—R4; 47 P—B4 ch, P×P e.p. ch; 48 K×P, Drawn.

The Lasker v. Tarrasch Match

Dr. S. Tarrasch

Lasker's second opponent, Dr. S. Tarrasch, was in every way worthy of his steel and indeed his tournament record was superior to that of the champion himself. Born in 1862, he was six years older than his rival and by 1908, when the match under consideration was played, he had already won no less than seven big international tournaments, a record unequalled by any other master. These successes were gained at Breslau 1889, Manchester 1890, Dresden 1892, Leipzig 1894, Vienna 1898, Monte Carlo 1903, and Ostend 1907. Besides them he had won many smaller events as well as numbers of lesser prizes. A match between Tarrasch and Lasker might well have taken place at an earlier date, but a number of considerations, not the least of which was the personal hostility between them, made it difficult to bring them together. When at last the match was arranged, it was felt that here, if anywhere, was the

opponent to take the crown from Lasker, and the final
score was a great disappointment to Tarrasch and his
supporters.

Tarrasch, like Marshall, loved chess and was inclined to
put the quality of his games above the result, although in
his case scientific accuracy rather than brilliancy was the
ideal at which to aim. Like all players of his generation he
was naturally much influenced by Steinitz, but he had a
more practical mind than that great theorist and he was
able to improve and develop the Steinitzian ideas, eliminating the old champion's eccentricities, and establishing in
his own play a happy synthesis between the profound
concepts of Steinitz regarding the framework of the
position and a rapid mobility of pieces, the importance of
which had been neglected by the old champion. His play
is a model of purity and logic and there is no better guide
for the student to follow. Nevertheless, he had the defects
of his qualities. He loved the tried and well-beaten paths,
and whenever a game deviated from the courses with which
he was familiar he was apt to lose his sense of balance and
become flustered. Such opponents as Lasker and later
Alekhine and Niemzovitch were, of course, quick to take
advantage of this temperamental weakness. He was a
brilliant writer on the game, his annotations being models
of accuracy and depth while his two main books, *Three
Hundred Games*, and *The Game of Chess*, are real classics.
The section of the latter work which deals with the middle
game is the best that I have seen, and he also sheds a great
deal of valuable light on the difficult, though vitally important, subject of Rook and pawn endgames.

Although he contributed a great deal to the theory of the
openings, his views on this branch of the game have to be
treated with caution. He carried consistency of opinion to
the length of stubbornness and once he had taken a variation under his wing he could never be induced to relinquish

it, even when the iron test of tournament practice had proved its inferiority. In consequence, his treatment of certain openings is that of a special pleader rather than an impartial judge. In addition, he entirely failed to grasp the ideas behind the new opening systems introduced by Niemzovitch, Tartakover, and Réti, which he regarded as mere temporary excrescences and could never understand why he lost against them. In the earlier part of the century, however, he was the ideal chess mentor and, as he always published the result of his researches, he must take a great deal of credit for the general improvement in chess standards which has taken place during the last fifty years.

In character he had the reputation of being somewhat irascible and certainly he had strong likes and dislikes, noteworthy among the latter being Lasker, although it is greatly to his credit that he always expressed a proper appreciation of his rival's play. In later life he seemed to mellow and was in great demand as a tournament director, a position for which his strong personality and complete knowledge of the game made him entirely suitable. He possessed also a caustic sense of humour, as shown in his attitude to an incident which occurred at a tournament where he was acting as director. Informed by a horrified attendant that one of the spectators was asleep, Tarrasch hurried to the scene, but, after surveying the dull position and watching a few inept moves, he turned away with the remark: "Ah, an acute critic!"

Personally, I met him at only one tournament, London 1927. He had made himself unpopular in this country by his opposition to the entry into the Hamburg Tournament of the British Champion, whom he called caustically, "A certain Mr. Yates," a taunt to which Yates replied by brilliantly defeating him, and I felt rather nervous in his presence. However, he did me the honour of sitting on my hat for three hours while he analysed an adjourned game.

I kept that hat till my hair came through the crown, and since then I have worn no other.

THE MATCH

The match between Lasker and Tarrasch was played at Düsseldorf and Munich, the conditions being the same as those in the Marshall match, viz. that the first to win eight games should be the victor.

In the early part of the struggle there seemed a possibility that the hopes of the challenger's supporters might be realized, but he seemed to lose heart when his carefully prepared system of defence to the Ruy Lopez was defeated in the fifth game and, quite unnecessarily, abandoned the variation. From then onwards Lasker was always winning, although Tarrasch put up a stout resistance to the very end. In fact, the games of this match were of a very high quality and several of them appear in most collections of classic games. I have deliberately refrained from giving one or two of the best known.

Final score: Lasker 8; Tarrasch 3; Drawn 5.

SECOND MATCH GAME

White: Dr. S. Tarrasch. Black: Dr. E. Lasker.

1	P—K4	P—K4
2	Kt—KB3	Kt—QB3
3	B—Kt5	Kt—B3
4	Castles	P—Q3

The Steinitz Defence. This must have come as a surprise to Tarrasch as Lasker had repeatedly smashed up this variation in his matches with Steinitz himself, and was reputed to hold a low opinion of it.

5	P—Q4	B—Q2
6	Kt—B3	B—K2

7 R—K1	P×P

Of course he does not fall into the "Tarrasch trap," 7 ...
Castles; 8 B×Kt, B×B; 9 P×P, P×P; 10 Q×Q,
QR×Q (if 10 ... KR×Q; 11 Kt×P, B×P; 12 Kt×B,
Kt×Kt; 13 Kt—Q3, P—KB4; 14 P—KB3 and wins);
11 Kt×P, B×P; 12 Kt×B, Kt×Kt; 13 Kt—Q3, P—
KB4; 14 P—KB3, B—B4 ch; 15 Kt×B, Kt×Kt; 16
B—Kt5 followed by B—K7, winning the exchange.

8 Kt×P	Castles
9 Kt×Kt	

More usual is 9 B×Kt, P×B; 10 B—Kt5, but Tarrasch
had a great affection for Bishops. Gaining a Bishop for a
Knight he termed "Winning the minor exchange."

9 ...	B×Kt

This move was widely condemned and certainly 9 ...
P×Kt seems much better. After the exchange of Bishops
the White Knight is able to settle on KB5.

10 B×B	P×B
11 Kt—K2	

En route for the important square. Black cannot reply
11 ... Kt×P because of Kt—Q4 with the double threat of
R×Kt and Kt×P. White would eventually win a piece.

11 ...	Q—Q2
12 Kt—Kt3	KR—K1

Intending to play B—B1 followed by P—KKt3 and B—
Kt2, but White's excellent next move gives him no time
to complete the manœuvre.

13 P—Kt3	QR—Q1
14 B—Kt2	Kt—Kt5

Had anyone else but Dr. Lasker made this move it would
be put down as a blunder, but White has already secured a
very strong game of the type which he played perfectly,

and it is quite possible that the champion deliberately made the move in order to bring about complications in which his opponent might go astray.

15 B×P	Kt×BP

Of course, if 15 ... K×B; 16 Kt—B5 ch and 17 Q×Kt wins easily.

BLACK

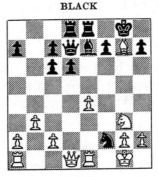

WHITE

16 K×Kt

And here at once is the mistake. With this move White wins a pawn but Black obtains counter chances. Much stronger was 16 Q—Q4, Kt—Kt5 (if 16 ... P—QB4; 17 Q—B3, Kt—Kt5; 18 Kt—B5 and Black has no good answer to the threat of Q—Kt3); 17 Kt—B5, P—B3 (what else?); 18 P—KR3, Kt—K4; 19 R—K3 with a winning attack.

16 ...	K×B
17 Kt—B5 ch	K—R1
18 Q—Q4 ch	P—B3
19 Q×RP	B—B1

Threatening R×KP followed by Q×Kt ch. The pressure Black is able to exert on the King's file gives him good counter play which Lasker exploits in splendid style.

| 20 Q—Q4 | R—K4 |
| 21 QR—Q1 | |

A routine move which does not help much. The position of the White Knight at B5 appears strong, but is not so actually as his support can be undermined by P—Q4. A good line therefore seems to be 21 Kt—R4 and if 21 ... P—Q4; 22 Kt—B3, R×P; 23 R×R, P×R; 24 Q×P, B—B4 ch; 25 K—B1 and White is safe enough. Against other 21st moves of Black, White can equally play the consolidating 22 Kt—B3.

| 21 ... | QR—K1 |
| 22 Q—B3 | |

22 K—Kt1 would not be good on account of 22 ... Q—K3; 23 Kt—Kt3, P—Q4 and Black will win the QP.

| 22 ... | Q—B2 |
| 23 Kt—Kt3 | |

After this retreat White's game rapidly disintegrates. Better chances appear to be offered by the apparently risky 23 Q×P, R—B4; 24 Q—R6, R×P ch; 25 R—K2.

23 ...	B—R3
24 Q—B3	P—Q4
25 P×P	

There is nothing satisfactory now. If 25 K—Kt1, Q—Kt3; 26 R—Q4, P—KB4, etc.

25 ...	B—K6 ch
26 K—B1	P×P
27 R—Q3	Q—K3
28 R—K2	P—KB4

Lasker conducts the counter-attack with superb vigour. White's last move indicated his intention of escaping with his King to the Queen's side, but if now 29 K—K1, P—B5; 30 Kt—B1, B—B7 ch and wins.

| 29 R—Q1 | P—B5 |

30	Kt—R1	P—Q5
31	Kt—B2	Q—QR3

Threatening B×Kt.

32	Kt—Q3	R—KKt4
33	R—R1	

If 33 P—QR4, 33 ... Q—R3 is even stronger than in the game as White has no escape for the King at Q1.

33	...	Q—R3
34	K—K1	

Of course not 34 P—KR3, R—Kt6; 35 Q—Kt7, Q×P; 36 P×Q, R—Kt8 mate.

34	...	Q×P
35	K—Q1	Q—Kt8 ch
36	Kt—K1	R(Kt4)—K4
37	Q—B6	

Hoping for the reply 37 ... P—Q6; 38 P×P, B—Q5; 39 Q×R ch, but Lasker is not to be caught in such traps.

37	...	R(K4)—K3
38	Q×P	R(K1)—K2
39	Q—Q8 ch	K—Kt2
40	P—R4	P—B6
41	P×P	B—Kt4
	Resigns	

A fine finish to a typical Lasker counter-attack. After 42 R×R, R×R; 43 Q—R5, B—R5 wins everything.

THIRD MATCH GAME

White: Dr. E. Lasker. Black: Dr. S. Tarrasch.

1	P—K4	P—K4
2	Kt—KB3	Kt—QB3
3	B—Kt5	P—QR3
4	B—R4	Kt—B3

5 Castles	B—K2
6 R—K1	P—QKt4
7 B—Kt3	P—Q3
8 P—B3	Kt—QR4

Nowadays these Queen's side manœuvres are usually preceded by Castling.

| 9 B—B2 | P—B4 |
| 10 P—Q4 | Q—B2 |

For now White can interfere with Black's plan by 11 P—QR4, to which there is no better answer than 11 ... P—Kt5. A game, Keres *v.* Reshevsky, Stockholm 1937, proceeded 11 P—QR4, P—Kt5; 12 P×KtP, P×KtP; 13 P—R3, Castles; 14 QKt—Q2, B—K3; 15 Kt—B1, KR—B1; 16 Kt—K3 and White has more space for manœuvring than his opponent.

11 QKt—Q2	Kt—B3
12 P—KR3	Castles
13 Kt—B1	

A pawn sacrifice which was a favourite of Lasker's, who always maintained that it was sound. It has now gone out of fashion and seems unnecessary as White can secure an excellent game by 13 P×BP, P×P; 14 Kt—B1, B—K3; 15 Kt—K3, QR—Q1; 16 Q—K2, P—Kt3; 17 Kt—Kt5 (Dr. Euwe *v.* Smyslov, World Championship, 1948).

| 13 ... | BP×P |
| 14 P×P | Kt×QP |

14 ... P×P is perhaps even better. The Knight may find a useful opportunity of playing to K4.

15 Kt×Kt	P×Kt
16 Kt—Kt3	Kt—Q2
17 B—Kt3	Q—Kt3
18 Kt—B5	

The great Austrian master, Carl Schlechter, suggested

what seems to be a preferable alternative in 18 B—Q5, R—R2; 19 P—Kt3. After 19 ... P—Kt3 (if 19 ... B—B3; 20 Kt—R5); 20 B—Kt2, B—B3; 21 Q—Q2, Black will find it impossible ultimately to preserve the pawn at Q4. Lasker prefers to rely on direct King's side attack.

18 ...		B—B3
19 B—KB4		Kt—K4

Finely played. If White replies 20 Kt×QP, there follows 20 ... B×P; 21 P×B, Q×Kt; 22 Q×Q, Kt—B6 ch; 23 K—Kt2, Kt×Q; 24 B×P, Kt×B; 25 P×Kt, B×P with a safe pawn ahead.

20 B—Q5		R—R2
21 Q—Kt3		R—B2
22 P—Kt4		P—Kt3
23 Kt—R6 ch		K—Kt2
24 P—Kt5		B—Q1
25 Q—Kt3		P—B3

BLACK

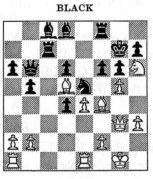

WHITE

A very fine move which transforms the game. White's attacking chances are cut down to a minimum and Black begins to exercise pressure against White's KBP. If White replies 26 P×P ch, R×P (threatening P—Kt4); 27

B×Kt, P×B; 28 Kt—Kt4, B×Kt; 29 P×B, P—Q6 with an overwhelming position.

26	Kt—B5 ch	K—R1

Not 26 ... P×Kt; 27 P×P db ch, K—R1; 28 B—R6 and wins.

27	Kt—R4	P×P
28	B×P	B×B
29	Q×B	P—Q6
30	K—R1	

Lasker, as always, chooses the line which affords the best tactical chances. Purely defensive play is of no avail either. If 30 R—K3, R—B7; 31 R—KB1, B×P. If 30 Q—Kt3, P—Kt4 wins and if 30 Q—K3, Q×Q; 31 R×Q, P—Q7 and wins.

30	...	R—B7
31	R—K3	

He must prevent 31 ... Q×P.

31	...	KR×P
32	Kt—Kt2	P—Q7

Of course not 32 ... R×Kt; 33 Q—B6 mate.

33	R—KKt1	R—QB8
34	Q—K7	

The last remote chance. If 34 B—Kt3, Kt—B5 wins at once.

34	...	R×R ch
35	K×R	P—Q8=Q ch
36	K×R	Q—B6 ch
37	K—K1	Q—R4 ch
38	R—B3	B×P

A delightfully cool move which makes possible the long combination that follows.

39	Q×P	Q(R4)×R ch

41

Black now forces the win of the Queen or mate.

40	P×Q	Q×BP ch
41	K—K2	Q—B7 ch
42	K—K3	

Other King moves lead to mate.

42	...	Q—Q6 ch
43	K—B4	

If 43 K—B2, Q—Q7 ch; 44 K—Kt3, Q×Kt ch; 45 K—B4, Q—B6 ch; 46 K—Kt5 (if 46 K×Kt, Q—Kt6 ch wins the Queen); 46 ... P—R3 ch and mates next move.

43	...	P—Kt4 ch
44	K×P	Kt—B2 ch
	Resigns	

A splendidly-played game by Tarrasch.

FIFTH MATCH GAME

White: Dr. E. Lasker. Black: Dr. S. Tarrasch.

1	P—K4	P—K4
2	Kt—KB3	Kt—QB3
3	B—Kt5	P—QR3
4	B—R4	Kt—B3
5	Castles	B—K2
6	R—K1	P—QKt4
7	B—Kt3	P—Q3
8	P—B3	Kt—QR4
9	B—B2	P—B4
10	P—Q4	Q—B2
11	QKt—Q2	Kt—B3
12	P—KR3	Castles
13	Kt—B1	BP×P
14	P×P	QKt×P
15	Kt×Kt	P×Kt
16	B—Kt5	

In the third game (*supra*), Lasker played 16 Kt—Kt3. Although the text is more immediately attacking and proved successful in this instance, it does not appear adequate against the best defence.

16 ...	P—R3

The correct move was 16 ... Kt—Q4. Of this Tarrasch writes: "After 17 B×B, Kt×B; 18 Kt—Kt3, B—K3; 19 Kt—K2, Kt—B3; 20 R—B1, Q—Kt3; 21 Q—Q2, White will ultimately capture the pawn at Q4, leaving Black with an isolated pawn at Q3." I. König, however, points out that after 21 Q—Q2, Black can play 21 ... P—Q4; 22 P×P, B×QP; 23 QR—Q1, QR—Q1, with an excellent game.

17 B—KR4	Q—Kt3
18 Q—Q3	

Threatening P—K5.

18 ...	P—KKt4

This creates a fatal weakness in the defences of Black's King. Better was 18 ... R—K1, but White can obtain the superior game either by the simple 19 QR—Q1, or by 19 P—K5, P×P; 20 R×P, B—K3; 21 QR—K1 followed by Kt—Kt3 with great pressure against Black's King's wing.

19 B—KKt3	B—K3
20 QR—Q1	KR—B1
21 B—Kt1	Kt—Q2
22 P—K5	Kt—B1
23 Q—KB3	

Preparing to attack the weak King's side. Regaining the pawn leads only to equality.

23 ...	P—Q4
24 Q—R5	K—Kt2
25 P—B4	

A splendid move which breaks the whole Black position wide open.

BLACK

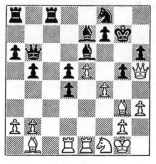

WHITE

25 ...	P—B4

Comparatively best. After the game Tarrasch suggested
the variation 25 ... Kt—Kt3; 26 P—B5, P—Q6 dis ch;
27 B—B2, B—B4; 28 Kt—K3, Kt—B5; but White can
then play 29 P—B6 ch, K—R2 (if 29 ... K—B1; 30
Q×P ch, K—K1; 31 Q×P winning easily); 30 B×P ch,
Kt×B; 31 Kt—Kt4 and Black must give up his Queen to
avoid mate.

26 P×P e.p. ch	B×P
27 P×P	P×P
28 B—K5	

Depriving Black of his last effective piece. The remainder
is a massacre.

28 ...	P—Q6 dis ch
29 K—R1	Kt—Kt3
30 Q×P	B—B2
31 Kt—Kt3	B×B
32 R×B	R—R1

If 32 ... Q—B2; 33 R—K7, Q×R; 34 Kt—B5 ch, etc.
The object of the text is to prevent the Queen playing to
KR6 after 33 Kt—B5 ch.

33 B×P	R—QR2
34 QR—K1	K—B1

35 B×Kt	Q×B

If 35 ... B×B; 36 R—K6.

36 Q—K3	R—B2
37 Kt—B5	

Threatening Q—R3 ch, etc.

37 ...	Q—QB3
38 Q—Kt5	Resigns

He cannot defend both the threatened mates. A fine example of Lasker's skill in attack.

LAST GAME OF MATCH

White: Dr. S. Tarrasch. Black: Dr. E. Lasker.

1 P—K4	P—K4
2 Kt—KB3	Kt—QB3
3 B—Kt5	Kt—B3
4 Kt—B3	B—Kt5
5 Castles	Castles
6 P—Q3	P—Q3
7 B—Kt5	B—K3

More usual is 7 ... B×Kt; 8 P×B and then either 7 ... Q—K2; 7 ... Kt—K2; or 7 ... B—Q2, followed by Kt—K2. The text creates great tactical complexities and was no doubt chosen by Lasker for that reason.

        8 P—Q4

The most aggressive continuation. A good alternative is the quieter 8 Kt—K2, followed by P—B3 and then P—Q4.

8 ...	P×P
9 Kt×P	P—KR3

A very complicated position. White could win a pawn by 10 B×KKt, Q×B; 11 Kt×Kt, P×Kt; 12 B×P, but Black secures good counter play after 12 ... R—QKt1; 13 Q—Q3, best B—R4; 14 Kt—Q1, R—Kt5. Another alternative is 10 B × QKt, B × Kt; 11 P × B (if 11 B × KtP, B × KtP); 11 ... KtP × B; 12 Kt × P, Q—Q2; 13 B × Kt, Q × Kt and Black regains the pawn with a good game.

10 B—R4	Kt—K4
11 P—B4	B—QB4

The point of Lasker's plan of defence. Black loses a piece but secures a strong counter-attack.

12 B × Kt

Winning a piece but allowing Black his strong counter-attack. Much to be preferred is Teichmann's suggestion, 12 K—R1. If, then, 12 ... Kt(K4)—Kt5; 13 Q—Q3, threatening P—KR3, and if 12 ... Kt—Kt3; 13 B × Kt, Q × B; 14 Kt—Kt3. In either case White has by far the better game. However, it is easy to be wise after the event, and it is not surprising that Tarrasch was unable to resist the immediate win of material.

12 ...	Q × B
13 P × Kt	Q × P
14 Kt—K2	B—KKt5
15 R—B3	

The only move.

15 ...	B × R
16 P × B	P—B4

A fine move which brings both Black's Rooks into immediate action.

17 Q—Q3

Apparently best. If 17 P × P Lasker gives the variation 17 ... R × P; 18 K—R1, R—R4; 19 Q—Kt1, R—KB1; 20 R—KB1, B × Kt; 21 Kt × B, R—B5; 22 P—B3, R × Kt, etc.

17 ...	P—B3
18 B—B4 ch	K—R1

19	K—R1	P—QKt4
20	B—Kt3	P×P
21	Q×KP	Q×Q
22	P×Q	QR—K1
23	Kt×BP	R×P
24	Kt—Kt3	QR—K1
25	R—Q1	

If 25 R—KB1, R×R ch; 26 Kt×R, R—K8; 27 K—Kt2, R—K7 ch; 28 K—R1 (if 28 K—Kt3, R—B7 wins the Knight); 28 ... P—KKt4, and the Black pawns on the King's side advance with the aid of the King while White's pieces remain disconnected. Nevertheless, this perhaps represents White's best chance.

25	...	R—B7
26	Kt—Q4	B×Kt

And White resigned the game and the match. White's 26th move was an unfortunate blunder, but it is doubtful if he can save the game. Black threatens P—KR4 and R5, forcing the entry of the Queen's Rook at K7. Comparatively best for White seems to be the sacrifice of a second pawn by 26 P—B3 followed by Kt—Q4, but his position remains very difficult.

Position after 16 P×B, P—B4

BLACK

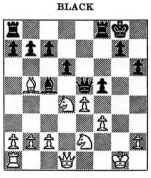

WHITE

47

THE LASKER *v.* JANOVSKY MATCH

D. JANOVSKY

Although Janovsky, a Pole naturalized as a French citizen, had a good tournament record, his qualifications as a world championship contender were considerably less than those of such players as Maroczy and Rubinstein, and the match with Lasker was entirely due to the financial backing provided by his patron, the wealthy Monsieur Nardus. In his early career Janovsky was extremely lucky in obtaining the support of this gentleman who assisted him in his tournament expenses and arranged several matches, including a short one with Lasker, which resulted in a tie 2–2. Lasker, however, was a very different opponent when the World Championship was at stake.

The one fly in Janovsky's ointment was that Nardus insisted on playing numbers of friendly games with him, and their relationship terminated when, at the conclusion of one such session the master broke out with: "Of all the bad players I have ever met you are the very worst." Nardus, who appears to have had a very good idea of his own abilities, did not take this criticism kindly, and Janovsky was henceforth left to his own devices. It was a sad blow to him. In the days of patronage the living of a professional chess master depended on his ability to make himself popular, and this Janovsky could never do. His supreme confidence in his own abilities—he is reported to have said: "There are only three chess masters, Lasker, Capablanca, and the third I am too modest to mention"—produced an arrogance of manner which jarred upon most of those with whom he came in contact, and he fell into very low water. A trip to America, where he did not meet with any great success although he was one of the few to win a game from Capablanca, brought him little reward, and he unfortunately developed the germs of consumption from which he eventually died. I met him in Paris in 1926, shortly after his return to Europe. He took a great fancy to my wife who shared with him a passion for strong tea, and they sat together for hours in a corner of the Café Rotonde in the Palais Royale, Janovsky boiling water on a small spirit lamp while he discoursed on his past glories and his plans for the future. He never realized that he was a dying man.

Janovsky's principal tournament successes were: 2nd to Lasker, London 1899; 1st, Hanover 1902; 3rd, Monte Carlo 1902, where he took his prize of £150 to the tables, turned it into £3,000 in one day and then had to borrow his fare home; 2nd with Lasker to Marshall at Cambridge Springs in 1904; 1st, Barmen 1905; and 2nd at Ostend in the same year. He also played three matches with Marshall, winning one and losing two, all by a narrow margin.

After his break with Nardus he accomplished comparatively little so far as results were concerned, although he played in a large number of tournaments and could always be relied upon to produce at least one brilliant game. In these later tournaments he developed the unfortunate habit of refusing to resign, due, no doubt, to his supreme optimism which made it impossible for him to realize that he could be beaten, a quality useful up to a point but which, in his case, degenerated into sheer obstinacy. In style he was combinative to the point of recklessness, attacking, as has been said, from the very first move, and his best games are extremely beautiful although he played too many bad ones for a master of the very top rank. One of his weaknesses was his refusal to recognize when a position was, by its nature, drawn, and he must have lost more games by trying to win such positions than any other grand master.

Lasker said that Janovsky loved playing chess so much that he could not bear a game to finish and preferred to lose rather than bring it to an untimely end. In point of fact, his confidence in his own abilities made him sure, in spite of many lessons to the contrary, that he could always outplay his opponents somewhere and somehow.

In spite of his faults, which only injured himself, Janovsky was a great personality and the quality of his best games will always give him a place in the hearts of those who love and admire a true chess artist.

THE MATCH

The match between Lasker and Janovsky was played in Paris in 1909. Although Janovsky did win one fine game, the match was really the easiest the champion played. He was, of course, fully aware of his opponent's temperamental weaknesses and their effect on his play, and took full advantage of his knowledge. Again and again Janovsky found himself forced into positions where his combinative genius had no possible scope and his attempts to transform such positions into types more to his liking usually resulted in material loss and speedy disaster. With more conservative play he could probably have made a better score, but had he adopted such tactics he would not have been Janovsky. The result came as a surprise to no one except the challenger.

Final score: Lasker 7; Janovsky 1; Drawn 2.

SECOND MATCH GAME

White: D. Janovsky. Black: Dr. E. Lasker.

1	P—K4	P—K4
2	Kt—KB3	Kt—QB3
3	Kt—B3	Kt—B3
4	B—Kt5	B—Kt5
5	Castles	Castles

50

6 P—Q3		P—Q3
7 B—Kt5		B×Kt
8 P×B		

So far a normal Four Knights' game, which has now gone out of fashion, as Black has several lines which secure equality. Besides the move chosen by Lasker, 8 ... B—Q2, followed by Kt—K2 or 8 ... Q—K2 are quite satisfactory.

8 ...		Kt—K2
9 B—QB4		

After 9 B×Kt, P×B, White does not seem able to take advantage of the weakness on Black's King's wing because of the absence of his Queen's Bishop, whereas Black may be able to make good use of his control of the black square at his KB5 in conjunction with the open KKt file. Marshall v. Capablanca played 9 Kt—R4, P—B3; 10 B—R4, Kt—K1; 11 B—Kt3, B—K3, but secured no advantage. Nevertheless, the line is preferable to that chosen here.

9 ...		Kt—Kt3
10 Kt—R4		Kt—B5
11 B×QKt		

He cannot play 11 Q—Q2 on account of 11 ... Kt×KP.

11 ...		P×B
12 Kt—B3		

The Knight must retreat in view of the threat 12 ... Kt×P.

12 ...		B—Kt5
13 P—KR3		B—R4
14 R—Kt1		P—QKt3
15 Q—Q2		

The only logical continuation. He cannot remain in the pin indefinitely and the open KKt file gives him some compensation for the doubled pawn.

51

15 ...	B×Kt
16 P×B	Kt—R4
17 K—R2	Q—B3
18 R—Kt1	QR—K1
19 P—Q4	

Preventing 19 ... R—K4.

| 19 ... | K—R1 |
| 20 R—QKt5 | |

Janovsky's last four moves have been strongly played and with this he brings his QR to the King's wing without loss of time. Unfortunately for him the attack is not strong enough.

| 20 ... | Q—R3 |

20 ... P—B4 would lead to complications tending in favour of White after 21 P—K5, and if 21 ... QP×P; 22 P×BP with greatly improved attacking chances.

21 QR—Kt5	P—KB3
22 QR—Kt4	P—Kt3
23 B—Q3	R—K2
24 P—B4	

BLACK

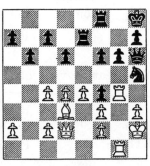

WHITE

To this move the loss of the game may be directly attributed as it allows Black to bring his Knight, whose function at present is purely defensive, into a strong attacking position. It is not easy, however, to suggest a constructive plan for White.

24 ...   Kt—Kt2

Lasker takes immediate advantage of the opportunity to bring his Knight to an attacking post. If White now plays 25 Q×P, Q×Q; 26 R×Q, Kt—K3; 27 R(B4)—Kt4, Kt×QP and White's Queen's wing is hopelessly weakened. Comparatively best seems 25 P—Q5, although this yields Black a valuable square at K4.

25 P—B3   Kt—K3

26 B—B1   P—KB4

27 R(Kt4)—Kt2

If 27 P×P, R×P; 28 P—Q5 (otherwise Black plays R—R4 and Kt—Kt4); 28 ... Kt—Kt4; 29 Q—Q3, R—K8, and if 30 B—Kt2, R×R; 31 K×R, Kt×RP ch; 32 B×Kt, Q×B; 33 Q—Q4 ch, K—Kt1; 34 R×P, R—R4 and wins.

27 ...   R—B3

28 B—Q3

If 28 P—K5, P×P; 29 P×P, R—KB1, the isolated KP cannot ultimately be defended and Black also obtains possession of the Queen's file.

28 ...   P—KKt4

Threatening Q×P ch and R—R3 mate.

29 R—KR1   P—Kt5

Decisive. There is no possible answer to the threat of Kt—Kt4.

30 B—K2   Kt—Kt4

31 BP×P   P—B6

32 R—Kt3   P×B

Resigns

Lasker's defensive play was impeccable and his counter-attack after White's weak 24th move remorseless in its energy.

THIRD MATCH GAME

White: Dr. E. Lasker. Black: D. Janovsky.

1	P—K4	P—K4
2	Kt—KB3	Kt—QB3
3	B—Kt5	P—QR3
4	B×Kt	

This line was a favourite of Lasker's who adopted it on many important occasions, including the decisive game against Capablanca in the Petrograd Tournament of 1914. The *motif* which stands out clearly right through the present game, is that White's four pawns to three on the King's side give an endgame superiority over Black's doubled Queen's side pawns.

4	...	QP×B
5	P—Q4	P×P
6	Q×P	B—Kt5

Janovsky's handling of the opening shows that he does not clearly understand its implications. Black's compensation for the inferiority of his pawn position lies in the possession of the two Bishops and these should be preserved as long as possible. Instead, Black deliberately abandons this advantage in order to split White's Queen's side pawns (*vide* his 10th and 11th moves), a matter of minor importance as the role of these pawns in Lasker's strategic plan is a purely defensive one. The right line is 6 ... Q×Q; 7 Kt×Q, B—Q3, with the continuation 8 Kt—QB3, Kt—K2; 9 Castles, Castles; 10 P—B4, R—K1, as in the game Lasker *v.* Capablanca, previously mentioned.

7	Kt—B3	Q×Q
8	Kt×Q	Castles
9	B—K3	B—Kt5

10	Kt—K2	B×Kt
11	K×B	B×Kt
12	P×B	Kt—B3
13	P—B3	Kt—Q2
14	QR—Q1	Kt—K4
15	R—Q4	P—QKt3

Rather better would be 15 ... P—QKt4 followed by Kt—B5, but even the excellent Knight post thus achieved would not compensate for White's King's side advantage.

16	P—KB4	Kt—Q2

16 ... Kt—Kt5; 17 P—KR3, Kt×B; 18 K×Kt is no better as White will have no difficulty in forcing a passed pawn in the centre.

17	KR—Q1	P—QB4
18	R(Q4)—Q3	Kt—Kt1

BLACK

WHITE

19 K—B3

The double exchange of Rooks followed by P—K5 looks tempting but is insufficient, i.e. 19 R×R ch, R×R; 20 R×R ch, K×R; 21 P—K5, Kt—Q2; 22 K—B3, P—QKt4; 23 K—K4, P—QB3; 24 P—B5, K—K2, and Black has some counter chances on the Queen's wing.

After the text move the threat of P—K5 followed by K—K4 becomes dangerous, and Black decides that his best chance is to keep the Rooks on the board.

| 19 ... | QR—K1 |
| 20 P—B5 | |

If now 20 P—K5, Kt—B3, and 21 R—Q7 is met by 21 ... R×P; 22 R×P, KR—K1.

20 ...	R—K2
21 B—B4	Kt—B3
22 P—Kt4	KR—K1
23 R—K3	P—B3
24 P—Kt5	Kt—R4

24 ... Kt—K4 ch; 25 B×Kt, R×B; 26 P×P, P×P; 27 R—KKt1 equally leads to a win for White. For instance, 27 ... K—Q2; 28 P—KR4, R(K1)—K2 (otherwise White advances RP to the 6th and then plays K—B4 and R—Kt7); 29 R—Kt8, R—K1; 30 R—Q3 ch, K—B3 (if 30 ... K—K2; 31 R—Kt7 ch, K—B1; 32 R(Q3)—Q7 and wins); 31 R×R, R×R; 32 K—B4 winning easily either by 33 R—KKt3 or if Black plays 32 ... R—KKt1; 33 P—K5.

25 P—KR4	Kt—B5
26 R—K2	R—B2
27 R—KKt1	K—Q2
28 P—R5	Kt—Q3
29 P—R6	

Decisive. Black must either lose a pawn or allow his opponent two passed pawns. Obviously 29 ... KtP×P, is answered by 30 P×BP.

| 29 ... | BP×P |
| 30 R×P | P—Kt3 |

If 30 ... P×P; 31 R—R5 and the two passed pawns must win.

31	P×P	P×P
32	R×KtP	R(K1)—KB1
33	R—Kt7	R×R
34	P×R	R—KKt1
35	R—Kt2	Kt—K1
36	B—K5	K—K3
37	K—B4	Resigns

In most of the previous games in this book we have seen Lasker's genius in complicated positions. In this game we have a different Lasker, a monument of precision in exploiting a minute technical advantage. Janovsky, after his poor opening, deserves every credit for his stout and accurate defence.

SIXTH MATCH GAME

White: D. Janovsky.   Black: Dr. E. Lasker.

1	P—K4	P—K4
2	Kt—KB3	Kt—QB3
3	Kt—B3	Kt—B3
4	B—Kt5	P—Q3

Transposing the game into the Steinitz Defence to the Ruy Lopez.

5	P—Q4	B—Q2
6	Castles	B—K2
7	R—K1	P×P
8	Kt×P	Castles
9	KKt—K2	

An unusual move which makes a welcome change from the conventional 9 B×Kt. The idea is probably Kt—B4 and QKt—Q5.

| 9 ... | | Kt—K4 |

Not a good move (a) because the Knight is susceptible to attack by White's KBP, and (b) because the square

KB5 becomes weak after the exchange of Bishops. Best appears to be 9 ... P—QR3, after which White must exchange his KB for a Knight since 10 B—R4 loses the KP.

10	Kt—Kt3	B×B
11	Kt×B	R—K1
12	P—Kt3	B—B1
13	B—Kt2	P—KKt3
14	P—KB4	QKt—Q2
15	Q—B3	

Janovsky has played the whole opening with great skill and has now brought all his pieces into their ideal attacking positions. 15 P—K5 looks strong but would have been premature on account of 15 ... P×P; 16 P×P, P—QR3; 17 P×Kt, R×R ch; 18 Q×R, P×Kt with approximate equality.

15 ...	P—QR3

But now 15 ... B—Kt2 would be a bad error because of 16 P—K5.

16	Kt—Q4	B—Kt2
17	QR—Q1	Q—K2

BLACK

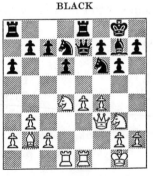

WHITE

This gives Janovsky the opportunity for a brilliant combination, but Black's position is cramped and difficult. Some contemporary analysts have suggested 17 ... R—K2 followed by Q—KB1, but after 18 P—B4, Q—B1; 19 B—R3 is difficult to meet. The best chance seems to lie in 17 ... Kt—B4, and if then 18 P—K5, KKt—Q2.

    18 Kt(Q4)—B5

A beautiful move. Black must accept the sacrifice for if 18 ... Q—B1; 19 Kt×B, Q×Kt; 20 P—K5 is decisive.

18 ...	P×Kt
19 Kt×P	Q—K3

Again, if 19 ... Q—B1 there is no answer to 20 Kt×B, Q×Kt; 21 P—K5.

20 Kt×B	K×Kt
21 P—K5	K—B1

He must return the piece. If 21 ... P×P; 22 P×P, Kt—Kt1 or Kt5; 23 R×Kt with a winning position.

    22 P×Kt   Q×R ch

The exchange of Queen for two Rooks is Black's best chance. If 22 ... Q—B4 White has a number of good continuations, the simplest of which is probably 23 Q×P, Q×QBP; 24 B—Q4 with a pawn ahead and much the superior position.

23 R×Q	R×R ch
24 K—B2	QR—K1
25 Q×P	

Here 25 Q—Kt4 looks very strong but Black can just save himself by 25 ... KR—K7 ch; 26 K—Kt3, QR—K6 ch; 27 K—R4, K—K1. The game will now be decided on pawns.

25 ...	KR—K7 ch
26 K—B3	R×BP

26 ... P—KR4 threatening 27 ... QR—K6 mate is met by 27 B—K5, R×BP; 28 Q—K4 followed by Q—R7.

27 B—Q4	P—QR4
28 Q—Kt5	

Threatening 29 Q—Kt5 as well as Q×Kt.

28 ...	Kt—B4
29 Q×P	Kt—Q6

Preventing 30 Q—Kt5 because of 30 ... Kt—K8 ch; 31 K—Kt3, R×P ch.

30 B—K3	P—Q4
31 B—Q2	P—B4
32 K—Kt3	Kt—B8

32 ... R—K7 fails against 33 Q—Q8 ch, R—K1; 34 Q—Q6 ch, K—Kt1; 35 Q×QP. The text also loses quickly but there is nothing good left.

33 B×Kt	Resigns

For if 33 ... R×B; 34 Q—Q2, R(B8)—K8; 35 Q×P, Black's game is absolutely hopeless. A fine win for Janovsky who, for once, was allowed to get a position that offered scope for his combinative talent.

TENTH AND FINAL GAME

White: D. Janovsky. Black: Dr. E. Lasker.

1 P—K4	P—QB4
2 Kt—QB3	

This move is now only seen when followed by the close variation 3 P—KKt3. If he intends to play the open game with P—Q4, it is decidedly premature as it deprives him of the possibility of P—QB4 in certain eventualities.

2 ...	Kt—QB3
3 Kt—B3	P—KKt3

Lasker plays the opening sequence cunningly in order to save the move P—Q3 which is indispensable in the normal variation.

4	P—Q4	P×P
5	Kt×P	B—Kt2
6	B—K3	Kt—B3
7	B—K2	

With 7 Kt×Kt, KtP×Kt (Lasker has also tried 7 ... QP×Kt); 8 P—K5, White drives the Knight back to his stable, but he comes out again with a good game after 8 ... Kt—Kt1; 9 P—B4 (or 9 B—Q4, P—QB4; 10 B×P, Q—B2); 9 ... P—B3; 10 P×P, Kt×P.

7	...	Castles
8	Q—Q2	

Here White should play 8 Kt—Kt3, P—Q3; 9 Castles, B—K3; 10 P—KB4, returning to present-day normality, but this variation was not known when the match was played. 8 Castles would also be better than the text although Black can then obtain a good game by 8 ... P—Q4; 9 P×P, Kt—QKt5.

8	...	P—Q4

Lasker has achieved his object and has now gained an important tempo on the regular line in which the **QP** reaches this square in two steps.

9	P×P

9 Kt×Kt, P×Kt; 10 P—K5, Kt—Kt5; 11 B×Kt, B×B; 12 P—B4, P—B3 is much in favour of Black.

9	...	Kt×P
10	Kt×KKt	

This move would be very good if White were Castled, but here it seems inferior to 10 Kt×QKt, P×Kt; 11 Kt×Kt, although even then Black's centre gives him a slight pull.

10	...	Q×Kt

Although only ten moves have been played White is already faced with a crisis owing to the threat against both his Knight's pawns. His best course seems to be to give up a pawn by 11 Kt×Kt, Q×Kt (if 11 ... P×Kt; 12 Q×Q, P×Q; 13 Castles QR); 12 Castles KR, B×P; 13 B—B3, Q—B2; 14 QR—Kt1 with pressure against Black's Queen's wing.

BLACK

WHITE

11 B—B3		Q—B5
12 P—QKt3		

And this is an error after which he must lose material. The only line was 12 Kt×Kt, P×Kt; 11 P—B3, R—Kt1; 12 B—K2 (not 12 B×RP, R×P); 12 ... Q—QR5; 13 Castles, B—B4; although even then Black has an advantage in mobility, and an attack along the QKt file.

12 ...		Q—R3
13 B—K2		Q—R6
14 P—QB3		

If 14 Castles, Kt×Kt; 15 B×Kt, R—Q1 wins a piece.

14 ...		R—Q1
15 R—Q1		

Whatever he plays at least a pawn is now lost, and the line chosen gives more chances of complications than 15 Q—B1, Kt×Kt; 16 B×Kt, Q×Q ch; 17 R×Q, B×B; 18 P×B, R×P.

15 ...		P—K4

| 16 Kt—Kt5 | R × Q |
| 17 Kt × Q | R × P |

A remarkable position for the King's Rook at this early stage of the game.

18 Kt—Kt5	B—B4
19 B—QB4	Kt—R4
20 B—Q5	B—B7
21 Castles	

Janovsky was always a gallant loser. The alternative 21 P—QKt4, Kt—Kt6; 22 B × Kt, B × B; 23 R—QKt1, B—B5 is quite hopeless.

21 ...	B × R
22 R × B	R—Q1
23 P—Kt3	Kt—B3
24 P—QB4	Kt—Q5

Simplest. The ending which would arise from 25 Kt × Kt, P × Kt; 26 B × P, B × B; 27 R × B, K—Kt2, is easy to win.

25 Kt—B3	R—Kt7
26 Kt—K4	R × KtP
27 B—Kt5	Kt—B6 ch
28 K—Kt2	Kt × B
29 Kt × Kt	R—Q2
Resigns	

Janovsky was in indifferent form in this game, and its principal interest lies in Lasker's astute handling of the opening and his skill in avoiding complications once his advantage was secure.

The Lasker v. Schlechter Match

Carl Schlechter

As I have mentioned in the Introduction, Schlechter was the only World Championship contender of the present century whom I did not meet personally. He died com-

paratively young, just after the first world war, a victim
of the famine conditions then prevailing in the Austrian
Empire.

From all accounts he was a delightful man, modest and
self-effacing, and was highly popular among his fellow
masters. From his games we can see that he was the
complete chess player, profound in his concept of strategical
necessities, accurate in analysis, and possessed of a deep
though perhaps rather limited theoretical knowledge. His
best games have that deceptive simplicity which conceals
supreme mastery. An almost total lack of ambition,
typically Viennese, marred his record. After his partial
success against Lasker he made no attempt to secure a
return match, and in his later tournaments was always
willing to draw provided his opponent was content to play
a placid game. But woe betide the player who ventured to
disturb his apparent lassitude. As many a young master
found, attempts to stir up the sleeping lion usually resulted
in dire disaster. All this does not mean that Schlechter was
a dull player—far from it. His best games are among the
most beautiful on record, while even in his later and more
passive days his play abounds in pretty points. The genius
was always there, though disinclined to show its full force
unless provoked. On the theoretical side he did not con-
tribute much, but his notes to games, published in the
Wiener Schachzeitung and elsewhere, are models of lucidity.

The weakest part of his play lay in the openings which
were inclined to be conventional and rather lacking in
variety. He had, however, a deep knowledge of the Ruy
Lopez in which he is responsible for several variations which
have survived the test of analysis and practice until to-day.
One of these was used with success in the match under
review. His principal victories, apart from his Lasker
match, were: Munich 1900, equal 1st and 2nd; Ostend
1906, 1st; Ostend 1907, 2nd; Vienna 1908, equal 1st to

3rd; Prague 1908, equal 1st to 2nd; Hamburg 1910, 1st.
He also regularly won native Austrian tournaments and
in 1912 created a record by playing through three big international tournaments, one of them double round, without
losing a game.

In matches he beat Janovsky by 6–1 and played a draw
with Tarrasch. Undoubtedly this record, fine though it is,
could have been improved upon had he possessed more
push and go, but it is very questionable whether he would
have been happier and I think Schlechter was a happy man.
In between his chess struggles he lived in the country,
preferring communion with nature to the stresses and
strains of city life. His means were sufficient to satisfy his
simple tastes and he was esteemed by all who knew him.
It is difficult to know what man could want more. I think
it was as well that he died when he did. The hurly-burly
of modern existence would have been anathema to this
simple soul, a true product of the culture of old Vienna,
gone, alas, never to return.

THE MATCH

The match between Dr. Lasker and Schlechter was
unique in that it was the only World Championship contest
to be inaugurated by the players themselves. It came about
as the result of a letter published in the chess Press in
October, 1909, in the following terms: "We are prepared
in December, January, February, and March next to fight
to a decisive issue a contest for the World's Championship
and ask the chess world to testify their interest in the
undertaking by the provision of a prize. The match will be
a public one. Care will be taken that all friends of chess,
wherever they may dwell, will be able to entertain themselves with the games of the match by playing them over.
Whoever feels that an enterprise which arouses public
interest and promises to give himself delight, deserves from

him more than merely moral support, should send a contri-
bution to the prize fund, etc., etc." This was signed by
Lasker and Schlechter. It is extremely interesting as it was
the first time that the general chess playing public, as
distinct from an individual or small group, had been asked
to make themselves responsible for a World Championship
match, and is highly significant in view of what was to
come. The chess players of Austria, Germany, England,
and Russia responded favourably to the appeal, but only
the two first-named actually did anything practical. The
City of London Chess Club, which undertook the organization in this country, announced that it was unable to
proceed through shortage of money, the common complaint
of British chess players, and the Russians cried off at the
last moment for unspecified reasons. Consequently the
match was limited to ten games, to be played in Berlin and
Vienna. This is far too small a number for a World Championship, but they made up in quality what they lacked in
quantity. For the first time since he won the Championship
Lasker was meeting an opponent with no psychological
weaknesses, and fully his equal in technical skill. In fact,
but for Schlechter's chivalry in declining to win the
championship by the odd point and consequently refusing
to draw the last game, the champion would have lost his
title.

These ten games are some of the very finest ever played
in a World Championship match, and it is a great pity that
it was not renewed.

Final score: Lasker 1; Schlechter 1; Drawn 8.

SECOND MATCH GAME

White: Dr. E. Lasker. Black: C. Schlechter.

1	P—K4	P—K4
2	Kt—KB3	Kt—QB3

3 B—Kt5	P—QR3
4 B—R4	Kt—B3
5 Castles	Kt×P
6 P—Q4	P—QKt4
7 B—Kt3	P—Q4
8 P—QR4	

First introduced by Tchigorin. It maintained its popularity over a number of years, but rightly went out of fashion when it was discovered that, after the reply made in this game 8 ... Kt×QP, it is White who is struggling for equality.

8 ...	Kt×QP
9 Kt×Kt	P×Kt
10 Q×P	

In the eighth game of the match Lasker played the better move 10 P×P with the continuation 10 ... B—QB4; 11 P—QB3, Castles; 12 BP×P, B—Kt3; 13 Kt—B3, B—Kt2; 14 P×P, R×P; 15 R×R, B×R, with approximate equality.

10 ...	B—K3
11 P—QB3	

Gunsberg suggests that White should first exchange pawns and Rooks, i.e. 11 P×P, P×P; 12 R×R, Q×R; 13 P—QB3, and now if 13 ... P—QB4; 14 Q—K5 and Black cannot reply 14 ... Q—Kt1 as in the game.

11 ...	P—QB4
12 Q—K5	Q—Kt1
13 Q×Q ch	R×Q
14 P×P	P×P
15 Kt—R3	B—K2

Better is 15 ... P—B5; 16 B—B2, Kt—B4 (Black also retains his material advantage by 16 ... B×Kt; 17 R×B, Castles, but after 18 B×Kt, P×B, the win is very difficult on account of the Bishops of opposite colour); 17 B—B4, R—Kt2, and White has little compensation for his sacrificed pawn.

> 16 B—KB4   R—Kt2

Schlechter points out that 16 ... B—Q3 is preferable. Then 17 B×B, Kt×B; 18 B×P, B×B; 19 KR—Q1 is met by 19 ... P—Kt5; 20 P×P, P×P; 21 Kt—Kt1 (if 21 Kt—B2, B—Kt6); 21 ... B—Kt6; 22 R×Kt, K—K2 with a decisive advantage.

> 17 P—B3   Kt—B3
> 18 Kt×P

BLACK

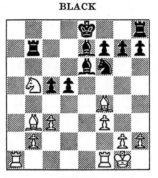

WHITE

With this brilliant stroke Lasker restores the balance. If Black plays 18 ... R×Kt; 19 B—R4 (not 19 R—R8 ch, K—Q2, and Black should win); 19 ... B—Q2; 20 B×R, B×B; 21 KR—K1 with the double threat of R—R8 ch and R—R7. Black has no way of avoiding the loss of a piece. If 21 ... K—B1; 22 R—R7, Kt—Kt1; 23 B—Q6 and wins, and other moves are just as hopeless.

> 18 ...   Castles
> 19 B—R4   P—B5

A very strong move after which White has to exercise the

greatest care. His pieces on the Queen's side are awkwardly placed and his QKtP is backward. However, there is always a saving clause which White invariably finds.

20	R—R2	B—B4 ch
21	K—R1	B—Q2
22	B—Q6	

The only move to avoid material loss. If 22 Kt—Q6, R—R2, etc.

22	...	B×B
23	Kt×B	R—Kt3

If 23 ... R—R2; 24 KR—R1, KR—R1; 25 B—Kt3 and draws. The text keeps up the pressure on the QKtP.

24	B×B	Kt×B
25	Kt—B5	R—K1
26	R—R7	

An important move which drives the Knight to the innocuous square KB3.

26	...	Kt—B3
27	R—R2	P—Kt3
28	Kt—Q4	KR—Kt1
29	R—B2	Kt—Q2
30	P—R3	Kt—B4
31	R—Q2	Kt—Q6

This leads to an immediate draw, but Black has no means of improving his position. Lasker's defence from the 18th move onwards was superbly accurate.

32	P—QKt4	P×P e.p.
33	Kt×P	R×Kt
34	R×Kt	R—QB1
35	R×P	R(Kt6)×P

Drawn

An extremely interesting and difficult game.

FIFTH MATCH GAME

White: C. Schlechter.   Black: Dr. E. Lasker.

1	P—K4	P—K4
2	Kt—KB3	Kt—QB3
3	B—Kt5	Kt—B3
4	Castles	P—Q3
5	P—Q4	B—Q2
6	Kt—B3	B—K2
7	B—Kt5	

A novelty which seems no improvement on the normal 7 R—K1. The usual effect of B—KKt5 in this opening is a series of exchanges leading to a heavy drawish game.

   7 ...   Castles

Here it is safer to exchange pawns.

   8 P×P

For Dr. Bernstein pointed out that White could secure a slight advantage by 8 B×QKt, B×B; 9 P×P, Kt×P (after 9 ... P×P; 10 Kt×P, Black cannot capture the KP without loss of material); 10 Kt×Kt, B×Kt; 11 B×B, Q×B; 12 P×P, Q×P; 13 Q×Q, P×Q; 14 Kt—Q4, and the isolated QP is a distinct weakness.

   8 ...   QKt×P

With this Black secures equality.

9	B×B	KKt×B
10	B×B	Kt×Kt ch
11	Q×Kt	Q×B
12	Kt—Q5	Q—Q1
13	QR—Q1	R—K1
14	KR—K1	Kt—Kt3
15	Q—B3	Kt×Kt
16	R×Kt	

16 P×Kt, Q—Q2, will eventually lead to an exchange of

both Rooks on the King's file with an almost certain draw. Schlechter considers that the position is worth more.

16	...	R—K3
17	R—Q3	Q—K2
18	R—Kt3	R—Kt3
19	R(K1)—K3	R—K1
20	P—KR3	

It is customary in this type of position to provide a way of escape for the King, but this creates a slight weakness of which Lasker takes advantage later on. The best plan seems 20 R×R, RP×R; 21 P—B3, defending the KP, and allowing the Rook to co-operate with the Queen in an attack on Black's Queen's side pawns. The correct result of the game is a draw.

20	...	K—B1
21	R×R	RP×R
22	Q—Kt4	P—QB3
23	Q—R3	

The object of these Queen manœuvres is the displacement of Black's Queen's side pawns. It is, however, ineffective as long as the Rook is tied to the defence of the KP.

23	...	P—R3
24	Q—Kt3	R—Q1

So that the Rook may defend the QKtP from the flank and so free the Queen for higher activities.

25	P—QB4	R—Q2
26	Q—Q1	

He cannot prevent Black's next move by 26 P—B4 because of 26 ... Q—R5, an unfortunate consequence of his 20th move P—KR3.

26	...	Q—K4

A dominating position for the Queen.

71

27	Q—Kt4	K—K1

The beginning of a profound plan to bring his King to the Queen's side where he not only defends that wing but may become an aggressive piece in the event of an exchange of Queens. The idea shows the influence of Steinitz on Lasker's play.

28	Q—K2	K—Q1
29	Q—Q2	K—B2
30	P—R3	R—K2
31	P—QKt4	P—QKt4
32	P×P	RP×P
33	P—Kt3	P—Kt4
34	K—Kt2	R—K1
35	Q—Q1	P—B3
36	Q—Kt3	Q—K3
37	Q—Q1	

If he exchanges Queens, the advance of the QBP supported by the King would give Black a winning ending.

37	...	R—KR1

Compelling White to block the King's side while he remains with the initiative on the other wing. Lasker's conduct of this part of the game is beyond praise.

38	P—Kt4	Q—B5

BLACK

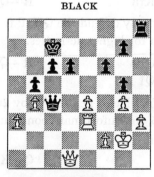

WHITE

72

39 P—QR4

Without making any real mistake Schlechter has drifted into a distinctly inferior position. The Black Queen has found a second dominating post and, as already pointed out, White cannot afford to offer an exchange, while, if he contents himself with waiting moves, Black, after proper preparation, can force a break-through on the Queen's wing by P—QB4. White, therefore, decides on a pawn sacrifice which gives him counter play against the Black King, and affords many chances of perpetual check or even more. The remainder of the game is intensely difficult and interesting.

39 ...	Q×KtP
40 P×P	Q×P

If 40 ... P×P the White Queen penetrates into the heart of Black's position after 41 Q—Q5, K—Kt3; 42 Q—B7.

41 R—QKt3	Q—R3
42 Q—Q4	R—K1

To bring the Rook to the defence of the King *via* K4. The alternative, 42 ... P—QB4; 43 Q—Q5, R—Q1; 44 Q—B7 ch, R—Q2; 45 Q—Kt8, Q—R2; 46 R—Kt2 followed by R—R2 is bad as Black is completely tied up.

43 R—Kt1	R—K4
44 Q—Kt4	Q—Kt4

If 44 ... R—Kt4; 45 Q—B4, K—Kt3; 46 Q—Q4 ch and White at least draws.

45 Q—K1	Q—Q6
46 R—Kt4	

Best. If 46 P—B3, R—Kt4 forces the exchange of Rooks.

46 ...	P—QB4

In view of the result of the game this move has been condemned by some annotators, unjustifiably so in my opinion. It forces the gain of a second pawn and Lasker had every reason to suppose that he could survive the attack. The alternative is 46 ... R—Kt4; 47 R—R4, K—Kt3; 48 Q—R1, and if then 48 ... R—Kt6; 49 R—R8, and Black seems to have nothing better than perpetual check.

47 R—R4	P—B5
48 Q—R1	

The only way to continue the attack. If 48 P—B3, Q—B7 ch wins the Rook.

48 ...	Q×KP ch
49 K—R2	R—Kt4
50 Q—R2	

Much stronger than 50 R—R7 ch, K—Q1, and he cannot take the KKtP because of 51 ... Q—K4 ch.

50 ...	Q—K4 ch
51 K—Kt1	Q—K8 ch
52 K—R2	P—Q4

Having provided against Q—R5 ch, after R—R7 ch, R—Kt2, Lasker must have considered that his King was safe enough.

53 R—R8	Q—Kt5
54 K—Kt2	

So as to play Q—R6 without being subjected to check at Q3.

54 ...	Q—B4

The position has suddenly become very difficult for Black, and this does not improve matters. Schlechter points out that 54 ... R—Kt1 is met by 55 Q—R7 ch, R—Kt2; 56 Q—K3, threatening Q—K8. Best was probably 54 ... R—Kt2; 55 R—KKt8 (if 55 Q—R6, Q—Kt3); 55 ... K—Kt3; 56 R—QR8, K—B2 with a draw.

Position after 54 K—Kt2

BLACK

WHITE

55 Q—R6	R—Kt1

The best of a bad lot. If 55 ... R—Kt2; 56 Q—K6 wins. If 55 ... R—Kt3; 56 Q—B8 ch, K—Q3; 57 Q—B8 ch wins the Queen.

56 R—R7 ch	K—Q1

There was still a little hope in 56 ... Q×R; 57 Q×Q ch, R—Kt2; 58 Q—B5 ch, K—Kt1; 59 Q×QP, R—QB2. After the text move Black is lost.

57 R×P	Q—Kt3
58 Q—R3	K—B1

If 58 ... Q—Kt5; 59 Q—R7 and wins.

59 Q—B8 ch and mates in two moves.

A truly remarkable game to arise from such a dull beginning. In a sense Lasker was unlucky to lose, but Schlechter deserves tremendous credit for the power with which he conducted the second half of the struggle.

SEVENTH MATCH GAME

White: C. Schlechter. Black: Dr. E. Lasker.

1 P—K4	P—QB4
2 Kt—KB3	Kt—QB3

3 P—Q4	P×P
4 Kt×P	Kt—B3
5 Kt—QB3	P—KKt3

It is generally recognized that 5 ... P—Q3 is necessary here. Compare Lasker's handling of the Sicilian in the tenth game against Janovsky.

6 B—QB4	

Also very good is 6 Kt×Kt, QP×Kt (if 6 ... KtP×Kt; 7 P—K5, Kt—Kt1; 8 Q—B3 with a tremendous attack); 7 Q×Q ch, etc. The text, however, may be even stronger.

6 ...	P—Q3
7 Kt×Kt	P×Kt
8 P—K5	Kt—Kt5
9 P—K6	

A stronger line is the Magnus-Smith variation: 9 B—B4, and if 9 ... P—Q4; 10 Kt×P, P×Kt; 11 B×P, B—K3; 12 B—B6 ch, B—Q2; 13 B×R, Q×B; 14 Castles.

9 ...	P—KB4
10 Castles	B—KKt2

Black cannot play P—Q4, either here or on the next move, because of Kt×P.

11 B—B4	Q—Kt3
12 B—QKt3	

This allows Black to force the exchange of Queens which greatly eases his position. Better was perhaps 12 P—KR3, Kt—K4; 13 B—QKt3, B—QR3; 14 R—K1, and if then 14 ... Kt—B5; 15 B×Kt, B×B; 16 B—K3 followed by B—Q4.

12 ...	B—QR3
13 Kt—R4	Q—Q5
14 Q×Q	B×Q
15 P—B4	Castles KR
16 QR—Q1	B—B3

16 ... B—K4 would have prevented the combination which follows. After 17 B—Kt5, B—B3; 18 B×B, R×B; 19 KR—K1, R—Q1 White has not got much. Not, however, 19 ... B—B1; 20 P—B5, P—Q4; 21 Kt—B3, B×P; 22 R×B, R×R; 23 Kt×P and White will win.

    17 KR—K1   P—Kt4

Again 17 ... QR—Q1 would have been safer. Lasker probably underestimated the strength of the combination which follows the text move.

BLACK

WHITE

    18 B×QP

A fine bold sacrifice which gives him at least three pawns for his piece, and a strong attack. It would almost certainly have succeeded against a lesser antagonist.

        18 ...   P×B
        19 R×P   B—K4
        20 P—B5

Excellent if Black replies 20 ... B×R; 21 P—K7 dis. ch, K—Kt2; 22 P×B, and wins.

        20 ...   KR—K1
        21 P—Kt3

77

It is unfortunate that White is compelled to this defensive move, but there is no alternative. If, instead, 21 P—KR3, B—R7 ch; 22 K—R1, B×R; 23 P×B, Kt×P ch; 24 K—Kt1, Kt—K5 and Black can hold up the passed pawns. 21 R×P is impossible because of 21 ... B—Kt4; 22 R—Q6, B×P ch with similar variations.

21 ...   B—B3

Now 21 ... B×R would be bad because of 22 P—K7 dis. ch, K—Kt2; 23 P×B, Kt—B3; 24 Kt—B5, B—B1; 25 B—R4, etc.

    22 R×P   B—Kt2
    23 R—B7   B—K5

Not 23 ... R—K2, because of 24 R×B, R×R; 25 P—K7 dis. ch, etc.

    24 Kt—B3   B×Kt

The right exchange which greatly reduces the power of White's Queen's side pawns and preserves the Queen's Bishop on his present powerful diagonal.

    25 P×B   Kt—K4
    26 R—Q1   Kt—B6 ch

Lasker, who was always on the look-out for the chance of snatching a win out of the most unpromising positions, cannot resist the gain of a pawn.

26 ... K—R1 would avoid the complications which follow.

    27 K—B1   Kt×P ch
    28 K—K1   Kt—B6 ch
    29 K—K2   Kt—K4
    30 R(Q1)—Q7

A terribly hard move to meet. Obviously the Rook cannot be taken and White is threatening a mating attack. The series of difficult moves which follow afford the only chance of saving the game.

30 ...	P—B5
31 R—Kt7 ch	K—R1
32 R×KtP	B—Q6 ch
33 K—Q1	P×P

The saving clause. Obviously, White cannot take the Kt on account of 34 ... P×P.

34 P×P	Kt—Kt3
35 R—Q5	B—K5
36 R—Q6	B—B4

White was threatening B—R4 followed by P—K7.

| 37 B—Q5 | QR—Kt1 |
| 38 P—B6 |

It is a moot point whether 38 R × P would be better. There is certainly no clear win.

| 38 ... | Kt—B1 |
| 39 R—QKt7 |

The alternative is 39 P—K7, Kt—Kt3; 40 R(Q6)—Q7 (not 40 B—B7, R×P; 41 B×Kt, B—Kt5 ch); 40 ... K—Kt2; 41 R×P, or R—Q8, K—B3 with a difficult ending which is probably drawn.

| 39 ... | QR—B1 |
| 40 P—K7 | Kt—Kt3 |
| 41 B—B7 |

Or 41 R(Q6)—Q7 as in previous note.

| 41 ... | R×KP |
| 42 B×Kt | B—Kt5 ch |
| 43 K—B1 |

Or 43 K—Q2, R—K7 ch; 44 K—Q3, P×B; 45 R×KtP, B—B4 ch; 46 K×R, B×R; 47 P—B7, K—Kt2 appears to draw.

| 43 ... | R—K8 ch |
| 44 K—Kt2 | P×B |

45	R×KtP	B—B4
46	R—B6	B—K5
47	R×P	R—Kt8 ch
48	K—R3	B×P

White draws by perpetual check 49 R—R6 ch.

A fine game, splendidly played by both antagonists and abounding in interesting situations.

One gets the impression that after 30 R(Q1)—Q7 White should have won but the most careful investigation fails to reveal the method. Lasker's defence was superb in its ingenuity.

Tenth and Final Match Game

In considering this game it is advisable to realize the circumstances under which it was played. Both players were determined not to draw, Schlechter because he did not wish to win the world title solely because of his rather lucky victory in the fifth game—a chivalrous attitude which must excite our admiration—and Lasker because he had at all costs to avoid losing the match. Consequently the game, almost from the start, takes on a wild character quite uncharacteristic of the two players' general style, and a number of mistakes are made. It is, however, intensely interesting.

White: Dr. E. Lasker. Black: C. Schlechter.

1	P—Q4	P—Q4
2	P—QB4	P—QB3

It is curious that nearly all the contemporary annotators condemned this move. It is, of course, one of the best methods of declining the Queen's Gambit.

3	Kt—KB3	Kt—B3
4	P—K3	P—KKt3

DR. E. LASKER

Schlechter's own system of defence, which is still known by his name.

5	Kt—B3	B—Kt2
6	B—Q3	Castles
7	Q—B2	Kt—R3

An eccentric move which does not turn out well. A sound method of play is 7 ... P×P; 8 B×BP, QKt—Q2; 9 Castles, Q—B2 with a view to P—K4.

8	P—QR3	P×P
9	B×P	P—QKt4

Now Black becomes "wild." The move is quite anti-positional on account of the weak backward QBP which can never be forced to the fourth rank.

10	B—Q3	P—Kt5
11	Kt—QR4	

Better than 11 B×Kt, P×Kt; 12 B×B, P×P; 13 B×P, R×B which furthers Black's development.

11	...	P×P
12	P×P	B—Kt2
13	R—QKt1	Q—B2
14	Kt—K5	

White, in his turn, abandons the path of positional play. With 14 Castles, QR—B1; 15 B—Q2, followed by KR—QB1 he has a clear advantage.

14	...	Kt—R4
15	P—Kt4	

In view of the circumstances, this must be regarded as a good move. White obtains many attacking chances on the open Knight's file.

15	...	B×Kt
16	P×Kt	B—Kt2
17	P×P	RP×P
18	Q—B4	

81

With the double threat of 19 R×B and 19 B×P.

18 ...   B—B1

An interesting, and indeed, the only defence. White can now win a pawn by 19 B×P, B—K3; 20 Q×Kt, P×B; but Black's two Bishops, coupled with pressure on the Bishop's file, give him good counter-chances.

19 R—Kt1

It would seem best to precede this by 19 B—Q2, preventing Black's manœuvre in the game.

19 ...   Q—R4 ch
20 B—Q2   Q—Q4
21 R—QB1   B—Kt2
22 Q—B2

Threatening 23 R×P followed by B—QB4.

22 ...   Q—KR4
23 B×P

BLACK

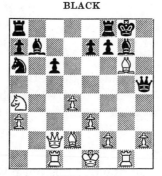

WHITE

This apparently strong move does not turn out well as Black obtains a powerful attack along the open KB file. The best line seems 23 R—Kt1, Q×P; 24 R—KB1, Q—B2 (if 24 ... B—B1; 25 Q×P); 25 B×P, P×B; 26 Q—Kt3 ch, R—B2; 27 Q×B, R—QKt1; 28 Q×Q,

R × R ch; 29 K—K2, Kt × Q; 30 R × R with the better endgame.

23 ...		Q × P
24	R—B1	P × B
25	Q—Kt3 ch	R—B2
26	Q × B	QR—KB1
27	Q—Kt3	

Not 27 Q × Kt, R × P; 28 R × R, R × R and wins. Marco condemns the text move but there seems no alternative if he wishes to keep winning chances. If 27 P—B4, 27 ... Q—Kt6 ch seems to draw. After 28 K—Q1, Q—Kt5 ch; 29 K—B2, Q—B4 ch; 30 K—B3 is too dangerous on account of 30 ... P—B4, and if 28 K—K2, Q—Kt5 ch; 29 R—B3, P—K4 is strong. Whether Schlechter, in view of his own determination to win, would have played this line is doubtful, but Lasker could not take the risk.

27 ...		K—R1
28	P—B4	P—Kt4

Now there is no draw. 28 ... Q—Kt6 ch; 29 K—Q1, Q—Kt5 ch; 30 K—B2, Q—B4 ch; 31 Q—Q3. The text move is very strong and it increases the pressure on the KB file.

29	Q—Q3	P × P
30	P × P	

If 30 Q × Kt, P × P wins.

30 ...		Q—R5 ch
31	K—K2	Q—R7 ch
32	R—B2	Q—R4 ch
33	R—B3	

The only way of escaping the incessant checks, but it is very risky to put the Rook into a pin. Black's initiative now becomes formidable.

33 ...		Kt—B2

34 R×P

The alternative 34 R—KR1, Q×R; 35 R—R3 ch, Q×R; 36 Q×Q ch is not very promising from the point of view of a win, but the text comes near to losing.

34 ...   Kt—Kt4

Schlechter says that 34 ... Kt—Q4, threatening to take the BP with Knight or Rook, according to White's play, would probably have won. It is certainly difficult to find an answer for White. 35 R—B5 is simply met by 35 ... Q—Kt5. A possibility is 35 R—B1, and if 35 ... Kt×P ch; 36 B×Kt, R×B; 37 R—KR1, Q×R; 38 R—R3 ch, R—R5; 39 R×Q, R×R; but the prospect is not a happy one. The move actually chosen, however, also looks very strong.

35 R—B4

Not 35 R—B5, because of 35 ... Kt×P ch; 36 Q×Kt, Q×R ch, nor 35 B—K3, Kt×P ch; 36 B×Kt, R×P; 37 B×B ch, K×B; 38 Q—B3 ch, P—K4; 39 R—B7 ch, K—R1, and wins the Rook on KB3.

BLACK

WHITE

35 ...   R×P

This sacrifice, if correctly followed up, should lead to a

draw. 35 ... R—Q1 still holds out slight chances of a win.
If 36 K—K1 threatening R—R3, 36 ... Q—R5 ch; 37
K—Q1, Q—Kt5, and after 38 K—B1, Kt×QP, the White
King is still exposed. He gains nothing by 39 R—R3 ch.

36	B×R	R×B
37	R—B8 ch	B—B1
38	K—B2	Q—R7 ch
39	K—K1	Q—R8 ch

39 ... Q—R5 ch would draw as White cannot escape to
Q1 because of 40 ... Q—Kt5.

After Schlechter misses this chance, his game is theoretically lost, although the limited number of pawns makes the
win for White a matter of great technical difficulty.

40	R—B1	Q—R5 ch
41	K—Q2	R×R

If 41 ... R×P; 42 QR×B ch, K—Kt2; 43 KR—B7 ch,
K—R3; 44 R—R8 ch, K—Kt4; 45 R—Kt8 ch, K—R3;
46 R—R7 mate.

42	Q×R	Q×P ch
43	Q—Q3	Q—B7 ch
44	K—Q1	Kt—Q3
45	R—B5	B—R3
46	R—Q5	K—Kt1
47	Kt—B5	Q—Kt8 ch
48	K—B2	Q—B7 ch
49	K—Kt3	B—Kt2
50	Kt—K6	Q—Kt7 ch
51	K—R4	K—B2
52	Kt×B	Q×Kt
53	Q—QKt3	K—K1

There is no way of saving the QRP.

54	Q—Kt8 ch	K—B2
55	Q×P	Q—Kt5 ch

56	Q—Q4	Q—Q2 ch
57	K—Kt3	Q—Kt2 ch
58	K—R2	Q—B3
59	Q—Q3	K—K3
60	R—KKt5	K—Q2
61	R—K5	Q—Kt7 ch
62	R—K2	Q—Kt5
63	R—Q2	Q—QR5
64	Q—B5 ch	K—B2

This facilitates White's task by allowing the exchange of Queens. After 64 ... K—Q1, Lasker would, no doubt, have won by gradually forcing the advance of the RP, but the task would be a laborious one.

65	Q—B2 ch	Q×Q ch
66	R×Q ch	K—Kt2
67	R—K2	Kt—B1
68	K—Kt3	K—B3
69	R—B2 ch	K—Kt2
70	K—Kt4	Kt—R2
71	K—B5	Resigns

The game could, of course, have been prolonged, but White's victory is certain. A curious game, containing more errors than are customary in World Championship contests, but extremely exciting in many of its phases. Like Lasker in the fifth game, Schlechter was a little unlucky to lose.

CHAPTER II

J. R. CAPABLANCA

CAPABLANCA himself tells the story of his introduction to the game of chess in his book *My Chess Career*. "I was not yet five years old," he says, "when by accident I came into my father's private office and found him playing chess with another gentleman. I had never seen a game of chess before; the pieces interested me and I went the next day to see them play again. The third day, as I looked on, my father, a very poor beginner, moved a Knight from a white square to another white square. His opponent did not notice it. My father won, and I proceeded to call him a cheat and to laugh. After a little wrangle, during which I was nearly put out of the room, I showed my father what he had done. He asked me how and what I knew about chess? I answered that I could beat him. We tried conclusions and I won. That was my beginning." Similar stories have been told about Morphy and others of the greatest players and have always been taken with a grain of salt. It seems incredible that anyone, by merely watching others play, could even grasp the object of the game, let alone such embroideries as Castling, pawn promotion and the *en passant* capture, the last two of which might not take place in a dozen games. One cannot help feeling that Capablanca must have forgotten one or two lessons he had received before he began to watch his father. However this may be, there is no doubt that at five years of age he was taken to the Havana Chess Club where the members attempted, without any success, to give him the odds of the Queen. Among those present at the time was the French master Taubenhaus, who used to boast in the Café de la Régence that he was the

87

only living master to have given Capablanca the odds of a Queen.

Capablanca was fortunate in his parents. He was encouraged to play chess, but was not overpressed, with the result that his game was allowed to develop naturally, and consequently he was not long in showing that he was indeed a genius of the highest order. At the age of eleven he proved himself superior to all the first-class players in the Havana Club with the exception of the Cuban Champion, J. Corzo, and one year later he defeated the latter in a set match with a score of four games to three with six draws. This was truly a remarkable performance for Corzo was a very strong player, fully up to international master standard. The games, too, speak for themselves, Capablanca exhibiting the cool position judgment of a veteran master, coupled with one or two touches of real brilliancy. He played little public chess afterwards until he completed his course at Columbia University, where he graduated with high honours in mathematics. On the conclusion of his University career Capablanca decided to give up most of his time to chess. He may be said to have graduated in the game at the Manhattan Chess Club of New York, then, as now, one of the strongest chess resorts in the world. Here he soon found himself head and shoulders above his rivals who included the best American amateurs, and it was evident that the highest honours were in store for him.

So great a reputation had he acquired that little difficulty was found in arranging a match with the American Champion, F. J. Marshall, veteran of a score of international tournaments, and rightly regarded as one of the strongest players in the world. Few thought that the youthful Capablanca could do more than put up a gallant fight against such a formidable opponent, but in the result he showed himself overwhelmingly superior, winning with a score of eight games to one with fourteen draws.

Like his predecessor, Morphy, with whom he had many points of resemblance, Capablanca now set out to conquer Europe. His victory over Marshall gave him the *entrée* to the San Sebastian Tournament of 1911, one of the strongest international contests ever held, in which the competitors were limited to those who had won at least two third prizes in previous first-class international events. The solitary exception was Capablanca, who was admitted on the strength of his match victory over Marshall. Even so, some of the experienced competitors resented the inclusion of the youthful Cuban, and Niemzovitch in particular, took exception to a remark he made during the course of a lightning game against Bernstein, saying that "Young players should keep quiet while acknowledged masters were playing." Capablanca promptly challenged him to a series of quick games for a stake which he won very easily and Niemzovitch was ever afterwards one of his most fervent admirers.

The result of the Tournament silenced all criticism, for Capablanca won the first prize, losing only one game to Rubinstein, who tied with Dr. Vidmar for second place. In this tournament Capablanca played superbly daring chess and his game against Dr. Bernstein contains one of the most brilliant and profound sacrificial combinations ever composed on the chess board. Negotiations were now begun for a World Championship match with Lasker, but the champion was unwilling to play, preferring to wait for the International Tournament at St. Petersburg, as it was then called, in which both he and Capablanca were due to take part. In view of age it would have been well for Lasker if he had played the match before 1914, but naturally he could not anticipate the world tragedy in the offing.

The St. Petersburg Tournament was Capablanca's first partial set-back. After leading from the start, he was beaten in the last round by Lasker and had to take second place to the old champion. Still he again played with superb brilliancy, notably in his games against Bernstein and Alekhine, and it was evident that a match between him and Lasker could not long be delayed. It was delayed by the world war. Capablanca spent the war years between his native Cuba and the United States, playing in a number of tournaments and completely changing his chess style. No longer do we see the brilliant combinations with which he electrified the chess world during his early career, but, in its place, the most perfect technique ever achieved by any player. In its essence the secret of Capablanca's technique seems to be that it was accompanied by an un-canny judgment of position which enabled him to anticipate his opponent's strategy before it had time to develop so that his pieces were always in the right place to thwart the hostile plans at the moment of their inception. As this judgment was coupled with an accuracy in endgame play only equalled by Lasker, it is no wonder that he soon achieved the name of the unbeatable. In fact, Capablanca's losses from the time of his match with Marshall to his defeat by Alekhine, a period of eighteen years, were eleven in all.

Probably the most important of his successes during the war period was the tournament organized by the Man-hattan Chess Club in 1918, in which he played a memorable game against Marshall. The latter, in the seclusion of his study, had evolved an ingenious sacrificial defence against the Ruy Lopez opening, leading to positions of tremendous complexity, all of which Marshall, of course, had at his finger tips. The American champion kept this variation up his sleeve for two years waiting for the chance to play it against Capablanca. The chance duly came. For ten or twelve moves the Cuban found the right move every time and emerged from the complications with a winning ending. After all these successes the Championship match with

Lasker, which would have aroused enormous excitement previous to the war, came almost as an anti-climax. In 1919 Capablanca came to England to take part in the Victory Tournament organized by the Hastings Chess Club, where I met him for the first time. The opposition, gathered from untried British players leavened by a few continentals from friendly or neutral nations, proved hardly worthy of his steel. He won ten games and drew only one. At this period of his career he gave the impression of being rather arrogant and aroused some criticism at Hastings by often making a move without sitting down at the board as if he were giving a simultaneous exhibition. This, however, wore off in later years. With this tournament ended the period of his unchallenged superiority. He found that the new openings introduced by what is called the hyper-modern school created difficulties for his technique, and a defeat by Réti in the New York Tournament compelled him to take second place to Lasker. In 1925, too, he could only finish third to Bogoljubov and Lasker in Moscow, where he lost his individual games to two unknown Soviet players. I think myself that the slight falling off was due to a change in his attitude to the game. He began to despise his medium. "Chess," he said, "was played out. Any master could draw when he liked against any other master and it was necessary to create a new game." This he attempted to do by increasing the size of the board and the introduction of two horrible monstrosities, but the "new game," fortunately, never found favour with the chess public.

In 1927 Capablanca seemed to recover his ascendancy with his victory in the four-round Tournament at New York where he did not lose a game to any of his five opponents, Alekhine, Niemzovitch, Vidmar, Spielmann, and Marshall. His defeat in the World Championship match with Alekhine in the same year created universal astonishment,

91

but perhaps in view of his declared attitude to chess it was scarcely so surprising as it seemed. It is an excellent thing to convince the world that you are unbeatable. It is a very dangerous one to believe it yourself.

During the following years Capablanca made strenuous efforts to recover his lost title, but was constantly thwarted by Alekhine's pertinacity in finding pretexts to avoid challenges. It is a great loss to the chess world that the return match was never played. It would certainly have provided an epic struggle. In these later years Capablanca seemed to regain all his powers, his victories at Moscow and Nottingham (equal with Botvinnik) in 1936 ranking among his greatest performances. His death during the war, when his powers seemed unimpaired, was a chess tragedy. Among his fellow masters he was extremely popular. When he got over the natural ebullience which springs from youthful success he seemed quite without conceit, he was courteous to all, free from mannerisms and always ready with helpful advice and criticism.

Although he came from a wealthy family and himself held a high ranking position in the Cuban diplomatic service, he was proud to consider himself a professional chess player and was always concerned to maintain the prestige of the profession, sometimes at considerable cost to himself. He was a veritable King among chess masters.

THE CAPABLANCA *v.* LASKER MATCH

The match was played at Havana in 1921. It was planned that the first to win six games should be declared the winner but, after the fourteenth game with the score four to nothing with ten draws against him, Lasker decided to abandon the contest.

There is no doubt that the dice were heavily loaded against the old champion. He was playing in his opponent's home town where climatic conditions necessitated unusual hours of play, he had played little or no chess during the war, and his health was none of the best. In addition, too, he was handicapped to a certain degree by *anno Domini*. Still, nothing can detract from the superb nature of the new champion's achievement. Lasker's play showed no signs of weakness but all his tactical efforts failed to shake his opponent's rock-like technique. In nearly all the games Lasker attacked in the first half, Capablanca in the second, with the inevitable result. It is unique among Championship matches in that the winner never seemed to have a lost position. That was Capablanca's own considered view and subsequent analysis has done nothing to shake it. Some of the games appear rather dull as Capablanca wisely sought simplification wherever possible, but his two wins published here are superb examples of the art of taking advantage of trifling weaknesses, and few players could have saved the two draws.

Final score: Capablanca 4; Lasker 0; Drawn 10.

SECOND MATCH GAME

White: Dr. E. Lasker.　Black: J. R. Capablanca.

1 P—Q4	P—Q4
2 P—QB4	P—K3
3 Kt—QB3	Kt—KB3
4 Kt—B3	QKt—Q2
5 P—K3	

The older form of the opening generally played before Steinitz and Pillsbury introduced the stronger B—Kt5. It has now almost disappeared from master practice as it is considered that Black should have little difficulty in obtaining equality.

　　5 ...　　　　　　　　　　B—K2

6	B—Q3	Castles
7	Castles	P×P
8	B×P	P—B4
9	Q—K2	P—QR3

A form of the Queen's Gambit Accepted has now arisen in which, however, White is one "tempo" behind as his Bishop has taken two moves instead of one to reach QB4. As against this, in the Gambit Accepted Black's Queen's Knight is often better placed at QB3 than at Q2.

10	R—Q1	P—QKt4
11	B—Q3	

In this type of position it is always a moot point whether the Bishop should play to Q3 or QKt3. Usually the former is preferred as it facilitates the advance of White's QP and exercises pressure on Black's KP. In this case Lasker probably did not care for the variation 11 B—Kt3, B—Kt2; 12 P—K4, P—Kt5; 13 P—K5, P×Kt; 14 P×Kt, B×P with quite a good game for Black.

11	...	B—Kt2
12	P—K4	P×P
13	Kt×P	Kt—K4
14	Kt—Kt3	

By allowing the exchange of his King's Bishop, White is able to bring his Rook to the King's side without loss of time but, in this opening, it is very difficult to force home an attack without the aid of the Bishop, and most players would have preferred 14 B—B2.

14	...	Kt×B
15	R×Kt	Q—B2
16	P—K5	Kt—Q4
17	R—Kt3	Kt×Kt
18	R×Kt	Q—Q2
19	R—Kt3	KR—Q1

20 B—R6	P—Kt3

Black is forced to weaken his King's side. If 20 ... B—B1; 21 B×P, B×B; 22 Q—Kt4 and wins.

21 B—K3	

This move is played with the idea of forcing the exchange of one of Black's Bishops, which Lasker actually accomplishes. A more attacking alternative was 21 Kt—R5, B—Q4; 22 Q—K3, threatening 23 R—R3 and B—Kt7.

21 ...	Q—Q4

Capablanca shows his excellent position judgment in making no effort to preserve his pair of Bishops. If he had played 21 ... QR—B1; 22 B—Kt6, R—K1; 23 Kt—R5, B—Q4; 24 R—Q1 with good attacking possibilities as Black's pieces are very cramped.

22 Kt—R5	QR—B1
23 Kt×B	Q×Kt
24 B—R6	Q—Q4
25 P—Kt3	Q—Q5
26 R—KB1	R—Q4
27 R—K3	B—R6

Position after 28 ... Q—Kt7

BLACK

WHITE

28 P—Kt3

It is necessary to provide an escape for the King in view
of Black's threat of R—B8.

| 28 ... | Q—Kt7 |
| 29 R—K1 | |

Sir George Thomas has pointed out a pretty variation in
28 Q—B3, and if 28 ... R×P; 29 P—QKt4, B×P; 30
Q—B6 and wins. Black, however, has an easy answer in
28 ... B—K2, leaving two White pawns subject to attack.

| 29 ... | R—B7 |
| 30 Q—B3 | B—K2 |

The same annotator has shown that it is unsafe for Black
to capture the QRP either here or on the next move. If
30 ... Q×RP; 31 Q—B6, B—B1; 32 R—B3, R—Q2;
33 B×B, K×B; 34 Q—R8 ch, K—K2; 35 Q×P and
wins.

| 31 R(K3)—K2 | R×R |

And now 31 ... Q×RP is met by 32 R×R, Q×R; 33
R—QB1, Q—KB4; 34 R—B8 ch, R—Q1 (if 34 ... B—
Q1; 35 Q×R); 35 Q—B6 forcing mate, or in this 33 ...
Q—Q6; 34 R—B8 ch, B—Q1; 35 Q×Q, R×Q; 36 B—
Kt5 and wins.

32 R×R	Q—Kt8 ch
33 K—Kt2	B—B1
34 B—B4	P—R3
35 P—KR4	P—Kt5
36 Q—K4	

All Lasker's ingenious attacks have failed against his
opponent's accurate defence and he now winds the game
up to a draw.

| 36 ... | Q×Q |
| 37 R×Q | K—Kt2 |

J. R. CAPABLANCA

38 R—B4	B—B4
39 K—B3	P—Kt4
40 P×P	P×P

Draw agreed.

Tenth Match Game

White: Dr. E. Lasker. Black: J. R. Capablanca.

1 P—Q4	P—Q4
2 P—QB4	P—K3
3 Kt—QB3	Kt—KB3
4 B—Kt5	B—K2
5 P—K3	Castles
6 Kt—B3	QKt—Q2
7 Q—B2	

Nowadays it is generally recognized that this move leads only to equality. Preferable is 7 R—B1 after which Black cannot safely advance P—QB4, or the Exchange variation 7 P×P.

7 ...	P—B4
8 R—Q1	Q—R4
9 B—Q3	

Threatening B×P ch.

9 ...	P—KR3
10 B—R4	BP×P
11 KP×P	P×P
12 B×P	Kt—Kt3
13 B—QKt3	B—Q2
14 Castles	QR—B1
15 Kt—K5	

Here 15 Q—K2 unpinning the Queen's Knight is suggested by Golombek, but it seems that Black gets a good game by 15 ... Q—R4.

15 ...   B—Kt4

16 KR—K1

Threatening 17 Kt—Kt6 followed, if 17 ... P×Kt, by 18 R×P.

16 ...   QKt—Q4

16 ... KKt—Q4 would have been safer in view of the continuation shown in the following note.

BLACK

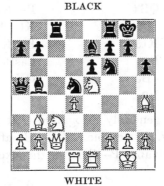

WHITE

Here the Hungarian master, Breyer, gave the following remarkable continuation, which appears to give White the better game: 17 B×KKt, B×B (if 17 ... Kt×B; 18 Kt—Kt6, R—K1 (if 18 ... P×Kt, R×P recovers the piece with a winning position); 19 R×P, P×R; 20 B×P ch, K—R2; 21 Kt—B8 dis. ch, K—R1; 22 Q—R7 ch, Kt×Q; 23 Kt—Kt6 mate); 18 B×Kt, P×B; 19 Kt—Kt4, B—Kt4 best; 20 P—B4, B×P; 21 Q—B5, B—Kt4; 22 Q×P, P—QR3; 23 P—QR4, QR—Q1; 24 Q—KB5, P—KKt3; 25 Q—K5, KR—K1; 26 Kt—B6 ch, B×Kt; 27 Q×B and the powerful passed QP gives White the advantage.

17 KB×Kt   Kt×B

18	B×B	Kt×B
19	Q—Kt3	B—B3
20	Kt×B	P×Kt

As a result of these exchanges White's chances of King's side attack are reduced to a minimum and his isolated **QP** proves weaker than Black's **QBP**. From now onwards White is fighting for a draw.

21	R—K5	Q—Kt3
22	Q—B2	KR—Q1
23	Kt—K2	

Against 23 Kt—R4, Black continues 23 ... Q—B2; 24 R—B5 (not 24 Kt—B5, R×P); 24 ... Kt—B4; 25 R—B4, R—Q3; 26 Kt—B3, Q—Kt3 with a strong attack on the QP.

| 23 ... | R—Q4 |
| 24 R×R | |

This exchange removes Black's only weakness. 24 R—K3 seems rather more promising. If then 24 ... Kt—B4; 25 R(K3)—Q3, QR—Q1; 26 P—KR3.

24 ...	BP×R
25	Q—Q2	Kt—B4
26	P—QKt3	P—KR4
27	P—KR3	

It would seem better to force an exchange of Knights by 27 Kt—Kt3, Kt×Kt; 28 RP×Kt, and if 28 ... Q—B2; 29 K—B1, Q—B7; 30 P—B3 but Black still retains the advantage owing to his domination of the QB file.

| 27 ... | P—R5 |

Very well played, ensuring that the Knight shall remain undisturbed as long as he wishes.

| 28 | Q—Q3 | R—B3 |
| 29 | K—B1 | P—Kt3 |

| 30 Q—Kt1 | Q—Kt5 |
| 31 K—Kt1 | |

White cannot form a plan of campaign and can only mark time.

| 31 ... | P—R4 |

Again a fine piece of strategy. Black will now force another weak isolated pawn on the Queen's wing. From now to the end Capablanca's play is a model.

| 32 Q—Kt2 | P—R5 |
| 33 Q—Q2 | |

Hoping to obtain relief by an exchange of Queens. The alternative 33 R—Q3 does not seem any better.

33 ...	Q×Q
34 R×Q	P×P
35 P×P	R—Kt3
36 R—Q3	

If 36 R—Kt2, R—Kt5 wins a pawn.

| 36 ... | R—R3 |

Now Black cannot be prevented from bringing his Rook to the rear of the White pawns.

37 P—KKt4	P×P e.p.
38 P×P	R—R7
39 Kt—B3	R—QB7
40 Kt—Q1	Kt—K2

The Knight has fulfilled his purpose on KB4 and now comes to join the attack on the QKtP.

41 Kt—K3	R—B8 ch
42 K—B2	Kt—B3
43 Kt—Q1	

With this Lasker lays a subtle trap into which his opponent declines to fall.

BLACK

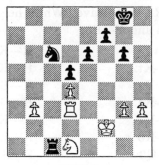

WHITE

For if now 43 ... Kt—Kt5; 44 R—Q2, R—Kt8; 45 Kt—Kt2, R×Kt; 46 R×R, Kt—Q6 ch; 47 K—K2, Kt×R; 48 K—Q2, White wins the Black Knight and remains with the superior game owing to his outside passed pawn. Black, however, can win the KtP by other means.

43 ...	R—Kt8
44 K—K2	

Possibly a slip, but it does not make much difference for if 44 K—K1, Kt—R4 wins the QKtP. In this case, however, Black would have to exchange Rooks.

44 ...	R×P
45 K—K3	R—Kt5

Capablanca prefers to keep the Rooks on the board, which probably makes his task easier. It would seem, however, that the Knight ending would also be won as Black could not ultimately be prevented from playing P—B3 and P—K4.

46 Kt—B3	Kt—K2
47 Kt—K2	Kt—B4 ch
48 K—B2	P—Kt4
49 P—Kt4	Kt—Q3
50 Kt—Kt1	Kt—K5 ch

51 K—B1

If 51 K—K3, R—Kt7, leaves White helpless against the threat of P—B4 and P—B5.

51 . . .	R—Kt8 ch
52 K—Kt2	R—Kt7 ch
53 K—B1	R—B7 ch
54 K—K1	R—QR7
55 K—B1	K—Kt2
56 R—K3	K—Kt3
57 R—Q3	P—B3

Black is now ready for the decisive advance of the KP which will ensure a passed pawn in the centre.

58 R—K3	K—B2
59 R—Q3	K—K2
60 R—K3	K—Q3
61 R—Q3	R—B7 ch
62 K—K1	R—KKt7
63 K—B1	R—QR7
64 R—K3	P—K4

The object of Black's last moves was to bring the White Rook to K3 instead of Q3 so that he can answer Kt—K2 by Kt—Q7 ch.

65 R—Q3	P×P
66 R×P	K—B4
67 R—Q1	P—Q5
68 R—B1 ch	K—Q4
Resigns	

Further resistance would be frivolous. A fine example of Capablanca's perfect technique which gave Lasker no opportunity of producing any of his characteristic complications.

For my notes to this game I am much indebted to the excellent analysis by Gerald Abrahams in his book *The Chess Mind*.

ELEVENTH MATCH GAME

White: J. R. Capablanca. Black: Dr. E. Lasker.

1	P—Q4	P—Q4
2	Kt—KB3	P—K3
3	P—B4	Kt—KB3
4	B—Kt5	QKt—Q2
5	P—K3	B—K2
6	Kt—B3	Castles
7	R—B1	R—K1

A poor move which not only loses time but creates a serious weakness at KB2 in certain variations. It is now well known that 7 ... P—B3; 8 B—Q3, P×P; 9 B×P, Kt—Q4; 10 B×B, Q×B, and if 11 Kt—K4, KKt—B3; 12 Kt—Kt3, P—K4 gives Black approximate equality.

8	Q—B2	P—B3
9	B—Q3	P×P
10	B×BP	Kt—Q4
11	B×B	R×B

Lasker evidently intends to adopt an idea of Steinitz and bring his Queen's Bishop, the development of which is the great problem of this opening, to K1.

After 12 ... Q×B; 13 Kt—K4, it is not easy for Black to force the liberating move P—K4 without disadvantage as 13 ... KKt—B3; 14 Kt—Kt3, P—K4 can be met by 15 Kt—Kt5, Q—Kt5 ch; 16 Q—Q2, Q×Q ch; 17 K×Q, Kt—Q4; 18 P—K4, etc.

12	Castles	Kt—B1
13	KR—Q1	B—Q2
14	P—K4	Kt—QKt3

14 ... Kt×Kt would give a slight relief to his cramped position.

15 B—B1

An excellent post for the Bishop.

15 ...		R—B1
16	P—QKt4	

Preventing the liberating P—QB4 and ensuring an advantage on the Queen's wing.

16 ...		B—K1
17	Q—Kt3	KR—B2
18	P—QR4	Kt—Kt3
19	P—R5	Kt—Q2
20	P—K5	

In order to bring the Knight *via* K4 to Q6, but the course of the game suggests that White may have overestimated the strength of this manœuvre. 20 P—Kt3 preventing Black's Kt—B5 would have maintained the bind on Black's position and retains the possibility of an alternative attack by Kt—K5 and P—KB4.

20 ...		P—Kt3
21	Kt—K4	R—Kt1
22	Q—B3	

At first sight this seems to lose a move (cf. his 24th move), but 22 Q—R3 could be met by 22 ... Q—K2; 23 Kt—Q6, P—QB4, with counter chances.

22 ...		Kt—B5
23	Kt—Q6	Kt—Q4
24	Q—R3	P—B3

A very good move which undermines the position of the Knight at Q6, and greatly relieves Black's position. The threat is 25 BP×P followed by Kt×KP.

25 Kt×B

It must have been with great reluctance that White parted with his beautifully-placed Knight. The only advantage left is a minute weakness in Black's pawn skeleton.

25 ...		Q×Kt

Position after 24 Q—R3

BLACK

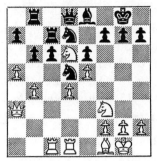

WHITE

26	KP×P	P×BP
27	P—Kt5	R(Kt1)—B1
28	P×BP	R×P
29	R×R	R×R
30	P×P	P×P
31	R—K1	

Threatening B—Kt5 followed by Q—Q6. Black's reply enables him to defend his weak KP by Kt—B1.

31	...	Q—QB1
32	Kt—Q2	Kt—B1
33	Kt—K4	Q—Q1
34	P—R4	R—B2
35	Q—QKt3	R—KKt2
36	P—Kt3	R—R2
37	B—B4	

Threatening 38 B×Kt, P×B; 39 Q×P, Q×Q; 40 Kt×P ch.

37	...	R—R4
38	Kt—B3	Kt×Kt

White must have been glad to see the end of this powerful Knight.

39	Q×Kt	K—B2
40	Q—K3	Q—Q3
41	Q—K4	R—R5

So far Black has defended his cramped position with true Lasker pertinacity, but here he makes a serious mistake. It was essential to defend the second rank by 41 ... R—R2. If then 42 P—Q5, P×P; 43 B×P ch, K—Kt2; 44 Q—Kt4 ch, K—R3 with a defensible game.

	42 Q—Kt7 ch	K—Kt3

When he made his 41st move Black probably overlooked that he could not now play 42 ... Q—K2 on account of 43 Q—B6, R moves; 44 P—Q5 and wins.

	43 Q—B8	Q—Kt5

This loses in a few moves. The only possible defence lay in 43 ... K—B2; 44 P—Q5, P—K4, but after 45 B—Kt5, R—R2 (best); 46 Q—K8 ch, there is not much hope for Black.

	44 R—QB1	Q—K2

If 44 ... K—B2; 45 P—Q5 is decisive.

45	B—Q3 ch	K—R3
46	R—B7	R—R8 ch
47	K—Kt2	Q—Q3
48	Q×Kt ch	Resigns

A pretty finish.

TWELFTH MATCH GAME

White: Dr. E. Lasker. Black: J. R. Capablanca.

1	P—K4	P—K4
2	Kt—KB3	Kt—QB3
3	B—Kt5	Kt—B3
4	Castles	P—Q3
5	P—Q4	B—Q2

106

6 Kt—B3	B—K2
7 R—K1	P×P
8 Kt×P	Castles
9 B—B1	

Recommended by Dr. Tarrasch who continued with 10 P—QKt3 and 11 B—Kt2. Its chief merit is that it avoids the exchanges associated with the normal 9 B×Kt, and was, no doubt, chosen by Lasker for that reason. At this stage of the match it was essential for him to force a win.

| 9 ... | R—K1 |
| 10 P—B3 | B—KB1 |

After this Black's game becomes very difficult. The best line was played by Capablanca himself in a subsequent game against Dr. Euwe (London, 1922): 10 ... Kt×Kt; 11 Q×Kt, B—K3; 12 Q—B2 (if 12 P—QKt3, Kt—Q2 followed by B—B3); 12 ... P—B3; 13 B—Q2, Q—Kt3, with easy equality.

| 11 B—KKt5 | P—KR3 |
| 12 B—R4 | P—KKt3 |

Apparently very risky, but it is difficult to find a satisfactory line. 12 ... P—KKt4 is possible but involves a serious weakening of the King's defences.

BLACK

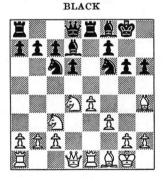

WHITE

13 Kt—Q5

This leads to a configuration probably unique in master chess which, apart from anything else, makes this game well worthy of preservation. A good alternative is 13 Kt×Kt, P×Kt (13 ... B×Kt; 14 P—K5 is inferior); 14 P—K5, P—Kt4 (obviously he loses a piece if he takes the KP); 15 P×Kt, P×B; 16 Q—Q4 with a fine position. Sir G. A. Thomas suggests here 16 ... Q—Kt1, which can be answered by 17 R×R, Q×R (if 17 ... B×R; 18 Q—Kt4 ch, K—R1; 19 B—Q3 with a winning attack); 18 Q×KRP, Q—K6 ch; 19 K—R1, P—Q4; 20 R—K1, with a pawn ahead and the superior position.

13 ...	B—Kt2
14 Kt—Kt5	

14 P—KB4 would be met by 14 ... P—KKt4; 15 P×P, Kt×P.

14 ...	P—Kt4
15 Kt(Q5)×P	P×B
16 Kt×QR	Q×Kt
17 Kt—B7	

Stronger seems 17 Q×P, threatening both P—K5 and Kt—B7. If Black replies 17 ... Q—Kt1; 18 P—K5, Q×Q; 19 P×Q with very strong pawns.

17 ...	Q—Q1
18 Kt×R	Kt×Kt

White has two Rooks and three pawns against three minor pieces which, calculated in units, amounts to a considerable material advantage. The configuration of the forces, however, makes this type of calculation of little material value and White finds it impossible to maintain his Queen's side pawns.

19 R—Kt1	B—K3
20 P—B3	

He must guard the square Q4. If 20 P—QKt3, for instance,
20 ... Q—R4; 21 P—QR4, Q—B4 ch; 22 K—R1, B—B6;
23 R—K2, Kt—Q5 with a dominating position. White's
Rooks are quite powerless against the swarming minor
pieces.

20 ...		B×RP
21 R—R1		B—K3

Not, of course, 21 ... Q—Kt3 ch; 22 K—R1, Q×P;
23 R—K2.

22 Q—Q2		P—R3
23 Q—KB2		P—KR4

Capablanca thought for over an hour before playing this
move. The position has become difficult for him, as White,
having secured his position, is ready for an attack by
P—KB4, and QR—Q1 followed possibly by R—K3, P—B5
and R—R3, etc. The text move weakens his rearmost KRP
but has the great merit of opening a new diagonal for his
King's Bishop whence it can attack the KBP after it has
played to B4.

24 P—KB4

White has no other means of carrying on the attack.

24 ...		B—R3
25 B—K2		

If 25 P—B5, B—Kt6; 26 B—K2, Kt—K4; 27 P—KR3
(he must prevent Kt—Kt5); 27 ... Q—Kt4 followed by
Kt—KB3 with a good game. 25 QR—Q1 is met by 25 ...
Q—B3.

25 ...   Kt—B3

Taking immediate advantage of the chance to exchange one
of his doubled Rook's pawns for White's more valuable
King's pawn. The loss of a pawn on the Queen's side is of
minor importance.

26 Q×P

There is nothing better.

26 ...	Kt×P
27 Q×Q ch	Kt×Q
28 B×QRP	P—Q4
29 B—K2	

If 29 B—Q3, Kt—B4; 30 B—K2, B×P, but not 29 ...
B×P; 30 B×Kt, P×B; 31 R—R8, B—Kt4; 32 R—Q1
and wins.

29 ...	B×P
30 B×P	B—B2
31 QR—Q1	

Draw agreed

There is, of course, plenty of play left in the game, but
it is impossible to say that either side has the advantage,
or even to suggest probable continuations. Capablanca's
play in the later stages was extremely accurate.

CHAPTER III

DR. ALEXANDER ALEKHINE

PAUL MORPHY used to be described as "The pride and the sorrow of chess." Alekhine may, in the same way, be be called its pride and shame; its pride for his splendid performances and the sheer beauty of his best games, and its shame on account of the weakening of moral fibre which led him into collaboration with the Nazis and, finally, to a miserable death, under obscure circumstances, in the most remote corner of Europe.

Alekhine was born in Russia of an aristocratic family in 1892. He played a good deal of chess as a schoolboy, chiefly by correspondence, and achieved sufficient prominence in his own country to be admitted into the Carlsbad International Tournament of 1911. Here he tied for eighth and ninth places, a good performance for so young a player, and displayed a vigour and originality in attack which made so good a judge as Amos Burn predict a bright future for him. In 1912 he won a tournament at Stockholm and one year later tied with Niemzovitch for the All Russian Championship. By far his best performance of his early years was his 3rd to Lasker and Capablanca in the St. Petersburg Tournament, above such famous players as Rubinstein, Tarrasch, Niemzovitch and Bernstein, to say nothing of the two British veterans J. H. Blackburne and I. Gunsberg. In these early days his *forte* was combination. He was always the young man in a hurry. Not for him the search for long and profound strategical plans when it was often possible by sheer analytical ability to evolve a sequence of moves ending in a decisive smash-up of the position. In consequence of this style he fared badly against the great strategists Lasker and Capablanca, but was often able to bring off surprises against the other masters, who were taken off their guard by the originality and vigour of his attacks.

When war broke out Alekhine was playing in a Tournament at Mannheim, in Germany, and was placed in an internment camp. He managed to escape, reached his own country after a series of exciting adventures, and joined the army. On the conclusion of hostilities he left Russia, reached Paris and soon became a naturalized French citizen. He also entered himself as a student at the Sorbonne where he was awarded a doctorate. He now decided to make chess his profession and soon ran up a remarkable series of tournament successes the chief of which are set out later in this biography. He soon established his position as the leading tournament player in the world, but he always had to play second fiddle to Capablanca on the few occasions on which they met. His style had matured considerably since the pre-war years and he had greatly improved his endgames, but he was still primarily a combinative player and the pundits shook their heads over his chances of winning six games against the invincible Capablanca. No combinative ability, however brilliant, they said, could beat that perfect technique. Still, on the virtual retirement of Lasker he was the only possible challenger, and in 1927 the match was arranged. A great surprise was in store. Alekhine had completely changed his style. Unknown to anyone he had secretly worked out a new approach to chess, and he went into the field a strategist equal to Capablanca himself, with greater vitality and physical vigour and possibly greater analytical powers. It must have required tremendous strength of character to change so utterly a style which had paid him so many dividends and, above all, to keep it secret from friends and foes alike.

Alekhine proved a busy champion. Almost as soon as he

returned from the match he recommenced his tournament round with even greater success than before. His best games at this period were models of all that is best in modern chess.

In the 1930's I knew him well and was his close companion in many an international event both in England and abroad. He was excellent company and full of good stories about his fellow-masters, all completely unmalicious. An excellent trait in his character was the generous praise he was always willing to bestow on any fine performance by one of his rivals. For instance, he described the game played by the British Champion, Yates, against Vidmar at San Remo, as "the greatest game since the war"; high praise indeed from one who had himself created so many beautiful specimens of the chess art.

The quality which specially endeared him to me in those days was his genuine devotion to chess. "You call me Grand Master," he said to me one evening in Prague. "I am not Grand Master, I am not even master. Chess will always be master of me and of all of us." Another thing which drew us together was a common passion for cats. He brought his beautiful Siamese to the Warsaw Team Tournament, where it became a regular *habitué* of the congress rooms. At first it caused a good deal of consternation but soon everyone loved the pretty furry little thing, with its plaintive "mew mew" when it thought it was not receiving sufficient attention.

As an opponent over the board Alekhine was rather nerve-racking. A restless soul, he could never keep still. When he had made his move he paced round the table like a caged tiger, looking at the position from every angle, and when it was his turn to play he sat glaring at the board as if he would see through it, twiddling all the while at a lock of hair which hung over his forehead. He also had an irritating habit of transferring to his pocket any box of matches which might be left unguarded in the vicinity of the chess board. These, however, were very minor peccadilloes, and we all admired and loved him.

The most serious blot on his character in these days in the 'thirties was his evasive attitude in regard to Capablanca's repeated challenges for a return Championship match. The abortive negotiations between the two were conducted with such acrimony that eventually the two great players were not on speaking terms, a state of affairs which did a good deal of harm to the cause of chess, and unpleasantness to those who, like myself, were friends with both of them. For this Alekhine was not solely to be blamed, but there was no doubt that he was primarily responsible as he had promised Capablanca a return match as one of the conditions of the previous encounter.

Alekhine's two matches with Bogoljubov and his match and return match with Euwe are dealt with later in this book. Of his activities during the war I will say nothing. His lamentable association with the Nazis is unfortunately too well known, and is too painful to discuss here. He died at Lisbon in 1946.

Alekhine's principal tournament successes were: Stockholm 1912, 1st; St. Petersburg 1914, 3rd; Triberg, Budapest and Hague 1921, 1st; London 1922, 2nd to Capablanca; New York 1924, 3rd to Lasker and Capablanca; New York 1927, 2nd to Capablanca; San Remo 1930, 1st, with the extraordinary score of thirteen wins and two draws; Bled 1931, 1st; Berne 1932, 1st; London 1932, 1st; Zürich 1934, 1st; Dresden 1936, 1st; an amazing and unequalled record which is by no means complete as only absolutely first-class master tournaments are included. Apart from World Championship encounters, he did not favour set matches, the only one of importance being a victory over Dr. Euwe by three games to two with five draws in 1926-7.

114

The Alekhine v. Capablanca Match

This match, played at Buenos Aires in 1927, was by far
the most sternly contested struggle in the history of the
World Championship. The conditions were the familiar
ones—the first to win six games to be the victor, but no
less than thirty-four games had to be played before this
result was reached. Alekhine caused general surprise by
winning the first game with the Black pieces, but Capablanca soon equalized and then took the lead by winning
the seventh. After this Alekhine played almost perfect
chess for game after game, slight weaknesses began to appear
in Capablanca's play, and after twenty-eight games the
challenger led by four games to two. Capablanca roused
the fading hopes of his spectators by winning the twenty-
ninth , but Alekhine struck back in the thirty-second and
finally clinched matters in the thirty-fourth a desperately
drawn-out struggle extending over eighty moves. As was
to be expected with two such protagonists, the general
standard of play was very high, but the match is marred
by a number of short draws, agreed upon just after the
opening, when the players were disinclined to struggle.
There is no disputing the right of chess players to agree to
draws when they wish, but such games are travesties of
chess and hardly fair to spectators, who may have travelled
long distances and paid considerable sums of money to
watch a match and then find that all there is to see is a
dozen or so "book" moves.

First Match Game

White: J. R. Capablanca. Black: Dr. A. Alekhine.

1	P—K4	P—K3
2	P—Q4	P—Q4
3	Kt—QB3	B—Kt5

Winaver's variation which has now achieved great popu-

larity owing to its consistent adoption by the present
World Champion, M. Botvinnik. It gives Black more
chances of counter-play than the conventional 3 ...
Kt—KB3.

4 P×P

After this White can expect no advantage from the opening. It is now generally agreed that 4 P—K5 is the only
move to yield lasting pressure. The text, however, is quite
consistent with Capablanca's general policy of keeping the
game as simple as possible in the opening, and relying
on his superb judgment in the later stages to produce the
required results.

4 ...	P×P
5 B—Q3	Kt—QB3
6 Kt—K2	KKt—K2
7 Castles	B—KB4
8 B×B	Kt×B
9 Q—Q3	Q—Q2
10 Kt—Q1	

The natural move here is 9 B—B4 to which Alekhine says
that he would have replied 9 ... Castles QR, after which
could follow 10 Kt—Kt5, B—Q3 (if 10 ... Kt—Q3; 11
P—QR3 with advantage); 11 Kt×B ch, Kt×Kt; 12
P—QB3, and both players have chances in a pawn advance
against the opponent's castled position.

10 ...	Castles KR
11 Kt—K3	Kt×Kt
12 B×Kt	KR—K1
13 Kt—B4	B—Q3

Inviting the continuation 14 Kt×P, B×P ch; 15 K×B,
Q×Kt after which White's King is exposed to an attack
by Black's heavy pieces.

14 KR—K1

Capablanca clearly under-estimates the strength of Black's next move. 14 P—QB3 was necessary here.

14 ...	Kt—Kt5

BLACK

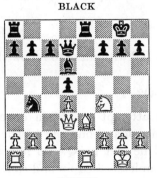

WHITE

15 Q—Kt3	

Better was 15 Q—Q2, Q—B4; 16 KR—QB1 against which Alekhine gives 16 ... P—KR4 followed by R—K5 and P—R5, with positional advantage for Black.

15 ...	Q—B4
16 QR—B1	

After this Black wins a pawn by a nice combination. The only chance lay in submitting to the doubled isolated pawns by 16 Kt—Q3.

16 ...	Kt×BP

The proper sequence. Neither 16 ... B×Kt; 17 Q×Kt nor 16 ... Kt×RP; 17 Q×Kt, B×Kt; 18 B×B, Q×B; 19 Q×QP leads to anything.

17 R×Kt	Q×Kt

The point of the combination. After 17 ... B×Kt; 18 R—B5 White recovers his pawn with an improved position.

18 P—Kt3	Q—B4

19 QR—K2	P—QKt3
20 Q—Kt5	P—KR4
21 P—KR4	

It is absolutely necessary to stop the further advance of the KRP.

| 21 ... | R—K5 |

Threatening R × RP with mate to follow the capture of the Rook.

22 B—Q2

An ingenious attempt to obtain counter-play by the temporary sacrifice of a second pawn. The purely defensive 22 Q—Q3 could be met by Q—B6 followed by QR—K1 and White is completely tied up and can only wait for the kill.

22 ...	R × QP
23 B—B3	R—Q6
24 B—K5	

After this White seems bound to win back one of his lost pawns. If 24 ... B × B; 25 R × B, Q—B6; 26 Q—B6, etc.

24 ...	R—Q1
25 B × B	R × B
26 R—K5	Q—B6
27 R × RP	Q × R

Of course not 27 ... R—K3; 28 Q—K8 ch followed by mate.

28 R—K8 ch	K—R2
29 Q × R ch	Q—Kt3
30 Q—Q1	R—K3

A fine idea which involves the sacrifice of a second pawn in order to utilize the passed Queen's pawn, combined with an attack by Queen and Rook. If White exchanges Rooks, the Queen ending is hopeless for him, as the Black King is

sufficiently protected against checks and the QP advances
to Queen.

31	R—QR8	R—K4

So as to bring the Queen behind the Rook and force an
entry to the seventh or eighth ranks when required.

32	R×P	P—QB4
33	R—Q7	Q—K3
34	Q—Q3 ch	P—Kt3
35	R—Q8	P—Q5
36	P—R4	

It matters little what White plays now. If 36 Q—KB3 with
the object of Q—R8; 36 ... R—B4; 37 Q—Q1, Q×P.

36	...	R—K8 ch

Alekhine points out that he could have won a Rook here
by 36 ... Q—K2; 37 R—QKt8, Q—B2; 38 Q—Kt3,
R—K3; 39 R—QR8, Q—Kt2 threatening mate by R—
K8 ch. The line chosen is equally decisive.

37	K—Kt2	Q—B3 ch
38	P—B3	R—K6
39	Q—Q1	Q—K3
40	P—KKt4	R—K7 ch
41	K—R3	Q—K6
42	Q—KR1	Q—B5

A neat finish. White has no answer to the threat of
R—KB7.

42	P—KR5	R—KB7
	Resigns	

This game was played with great power by Alekhine and
proved a forerunner of things to come. It destroyed once
and for all the legend of Capablanca's invincibility which
had sprung up since his match with Lasker and the New
York Tournament of 1927. Capablanca's play showed
signs of lack of practice and his famous position judgment

was less acute than usual, especially in the early middle game.

To Alekhine the result must have been stimulating to the highest degree as it was the first occasion on which he had ever beaten the great Cuban, and it was especially encouraging that he accomplished the feat with the Black pieces.

SEVENTH MATCH GAME

White: J. R. Capablanca. Black: Dr. A. Alekhine.

1	P—Q4		P—Q4
2	P—QB4		P—K3
3	Kt—KB3		QKt—Q2
4	Kt—B3		KKt—B3
5	B—Kt5		P—B3
6	P—K3		Q—R4

Alekhine had prepared the Cambridge Springs Defence for this match with a view to surprising Capablanca. It had never been a favourite with him in his earlier games.

7	Kt—Q2		B—Kt5
8	Q—B2		Castles

In later games Alekhine continued with 8 ... P×P which yields Black the advantage of two Bishops but gives White a powerful position in the centre. In my view the text is quite satisfactory if correctly followed up.

9 B—R4

A novelty which seems neither better nor worse than the customary 9 B—K2. It may lead to a simple transposition.

9 ...   P—B4

This is not the best reply. There seems no objection to the customary liberating move: 9 ... P—K4; 10 P×P, Kt—K5; 11 KKt×Kt, P×Kt. Alekhine may possibly have been afraid of the continuation 12 P—K6 but this can apparently be met by 12 ... Kt—B4; 13 P×P ch, R×P; 14 B—K2, Kt—Q6 ch; 15 B×Kt, P×B; and if 16 Q×P, B—B4; 17 Q—Q2, R—Q2; 18 Q—B1, B—Q6 with a winning attack. White might do a little better with 16 Q—Q2 instead of 16 Q×P but after 16 ... B—B4 Black could hardly lose the game.

10 Kt—Kt3	Q—R5

This results in the loss of a pawn, but was probably intentional as 10 ... Q—B2; 11 B—Kt3, Q—Kt3; 12 P—QR3, B×Kt ch; 13 P×B leaves Black with a poor game. As played he is able to hamper White's development for some time.

11 B×Kt	Kt×B
12 QP×P	Kt—K5
13 P×P	B×Kt ch
14 P×B	Kt×P(B5)

14 ... P×P is met with 15 B—Q3 after which Black has no compensation for the sacrificed pawn.

15 R—Q1	

Best. If 15 P×P, B×P; 16 Kt—Q4, Q×Q; 17 Kt×Q, Kt—K5, Black will eventually recover his pawn.

15 ...	P×P
16 R×P	Kt×Kt

Forced. If 16 ... P—QKt3; 17 R—Q4 and 18 Kt×Kt.

17 P×Kt	Q—B3
18 R—Q4	KR—K1
19 B—Q3	

Very well played. Although White's King is confined to the centre of the board he is quite safe there, and the pieces soon take up attacking positions. The alternative 19 Q—Q2 intending P—B3 is too slow on account of 19 ... B—K3; 20 P—QB4, P—QR4 followed by P—R5 with good counter chances.

19 ...	Q×KtP
20 B×P ch	K—B1
21 B—K4	Q—R6
22 Q—Q2	

A wise precaution. In some variations Black threatens
R×P ch. For instance, 22 R—Kt1, B—K3; 23 B×P (23
P—QB4 is better); 23 ... R—Kt1; 24 B—Q5, B×B;
25 R×B, R×P ch; 26 P×R, Q×P ch; 27 K—B1, Q—
B6 ch and wins.

| 22 ... | B—K3 |
| 23 P—QB4 | P—R4 |

Black's best chance is a break through by P—R5.

24 R—Kt1

BLACK

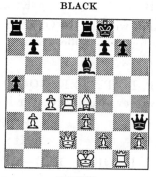

WHITE

24 ...   Q×RP

It is very dangerous to allow White the open KR file,
but it is difficult to find an alternative line. He cannot
play 24 ... P—R5 because of 25 Q—Kt4 ch and 26 P×P,
while if he makes the preliminary move 25 ... K—Kt1,
White obtains a strong attack by 26 Q—Kt2 threatening
R—Q5 and R—KKt5.

122

25 R—R1	Q—B2
26 Q—Kt2	

Threatening immediate destruction by R—R8 ch and Q—R3 ch.

26 ...	Q—B4
27 B—Q5	R—R3

If 27 ... B×B; 28 R×B, Q—Kt5 ch; 29 K—B1, P—B3; 30 R—Q7 (threatening Q×P ch), and wins.

28 R—K4	R—Q3

Black is lost now. For instance, 28 ... Q—Kt5 ch; 29 K—B1, P—R5; 30 R—R7 and wins.

29 R—R7	K—K2

If 30 ... P—KKt3; 31 Q—B6, or if 30 ... P—B3; 31 R—R8 ch wins a piece.

30 Q×P	K—Q1
31 B×B	P×B
32 Q×P	

Threatening mate by Q—R8 ch, and Q×P ch.

32 ...	Q—Kt5 ch
33 Q×Q	P×Q
34 P—B5	R—B3
35 R×KtP	R×P
36 R—QR7	Resigns

White can force the exchange of both Rooks. Alekhine lost the game through his inferior opening. Capablanca's remorseless style was seen at its best in the closing stages.

TWENTY-FIRST MATCH GAME

White: J. R. Capablanca. Black: Dr. A. Alekhine.

1 P—Q4	P—Q4
2 P—QB4	P—K3
3 Kt—QB3	Kt—KB3
4 B—Kt5	QKt—Q2

123

5 P—K3	B—K2
6 Kt—B3	Castles
7 R—B1	P—QR3

Alekhine played this move in eight games of the match, winning one and drawing seven. It was not until the twenty-third game that Capablanca chose the right reply, 8 P×P, after which 7 ... P—QR3 is revealed as loss of time.

| 8 P—QR3 | P—R3 |

An important move in this position. In some variations the possibility of playing P—KKt4 is useful for Black.

9 B—R4	P×P
10 B×P	P—QKt4
11 B—K2	

The alternative is 11 B—R2 with the idea of an attack along the long diagonal with B—Kt1 and Q—B2. Black can, of course, defend himself, but on the whole the line offers White more chances than the tame text move.

| 11 ... | B—Kt2 |
| 12 Castles | |

If now 12 ... P—QKt4 to hold back Blacks QBP, Black gets good counter-play by 12 ... P—QR4.

12 ...	P—B4
13 P×P	Kt×P
14 Kt—Q4	

The attempt to win a pawn by 14 B×Kt, B×B; 15 Kt×KtP loses material after 15 ... Q×Q; 16 KR×Q, Kt—Kt6; 17 R—B7, B×Kt; 18 B×B, P×Kt. White has failed to secure the slightest advantage in the opening and, as often happens in such cases, gradually drifts into inferiority.

| 14 ... | QR—B1 |
| 15 P—QKt4 | |

As will be seen later, this move seriously weakens the

square at White's QB4. Better was 15 B—B3, Q—Kt3;
16 B×B, Q×B; 17 Q—K2. The manner in which Alekhine
takes advantage of his opponent's slight inexactitude is a
model of position play.

15 ...	QKt—Q2
16 B—Kt3	Kt—Kt3
17 Q—Kt3	KKt—Q4

17 ... Kt—B5 at once would not be good on account of
18 KR—Q1 followed by P—QR4. The excellent text move
threatens to obtain a stranglehold on the vital square by
Kt×Kt and B—Q4.

18 B—B3	R—B5

Another fine positional move which makes way for the
Queen either at QB1 or QR1. Again 18 ... Kt—B5 would
be premature on account of 19 Kt×Kt, B×Kt; 20 B×B,
if 20 ... Q×B; 21 KR—Q1.

19 Kt—K4	Q—B1

BLACK

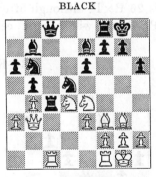

WHITE

20 R×R	

Alekhine considers this to have been White's decisive
positional error and suggests instead 20 Q—Kt1, R—Q1;
21 Kt—Q2, with the continuation 21 ... R×R; 22 R×R,
Q—R1; 23 B—B7.

20 ...	Kt × R
21 R—B1	Q—R1

Threatening Kt × KtP or Kt × KP.

22 Kt—B3

22 Kt—B5 would lead to the loss of a pawn by 22 ...
B × Kt; 23 P × B, R—QB1; 24 B—K2, R × P; 25 B × Kt,
Q—QB1.

22 ...	R—B1
23 Kt × Kt	B × Kt
24 B × B	Q × B
25 P—QR4	

This has been condemned by some annotators but it is hard
to suggest an alternative method of coping with Black's
threat of B—B3 followed by B—Kt7, or R—Q1 and
Q—Q6.

25 ...	B—B3
26 Kt—B3	

Slightly better is 26 P × P, although after 26 ... B × Kt;
27 P × B, P × P, Black will almost certainly win the
isolated QP.

26 ...	B—Kt7

BLACK

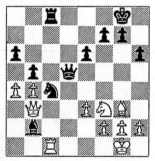

WHITE

A fine move which enables the KP to advance without obstructing the Bishop. White's reply is the best available.

>27 R—K1

Against other Rook moves Alekhine gives the following fine variations—

(*A*) 27 R—Q1, P×P; 28 Q×P, Kt—Kt3; 29 R×Q, Kt×Q; 30 R—Q1, Kt—B6; 31 R—K1, R—B5; 32 B—Q6, Kt—K5; 33 B—K7, P—B3; 34 R—Kt1, K—B2; 35 K—B1, B—B6 with a won ending.

(*B*) 27 R—Kt1, Kt—R6; 28 Q×B, Kt×R; 29 Q×Kt, Q—Kt6; 30 Q—KB1, P×P; 31 P—KR3, P—R6 and wins.

27 ...		R—Q1
28 P×P		P×P
29 P—R3		P—K4
30 R—Kt1		P—K5
31 Kt—Q4		

Other Knight moves are equally hopeless. Alekhine gives as possibilities 31 Kt—K1, Q—Q7; 32 Q—B2, Q×Q; 33 Kt×Q, R—Q7 or 31 Kt—R2, Q—Q6; 32 R×B, Q×Q; 33 R×Q, R—Q8 ch; 34 Kt—B1, Kt—Q7 with a comfortable win for Black in either case.

31 ...		B×Kt
32 R—Q1		

This loses at once but 32 P×B, Q×P is also a clear win for Black.

32 ...		Kt×P
Resigns		

In this game Alekhine outplayed Capablanca in the latter's own speciality, positional chess.

TWENTY-NINTH MATCH GAME

White: J. R. Capablanca. Black: Dr. A. Alekhine.

1 P—Q4		P—Q4
2 P—QB4		P—K3

3 Kt—QB3	Kt—KB3
4 B—Kt5	QKt—Q2
5 P—K3	P—B3
6 Kt—B3	Q—R4
7 Kt—Q2	B—Kt5
8 Q—B2	P×P

Alekhine also played this in the eleventh game. It is safer than 8 ... Castles, which he played in the seventh game, but he has to submit to a cramped position for some time.

9 B×Kt	Kt×B
10 Kt×P	Q—B2
11 P—QR3	B—K2
12 P—KKt3	

In the eleventh game Capablanca continued with 12 B—K2, but as he followed with B—KB3, it does not make a great deal of difference.

12 ...	Castles

A possibility here is 12 ... P—QB4 as White cannot reply 13 Kt—Kt5 because of 13 ... Q—B3.

13 B—Kt2	B—Q2
14 P—QKt4	

To prevent P—QB4.

14 ...	P—QKt3

With a view to securing action on the QR file by P—QR4. The plan does not turn out well and only results in the exchange of one of his pair of Bishops, his only compensation for his cramped position. A better idea was 14 ... KR—Q1, followed by the Steinitzian 15 ... B—K1 and QR—B1, after which his position is secure at all points.

15 Castles	P—QR4

A surprising move for Alekhine to make. In his notes to the eleventh game, in which the positions are identical except that White's Bishop was on KB3 and his pawn on KKt2, Alekhine says that P—QR4 would be bad because of 16 Kt—K5, P×P; 17 Kt—QKt5 with advantage to White. He must have had second thoughts about it but such are not always best.

16	Kt—K5	P×P
17	P×P	

Capablanca rejects 17 Kt—Kt5 in favour of a simpler line. After 17 ... Q—Q1; 18 Kt×QBP, B×Kt; 19 B×B, R—QB1 or 18 Kt×B, Kt×Kt; 19 Q×P, R—QB1, Black can probably defend himself.

17	...	R×R

Or 17 ... B×P; 18 Kt—Kt5, Q—Q1; 19 B×P, R—B1; 20 KR—B1 with much the better game for White.

18	R×R	R—B1

Now 18 ... B×P; 19 Kt—Kt5 would be very bad for Black.

19	Kt×B	Q×Kt

19 ... Kt×Kt providing an extra defence to the QKtP appears slightly better.

20	Kt—R4	Q—Q1
21	Q—Kt3	Kt—Q4
22	P—Kt5	

A very strong move which forces the gain of a pawn. If Black replies 22 ... P—B4; 23 P×P, P×P; 24 R—Q1, P—B5; 25 Q—B2 threatening P—K4.

22	...	P×P
23	Q×P	R—R1
24	R—B1	R—R4
25	Q—B6	

BLACK

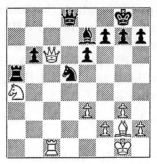

WHITE

25 ...	B—R6

If 25 ... P—QKt4; 26 Q—Kt7, B—B1; 27 R—B8, Q—Q3; 28 Kt—B5, Kt—B3; 29 B—B6, and if 29 ... P—K4; 30 B—K8, Kt×B; 31 R×Kt followed by Kt—Q7, or if in this, 28 ... R—R8 ch; 29 B—B1, Kt—B3; 30 K—Kt2, Q—Q4 ch; 31 Q×Q, P×Q; 32 B×P, winning comfortably as the QP must also fall.

26 R—Kt1	B—B1

26 ... R×Kt would be a mistake on account of 27 Q×R, Kt—B6; 28 Q×B, Kt×R; 29 Q—Kt2, trapping the Knight.

27 B×Kt	R×B
28 Kt×P	

The first phase of the game is over and White has won the QKtP. With all the pawns on the same side of the board, however, it is very difficult to bring the advantage to maturity, and Capablanca's methods deserve close study.

28 ...	R—Q3
29 Q—Kt7	P—R4
30 Kt—B4	R—Q2

130

31 Q—K4	R—B2
32 Kt—K5	Q—B1
33 K—Kt2	B—Q3
34 R—QR1	R—Kt2
35 Kt—Q3	

It is important, for the present, to conserve the Knight, which is superior to the Bishop in this type of game.

35 ...	P—Kt3
36 R—R6	B—B1
37 R—B6	R—B2

The exchange of Rooks is forced. If 37 ... Q—Kt1; 38 Kt—K5, followed by Kt×KtP, with an overwhelming mass of pawns.

38 R×R	Q×R
39 Kt—K5	

Again threatening Kt×KtP.

39 ...	B—Kt2
40 Q—R8 ch	K—R2
41 Kt—B3	

Threatening 42 Kt—Kt5 ch, and 43 P—R4 with a mating attack.

41 ...	B—B3
42 Q—R6	K—Kt2
43 Q—Q3	Q—Kt2
44 P—K4	

White's winning method is to secure a passed pawn on the Queen's file.

44 ...	Q—B3
45 P—R3	Q—B2
46 P—Q5	P×P
47 P×P	Q—B6

He has nothing better than the exchange of Queens. If 47 ... Q—Q3; 48 Q—B4 followed by Q—B6, or if 47 ...

B—K2; 48 Kt—Q4 and Kt—QKt5. The ensuing endgame is both difficult and interesting.

48	Q×Q	B×Q
49	K—B1	K—B3
50	K—K2	B—Kt5
51	Kt—Q4	B—B4
52	Kt—B6	K—B4
53	K—B3	K—B3
54	P—Kt4	

This is the only way to make any progress as his King is tied to the defence of his KBP. Against 54 K—K2, for instance, Black plays 54 ... K—B4; 55 P—B3, B—Q3.

54	...	P×P ch
55	P×P	

BLACK

WHITE

55 ...   K—Kt4

The late J. H. Blake gave 55 ... B—Q3; 56 K—K4, K—Kt4; 57 Kt—K5, P—B4 ch; 58 K—Q4, K—B5 (not 58 ... K—B3; 59 P—Kt5 ch, K—Kt2; 60 P—B4 and wins); 59 Kt—B7, B—R6; 60 P×P, P×P and draws as Black can give up his Bishop for the two White pawns. White, however, seems to win by 60 P—Kt5 instead of 60 P×P. If then 60 ... K—B6; 61 P—Q6, B×P (if 61 ...

K×P; 62 P—Q7, B—K2; 63 K—Q5 wins at once);
62 Kt×B, K×P; 63 Kt×P and wins.

	56 Kt—K5	B—Q5

A remarkable position. Black cannot avoid the loss of the
KBP. If 56 ... P—B4; 57 P—Q6, P×P ch; 58 K—Kt2
(best if 58 K—K4, B×P; 59 Kt—B7 ch, K—R5; 59
Kt×B, P—Kt6); 58 ... K—B4; 59 P—Q7, B—Kt3;
60 Kt—B6 and wins. If 56 ... P—B3; 57 Kt—B7 ch and
58 P—Q6, or if 56 ... B—R6; 57 P—Q6, K—B3; 58 P—
Q7, K—K2; 59 Kt×BP, K×P; 60 Kt—K5 ch and wins.

57	Kt×P ch	K—B3
58	Kt—Q8	B—Kt3
59	Kt—B6	B—B4
60	K—B4	

A nice *finesse*. 60 K—K2 is no use because of 60 ... K—
Kt4; 61 P—B3, K—B5, but if Black now plays 60 ...
P—Kt4 ch; 61 K—B3, followed by K—K2 and P—B3
leaves Black helpless.

60	...	B×P
61	P—Kt5 ch	K—B2
62	Kt—K5 ch	K—K2

If 62 ... K—Kt2; 63 P—Q6 and wins.

63	Kt×P ch	K—Q3
64	K—K4	B—Kt6
65	Kt—B4	K—K2
66	K—K5	B—K8
67	P—Q6 ch	K—Q2
68	P—Kt6	B—Kt5
69	K—Q5	K—K1
70	P—Q7 ch	Resigns

Capablanca showed his best form in this game and the
ending is in the nature of a classic of its kind.

Thirty-second Match Game

White: Dr. A. Alekhine.   Black: J. R. Capablanca.

1	P—Q4	P—Q4
2	P—QB4	P—K3
3	Kt—QB3	Kt—KB3
4	B—Kt5	QKt—Q2
5	P—K3	P—B3
6	P×P	KP×P
7	B—Q3	B—K2
8	KKt—K2	

A good place for the Knight which threatens to come to KB5 via KKt3. The move, however, is usually preceded by 8 Q—B2 in order to prevent the simplifying variation shown in the next note.

8 ...	Castles

A suggestion of Dr. Tartakover, 8 ... Kt—K5; 9 B×B, Kt×Kt; 10 P×Kt, Q×B, makes things a good deal easier for Black. Also 8 ... P—KR3 compelling White to commit himself with the Bishop seems preferable to the text.

9 Kt—Kt3	Kt—K1

If 9 ... P—KR3; 10 P—KR4.

10	P—KR4	QKt—B3
11	Q—B2	B—K3
12	Kt—B5	B×Kt
13	B×B	Kt—Q3
14	B—Q3	P—KR3
15	B—B4	

15 Castles QR looks tempting here as Black cannot safely take the Bishop, but Alekhine considered that there were dangers in the counter-attack 15 ... P—QKt4.

15 ...	R—B1

This is a tactical error which enables White to obtain a

strong attack by advancing the KKtP. 15 ... P—QKt4 might still have been tried.

16 P—KKt4

Seizing this opportunity. Black cannot reply 16 ... Kt×P because of 17 B×Kt, followed by B—B5, winning the exchange.

16 ...   Kt(B3)—K5

Although this loses a pawn it offers the only chance of a successful defence. The threat of P—Kt5 is a deadly one.

17	P—Kt5	P—KR4
18	KB×Kt	Kt×B
19	Kt×Kt	P×Kt
20	Q×KP	Q—R4 ch
21	K—B1	

If 21 K—K2, Q—Kt4 ch forces the White King on to dangerous squares.

21 ...   Q—Q4

An excellent continuation. After the forced exchange of Queens, Black is able to enter with his Rook on the seventh rank with good drawing chances. The following series of moves is played by both sides with consummate skill.

22	Q×Q	P×Q
23	K—Kt2	R—B7
24	KR—QB1	

Also excellent. If he tamely defends the pawn by 24 QR—Kt1, then KR—B1 followed by R—Q7, and White has more chance of losing than of winning.

24 ...   KR—B1

Better than 24 ... R×P; 25 KR—Kt1, R×R; 26 R×R, P—QKt3; 27 R—QB1, and the possession of the QB file gives White considerable endgame advantage.

25 R×R   R×R

135

26 R—QKt1   K—R2

Threatening to march his King into the centre along the white diagonal. White has to exercise great care hereabouts.

27 K—Kt3

The best square for the King. It is important to keep a watch on the KRP which Black threatens to put under pressure after K—Kt3 and P—B3.

27 ...   K—Kt3
28 P—B3   P—B3

28 ... K—B4 would be a mistake because of 29 P—K4 ch, P×P; 30 P×P ch, K×P; 31 R—K1 ch.

29 P×P   B×P
30 P—R4

Now that he has a moment's breathing space, White prepares a Queen's side advance which will relieve his Rook from its defensive role.

30 ...   K—B4
31 P—R5   R—K7

BLACK

WHITE

Now Black is developing threats against the KP and Alekhine decides to give up his extra pawn to get his Rook

into play. He points out that 32 P—QKt4 only draws after
32 ... P—KKt4; 33 P×P, B×P; 34 B×B, K×B; 35
P—B4 ch, K—B4; 36 K—B3, R—KR7; 37 R—Kt1,
R—R6 ch; 38 R—Kt3, R×R ch; 39 K×R, P—R3 with
a drawn ending, a curious position in which Black has to
be ready to play his King to B4 when White plays K—B3,
and to Kt3 when the King arrives at R4.

32 R—QB1

Alekhine considers that a better method of giving up the
pawn was 32 P—R6, P×P (if 32 ... P—Kt3; 33 B—Kt8);
33 R—QR1, R×KtP; 34 R×P, and if 34 ... R—Kt2;
35 R—R5 with "decisive positional advantage." It seems
to me, however, that Black could put up a good fight by
34 ... R—Kt4 (instead of 34 ... R—Kt2, and if 35 R×P,
P—Kt4.

32 ...	R×KtP
33 R—B5	K—K3
34 P—K4	B×QP

White's winning chances, of course, lie in the strength of
his centre pawns, for which reason this appears to be Black's
best move as 34 ... P×P; 35 P—Q5 ch, K—B4; 36 P—
Q6 ch, K—K3; 37 P×P yields White two passed pawns.

| 35 R×P | B—B6 |
| 36 R×P | P—QR3 |

He cannot regain the pawn by 36 ... B—K8 ch; 37 K—
R3, R—KB7, because of 38 R—K5 ch, K—Q2 (if 38 ...
K—B2; 39 R—B5 ch and 40 B—Kt8); 39 R—Q5 ch.

37 B—B7	B—K8 ch
38 K—Kt4	R—Kt7 ch
39 K—R3	

Not 39 K—B4, B—Q7 mate!

| 39 ... | R—KB7 |
| 40 K—Kt4 | |

To gain time on the clock.

40 ...	R—Kt7 ch
41 K—R3	R—KB7
42 P—B4	R—B6 ch
43 K—Kt2	R—B7 ch
44 K—R3	

More time-saving tactics.

44 ...	R—B6 ch
45 K—Kt2	R—B7 ch
46 K—Kt1	R—B7
47 B—Kt6	

BLACK

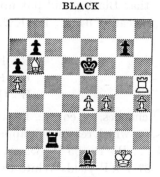

WHITE

47 ...	R—B5

It seems as if Capablanca must have overlooked White's clever tactical reply to this move. Correct, as Alekhine points out, was 47 ... B—Kt6 against which he says that he would "have tried to obtain the victory" by 48 R—K5 ch, K—Q3; 49 R—KKt5. The text move enables White to bring his King into play with decisive results.

48 K—Kt2

Very clever. Black cannot capture the KP because of 49 K—B3 followed by R—K5 ch winning the Bishop.

138

48 ...	P—Kt3
49 R—K5 ch	K—Q2
50 P—R5	

Again well played. White now obtains two irresistible passed pawns.

50 ...	P×P
51 K—B3	P—R5
52 R—R5	R—B6 ch
53 K—Kt4	R—B5
54 K—B5	

This apparently loses a pawn, but Alekhine has correctly calculated that his KBP will prove unstoppable.

| 54 ... | B×P |
| 55 R—R7 ch | |

Not 55 B×B, R—B4 ch; 56 K—Kt6, R×R; 57 K×R, P—R6 and Black wins.

| 55 ... | K—B3 |

55 K—K1 loses at once by 56 B×B, R—B4 ch; 57 K—K6.

56 B×B	R—B4 ch
57 K—K6	R×B
58 P—B5	R—R6
59 P—B6	R—KB6
60 P—B7	P—Kt4
61 R—R5	

Leading to a neat finish.

61 ...	P—R6
62 R—KB5	R×R
63 P×R	Resigns

For if 63 ... P—R7; 64 P—B8=Q, P—R8=Q; 65 Q—R8 ch.

A well-contested game, full of points of interest in all its phases.

THE MATCHES WITH BOGOLJUBOV

E. D. BOGOLJUBOV

Previous biographies in this book have dealt with the lives of deceased champions and their challengers. The subject of the present sketch and of all those to come are happily still with us, and details of their careers are necessarily incomplete.* Indeed, in the case of some of the young masters to be mentioned, their lives may be said to have just begun. No final judgment, therefore, can be passed either on their style as chess players or their general characteristics, and we must content ourselves with considering apparent trends.

E. D. Bogoljubov, Alekhine's first challenger, was born in Russia and was originally trained for the priesthood. Finding that he had no vocation for the religious life but a great gift for chess, he decided to follow the bent of his inclinations and embark on the perilous but entertaining career of a professional chess player. Like Alekhine, he was playing in the Mannheim Tournament when world war No. 1 broke out, and was interned at Triberg, where he spent the rest of the war years. Here he may be said to have completed his chess development. The internment camp at Triberg seems to have been a regular chess colony, a number of the Mannheim competitors were interned there and their captors put no obstacle in the way of their favourite pastime. Gifts of books and chess requisites were sent through the International Red Cross from chess players in allied countries and regular monthly tournaments were held in most of which Bogoljubov was successful. He emerged from captivity a master of the highest rank and soon showed his prowess by winning a strong tournament at Pistyan in which Alekhine himself was among the

* Since the above was written news has arrived of the death of Boguljubov at Triberg, on June 18th, 1952. He was sixty-five.

competitors. Other successes, the most notable of which were Moscow 1925, and Bad Kissingen 1928, followed, and his tournament prowess gave him every right to a match for the World Championship. By this time he had become domiciled in Germany, taken out naturalization papers, and married a German girl whom, I believe, he first met while a prisoner during the war. Responsibility for the match was therefore assumed by the German players, who hoped that their new acquisition might restore the past glories of Lasker and Tarrasch. Bogoljubov's tournament record justified these hopes, but tournament and match play are two very different things and it soon became evident that he stood little chance.

Brilliant in combination and revelling in complicated positions, he was yet deficient in the finer points of strategy, and the unbounded optimism which brought him so many tournament successes from unpromising positions degenerated into mere rashness when opposed by Alekhine's deep positional sense. In the first match he made a respectable score but the champion was clearly his superior, and the second match should not have been played.

Personally, Bogoljubov was a likeable man, friendly and good humoured—who seemed thoroughly to enjoy life. In appearance he was the antithesis of the popular conception of a chess master, which gave rise to an unfortunate incident when he was giving a blindfold display in Switzerland. A local photographer, called in to photograph the assembly, deleted the most important figure on the grounds that "that fat fellow with the mug of beer looked out of place in a chess picture so I cut him out!" Considering the many vicissitudes he had gone through Bogoljubov had kept up his playing strength remarkably well. In the Staunton Centenary Tournament, organized by the British Chess Federation in 1951, he played as vigorously and optimistically as ever and produced some sparkling games,

141

notably one against the powerful Yugoslav, Trifunovic, in which a brilliant Rook sacrifice snatched victory from the jaws of defeat.

Bogoljubov's principal successes have been: Pistyan 1922, 1st above Alekhine; Carlsbad 1923, 1st to 3rd with Alekhine and Maroczy; Moscow 1925, 1st above Capablanca; Berlin 1926, 1st; Bad Kissingen 1928, 1st again above Capablanca. In addition he was a consistent winner of smaller prizes, many times won the German Championship, and played with success on the top board in the International Team Tournaments. He was awarded the title of Grand Master by the International Chess Federation (F.I.D.E.).

The Alekhine v. Bogoljubov Matches

These matches were the first to be played on what is known as the perambulatory system, under which several towns combine together to bear the cost of the match, a number of games, determined in proportion to the amount subscribed, being played in each of them.

This system has the merit that it enables a large number of people to take a personal interest in the match and it eliminates the short agreed draws which marred the Alekhine v. Capablanca encounter. Its drawback is that the constant travelling and upsetting of routine involved is hard on the players, and was probably responsible for the occasional lifeless games which were played in both the matches under review.

The first match produced some interesting games, although it soon became evident that Alekhine had taken the measure of his opponent and that his victory was merely a matter of time. The second match, as I have said, should not have been played. Its only *raison d'être* seems to have been that it provided Alekhine with one more excuse for evading the challenge of Capablanca, while Bogoljubov was glad of the loser's end of the purse. As a sporting event it was of no value whatsoever.

The scores of the matches were—

First match, 1929: Alekhine 11; Bogoljubov 5; Drawn 9. Second match, 1934: Alekhine 8; Bogoljubov 3; Drawn 15.

THE FIRST MATCH

FIFTH MATCH GAME

White: Dr. A. Alekhine. Black: E. D. Bogoljubov.

1 P—Q4	P—Q4
2 P—QB4	P—QB3
3 Kt—KB3	Kt—KB3
4 Kt—B3	P×P
5 P—QR4	B—B4
6 Kt—K5	

At the time this match was played this move was all the rage. It has since been found that, correctly answered, it should yield White no advantage, and 6 P—K3 is now almost universally preferred.

6 ...   P—K3

The best reply. 6 ... QKt—Q2, as played in the first game of the 1935 match, Alekhine v. Euwe (q.v.), is also quite playable but sets Black more problems.

7 B—Kt5

If 7 P—B3, B—Kt5; 8 P—K4, B×P; 9 P×B, Kt×P, Black has a strong counter-attack which will yield him either a draw by perpetual check or a large preponderance of pawns in return for his piece.

143

7 ...	B—K2

Too defensive. The correct move is 7 ... B—QKt5, and
if then 8 P—B3 as in the game, 8 ... P—KR3; 9 P—K4,
P×B; 10 P×B, P—QKt4, and Black retains the Gambit
pawn.

8	P—B3	P—KR3
9	P—K4	B—R2

If now 9 ... P×B; 10 P×B, KP×P; 11 B×P, Castles;
12 P—KR4 with a fierce attack. The move played is,
for different reasons, almost equally bad. The Queen's
Bishop remains shut out of the game for many moves and
White is able to bring superior forces to bear on the Queen's
wing. It appears that, after his 7th move, Black's game is
theoretically lost.

10	B—K3	QKt—Q2
11	Kt×P(B4)	Castles
12	B—K2	P—B4
13	P×P	

Alekhine shows his fine judgment of position by welcom-
ing exchanges which will give him opportunities on the
Queen's wing before Black's out of work Bishop can come
into the game. One is apt to forget, in admiration for
Alekhine's genius for combinative attacks, that he was also,
when the occasion demanded, a very fine positional player.

13	...	B×BP
14	B×B	Kt×B
15	P—QKt4	Kt—R3

Alekhine gives the variation 15 ... Q×Q ch; 16 R×Q,
Kt×RP; 17 Kt×Kt, P—QKt4; 18 Kt(B4)—Kt6,
RP×Kt; 19 B×KtP with advantage to White as Black's
QKtP will eventually fall to the superior forces which his
opponent can bring to bear.

16	Q×Q	KR×Q

17 Kt—R2

A subtle move and undoubtedly the best. Alekhine rejected the obvious 17 R—QKt1 because of the possibility of 17 ... Kt—Q4; 18 P×Kt, P×P; 20 Kt—R5, B×R; 26 Kt×B, Kt×P, with many chances owing to the mobility of his Rooks. The text move threatens to win a pawn by Kt—R5.

17 ...	Kt—Kt1
18 K—B2	Kt—B3
19 KR—Q1	Kt—Q5

Undoubtedly best. After the double exchange of Rooks by 19 ... R×R; 20 R×R, R—Q1; 21 R×R, Kt×R, Black is, to all intents and purposes, a piece to the bad.

20 QR—B1	K—B1

Black plans to bring his unfortunate Bishop into the game by the moves Kt—K1, P—B3, P—K4, and B—Kt1. If he can accomplish this he will secure equality and it is therefore necessary for White to strike quickly.

21 B—B1	Kt—K1
22 Kt—B3	

Alekhine suggests 22 Kt—R5 as a good alternative, and certainly the move does appear even more effective than the line chosen. If Black replies 22 ... P—QKt3; 23 Kt—Kt7, R—Q2; 24 B—Kt5, R×Kt; 25 R×Kt with a big positional advantage as 25 ... R—B2 is met by 26 R×R, Kt×R; 27 R—Q7. If Black plays 22 ... QR—Kt1; 23 Kt—B3, P—QKt3 (23 ... P—B3; 24 Kt—Kt5 transposes into the game but 23 ... K—K2 is a possibility); 24 R×Kt, R×R; 25 Kt—B6, QR—Q1; 26 K—K3, R(Q5)→ Q3; 27 Kt×R, R×Kt; 28 Kt—Kt5 again with a very favourable position.

22 ...	P—B3

23 Kt—R5   QR—Kt1

BLACK

WHITE

This purely defensive move enables Alekhine to win a
pawn by a finely-calculated combination. Much better was
23 ... P—QKt3; 24 Kt—Kt7, R—Q2; 25 B—Kt5 (not
25 Kt—Kt5 because of 25 ... P—K4); 25 ... R×Kt;
26 R×Kt, R—B2 (the possibility of this move marks the
difference between this variation and that suggested in the
preceding note); 27 Kt—K2, R×R; 28 Kt×R, P—K4
best; 29 R—Q7, B—Kt1; 30 B—B6, B—K3 and Black is
out of his worst difficulties.

24 Kt—Kt5

This wins a pawn by force.

24 ...   Kt×Kt
25 R×R   R×R
26 Kt×P

The point of the combination.

26 ...   R—Kt1

26 ... R—Q7 ch is worse, i.e. 27 K—K3, Kt(Kt4)—Q3;
(if 27 ... R—QKt7; 28 B×Kt, K—K2; 29 B×Kt, K×B;
30 R—B7, R×KKtP; 31 Kt—Q6 ch, and 32 R×RP wins);

146

28 K×R, Kt×Kt; 29 R—B8 followed by R—R8 and R×RP winning with the two passed pawns.

27 Kt—B5

Threatening to fork the King and Rook and therefore regaining the sacrificed piece. The ensuing endgame is, of course, won for White and Alekhine's method of reducing his opponent's forces to impotence is a model of elegant simplicity.

27 ...   K—K2
28 P×Kt

Stronger than 28 B×Kt, Kt—Q3; 29 R—Q1, P—K4; with fair hopes of a successful defence.

28 ...	Kt—Q3
29 R—R1	Kt—B1
30 B—B4	B—Kt1

Other moves lose more material. If 30 ... P—K4; 31 B—K6, or 30 ... R—Kt3; 31 R—Q1 and R—Q7.

31 P—B4	B—B2
32 P—K5	

Depriving Black of his last hope, P—K4.

32 ...	P×P
33 P×P	R—Kt3
34 K—K3	B—K1
35 R—R5	B—Q2
36 K—Q4	B—K1
37 P—R4	B—Q2
38 B—K2	

If 38 Kt×B, K×Kt; 39 K—B5, Black can cause a little trouble by 39 ... R—Kt2 followed by R—B2 ch. White plans to bring his Bishop to the diagonal KR1, QR8.

38 ...   R—Kt1

If 38 ... B—K1 White wins by 39 B—Kt4, R×P (if 39 ... B—Q2; 40 Kt×B as in the game or 39 ... B—B2; 40 B—B3, B—K1; 41 B—Kt7); 40 R×R, B×R; 41 B×P with an easy minor piece ending. There are also other methods of winning, such as 39 P—Kt3, R—Kt1; 40 R—R6.

39 Kt×B	K×Kt
40 B—B3	R—Kt3
41 K—B5	R—Kt1
42 P—R5	K—Q1

Not 42 ... R—Kt3; 43 R×P ch.

43 B—B6	K—K2
44 R—R3	K—B2

If 44 ... K—Q1; 45 R—KKt3.

45 B—K4	K—K2
46 K—B6	K—Q1
47 R—Q3 ch	K—K2
48 K—B7	Resigns

A very fine positional game by Alekhine. It might have been played by Capablanca, the highest praise that can be given to this sort of game.

SEVENTEENTH MATCH GAME

White: Dr. A. Alekhine.   Black: E. D. Bogoljubov.

1 P—Q4	Kt—KB3
2 P—QB4	P—KKt3
3 P—B3	

This move, the object of which is to build up a strong chain of pawns on the white central squares, is not often seen nowadays, but gives White attacking chances unless Black plays with extreme exactitude.

148

3 ...	P—Q4

This seems to be playing White's game. A better line is
3 ... B—Kt2; 4 P—K4, P—Q3; 5 Kt—B3, Castles;
6 B—K3, P—K4.

4 P×P	Kt×P
5 P—K4	Kt—Kt3
6 Kt—B3	B—Kt2
7 B—K3	Kt—B3

Bogoljubov says that he rejected 7 ... Castles, on account
of 8 P—B4 after which his development is certainly a
matter of difficulty. The move played is not convincing
either, but already there seems no really satisfactory line.

8 P—Q5	Kt—K4
9 B—Q4	P—KB3

If 9 ... Castles; 10 P—B4, Kt—Kt5; 11 B×B, K×B;
12 P—KR3, Kt—B3; 13 Q—Q4, and White is ideally
placed to Castle Queen's Rook and storm Black's King's
side position with pawns.

10 P—B4	Kt—B2
11 P—QR4	

Very strong. If Black prevents the further advance of this
pawn by 11 ... P—QR4; 12 B × Kt, P × B; 13 B—Kt5 ch,
B—Q2; 14 Kt—B3 followed by Kt—Q4 with a stranglehold on the weak square at K6.

11 ...	P—K4
12 P×P e.p.	B×P
13 P—R5	Kt—Q2
14 P—R6	P—Kt3
15 B—Kt5	

Threatening B—B6 and Kt—Kt5 winning the RP.

15 ...	Q—K2

In order to answer 16 B—B6 by 16 Castles QR.

16	KKt—K2	P—QB4
17	B—B2	Castles QR

Very risky, but in conjunction with his sacrifice on the 20th move, it probably offers more chances than anything else. If 17 ... Castles KR; 18 Kt—Q5, Q—Q3 (18 ... B×Kt; 19 Q×B threatening Q—Kt7 is even worse); 19 KKt—B3, B×Kt; 20 Kt×B, QR—Q1 (not 20 ... KR—K1 because of 21 B×Kt winning a piece); 21 Castles with a dominating position.

18	Q—R4	P—B4
19	P—K5	P—Kt4
20	B—B4	

Threatening mate in two moves.

20	...	Kt(Q2)×P

A fine bold sacrifice, characteristic of Bogoljubov's fighting style. He obtains two pawns at once, with a good chance of a third, and White's attack is forced back. Purely defensive play would result in speedy disaster. If 20 ... Kt—B1; 21 Q—B6 ch, K—Kt1; 22 B×P, P×B; 23 B×B, Kt×B; 24 R—R5 and wins, or 20 ... Kt—Kt1; 21 B×B ch, Q×B; 22 Castles, P×P; 23 P—QKt4, with an overwhelming attack; for instance, 23 ... Kt×P; 24 P×P, Q—B5; 25 P×P, Q×Q; 26 R×Q, Kt(Kt1)—B3; 27 P×P, winning easily.

21	B×B ch	Q×B
22	P×Kt	Kt×P
23	Castles KR	Q—B5

The point of Black's combination. After 24 Q×Q, Kt×Q Black is bound to win a third pawn and has very good chances.

BLACK

WHITE

24 P—QKt4

With this brilliant rejoinder Alekhine retains the attack. If Black replies 24 ... P×P; 25 Kt—Kt5, Q×Kt(K7) (if 25 ... K—Kt1; 26 B×P, and wins); 26 KR—K1, Q—Q7 or Q6; 27 Kt×P ch, K—Kt1; 28 Kt—B6 ch, and wins, as 28 ... Kt×Kt; 29 Q×Kt leads to a forced mate.

24 ...	Q×P
25 Q—B2	

Threatening to win Black's Queen by 26 R—R4, Black finds the only possible reply.

25 ...	Kt—Q6
26 KR—Kt1	Q—B5
27 R—R4	Q—K3

At first sight 27 ... Q—B2 guarding the second rank appears better, but Alekhine points out the following fine rejoinder: 28 B—Q4, P×B (or 28 ... B×B ch; 29 Kt×B, R×Kt; 30 R×R, P×R; 31 Q×Kt, and Black cannot take the Knight while if 31 ... R—Q1 is met by 32 Kt—Kt5, K—Kt1; 33 Q—Kt3 ch, P—B5; 34 Q×KtP); 29 Kt—Q5 dis. ch, Kt—B4; 30 Kt×P ch, P×Kt; 31 R×KtP, and wins. With Black's Queen at K3, this variation is not possible on account of the check at K6.

| 28 Kt—Kt5 | K—Kt1 |

But here Black slips. He should play 28 ... Kt×B when, as Alekhine shows, 29 Kt×P ch would not be good because of 29 ... K—Kt1; 30 Q×QBP, R—Q8 ch. After 29 K×Kt, K—Kt1 White would still have the advantage, but the disappearance of the Bishop makes the win much more difficult.

| 29 Kt(K2)—Q4 | Q—K5 |

Taking the Knight would lose the exchange, i.e. 29 ... B×Kt; 30 B×B, R×B; 31 R×R, Q—K6 ch; 32 K—B1 and Black cannot play 32 ... P×R because of 33 Q—B7 ch with mate to follow.

30 Kt—QB3	Q—K1
31 Q×Kt	P×Kt
32 B×P	

The simplest way to win.

| 32 ... | Q—K3 |

Either here or at the next move B×B ch would prolong the agony.

| 33 Q—B3 | Q—B2 |
| 34 B×P | Resigns |

An exciting game, full of combinational points and creditable to both players.

EIGHTEENTH MATCH GAME

White: E. D. Bogoljubov. Black: Dr. A. Alekhine.

1 P—K4	P—K3
2 P—Q4	P—Q4
3 Kt—QB3	Kt—KB3
4 B—Kt5	P×P
5 Kt×P	B—K2
6 B×Kt	P×B

6 ... B×B is safer but Alekhine naturally preferred lines which enabled him to fish in troubled waters.

7 Kt—KB3   P—KB4

In the book of the New York Tournament, 1924, Alekhine condemned this move and suggested as best 7 ... P—QKt3 followed by B—Kt2. The drawback to the advance of the BP is that it allows White's KKt a powerful square at K5.

8 Kt—B3   P—QB3

Now 8 ... P—QKt3 would be bad because of 9 Kt—K5, B—Kt2 (if 9 ... Kt—Q2; 10 B—Kt5); 10 Q—R5, Castles; 11 Castles, with very strong attacking potentialities.

9 P—KKt3

A good line. The King's Bishop has more possibilities at KKt2 than at Q3.

9 ...   Kt—Q2

10 B—Kt2   Q—B2

11 Q—K2   P—Kt4

Anticipating that White will Castle on the Queen's side, he prepares for a pawn storm. The move has been condemned by some annotators but it certainly seems to hold out more possibilities than 11 ... P—Kt3; 12 Kt—K5, B—Kt2; 13 Castles QR, Kt×Kt; 14 P×Kt after which Black has a cramped and futureless game.

12 Kt—K5   B—Kt2

13 Castles QR   Kt—Kt3

14 Q—R5   R—KB1

14 ... Castles KR would, of course, be much too dangerous in view of the exposed position of his King, but there seems no objection to 14 ... B—B3; 15 KR—K1, B×Kt (not 15 ... P—Kt5, because of 16 Kt×QBP, threatening R× P ch); 16 P×B, P—Kt5; 17 Kt—K2, Kt—Q4. Probably

Alekhine hoped to make something out of the pair of Bishops.

> 15 P—B4

15 Q×RP would be dangerous. For example, 15 Q×RP, B—B3; 16 Q—R5, P—Kt5; 17 Kt—K2, B×Kt; 18 P×B, Kt—B5; regaining the pawn with attacking chances.

15 ...	P—Kt5
16 Kt—K2	Kt—Q4
17 B×Kt	

Again well played. In this broken position White's Knights prove stronger than the opposing Bishops.

| 17 ... | BP×B |
| 18 K—Kt1 | |

A necessary precaution. If 18 Q×RP, R—B1; 19 R—Q2, Q—R4; 20 K—Kt1, P—Kt6 and wins.

| 18 ... | P—R4 |

Alekhine says that this was his fatal error. He should have played 18 ... B—KB3 so as to enable him to capture the Knight when necessary.

> 19 P—Kt4

Bogoljubov now smashes up the position in a few powerful strokes. Black's next moves are forced.

19 ...	P×P
20 P—B5	P×P
21 Q×BP	P—R5
22 KR—K1	P—R6
23 P—Kt3	B—B1
24 Q×RP	B—K3
25 Q—Q3	Castles

Risky though this is, it offers the only chance of salvation.

If 25 ... R—B1; 26 QR—B1 with the deadly threat of
P—B3.

26	P—B3	K—Kt2
27	R—QB1	Q—Kt3
28	P × P	B × P
29	R—B6	

BLACK

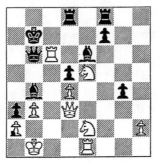

WHITE

29 ...   Q—R4

The exchange of the Queen for the two Rooks would be
disastrous for Black, i.e. 29 ... B × R; 30 R × Q ch, K × R;
31 Kt—B3, B × Kt (if 31 ... B—B4; 32 Q × B, B × Kt;
33 Q—B6 ch, winning the exchange or a piece); 32 Q × B,
R—B1; 33 Q—Kt4 ch, K—R2; 34 Q × P ch (not 34 Kt—
B6 ch, R × Kt; 35 Q × R, B—B4 ch and mates next move);
34 ... K—Kt2; 35 Q—Kt4 ch, K—R2 (if 35 ... K—R3;
36 P—QR4); 36 Kt—B6 ch, and wins.

30	KR—QB1	R—B1
31	Kt—KB4	B—Q3

After 31 ... R × R; 32 Kt × R, Q—Kt3; 33 Kt × QB,
P × Kt; 34 Q—R7 ch, K—R1; 35 Q—Q7, Black is helpless.

          32 Kt × B

Not 32 R × B, R × R ch; 33 K × R, Q—K8 ch, etc.

32 ...	P×Kt
33 Q—R7 ch	R—QB2

If 33 ... B—B2; 34 R(B6)—B5, Q—Kt3; 35 Kt—Q7 and wins.

34 R×R ch	B×R
35 Q—Q7	Q—Kt3
36 Kt—Q3	R—Q1
37 R×B ch	

Exchanging into a winning pawn ending.

37 ...	Q×R
38 Kt—B5 ch	K—Kt3
39 Q×Q ch	K×Q
40 Kt×P ch	K—Q2
41 Kt×R	K×Kt

Black could have resigned here.

42 P—Kt4	K—Q2
43 K—B2	K—B3
44 K—Kt3	K—Kt4
45 K×P	K—B5
46 P—Kt5	

The simplest. 46 K—R4, K×P; 47 P—Kt5, K—B4; 48 K—R5 is also good enough as, after both sides Queen, White wins with two checks.

46 ...	K×KtP
47 K—Kt3	K—R4
48 P—QR4	K—R3
49 K—Kt4	K—Kt3
50 P—R5 ch	K—B3
51 K—R4	Resigns

The whole of this game was played logically and energetically by Bogoljubov who, for once in a way, showed the form which won two great international tournaments.

TWENTY-SECOND MATCH GAME

White: E. D. Bogoljubov. Black: Dr. A. Alekhine.

1	P—K4	P—K4
2	Kt—KB3	Kt—QB3
3	B—Kt5	P—QR3
4	B—R4	P—Q3
5	P—B3	B—Q2
6	P—Q4	P—KKt3

For the alternative 6 ... Kt—K2 see the games Euwe *v.* Keres (p. 230) and Smyslov *v.* Reshevsky (p. 226) in the World Championship Tournament.

7	B—KKt5

Better is 7 B—K3, with the possible continuation 7 ... B—Kt2; 8 P×P, P×P; 9 B—B5. The text allows Black to bring his KKt to a favourable square at KB2.

7	...	P—B3
8	B—K3	Kt—R3
9	Castles	B—Kt2
10	P—KR3	

If 10 QKt—Q2, Kt—KKt5.

10	...	Kt—B2
11	QKt—Q2	Castles
12	P×P	QP×P

12 ... BP×P is also good. Alekhine preferred the capture with the QP because of the possibilities of a later P—KB4.

13	B—B5	R—K1
14	B—Kt3	P—Kt3
15	B—K3	

There is a good deal to be said for 15 B—R3, with the idea of Kt—B4, K3, and Q5.

15	...	Q—K2
16	Q—K2	QKt—Q1
17	B—Q5	B—B3

18 P—B4

White has gained nothing out of the opening and his best course here was 18 B×B, Kt×B; 19 QR—Q1 with a probable draw. After the text Black is able to develop a menacing attack against White's pawn centre.

18 ...   B×B
19 BP×B

If 19 KP×B, 19 ... P—KB4 is very unpleasant for White.

19 ...   P—KB4
20 Kt—B4

20 P×P would give Black opportunities of attack on the KKt file later.

20 ...   Kt—Kt2
21 QR—B1

21 QR—Q1, would be more to the point. There is no attack on the QB file and the Rook obstructs the flight square for his Bishop.

21 ...   QR—Q1

The best. Alekhine points out that 21 ... KR—Q1 would not have been so good because of 22 P×P, P×P; 22 B—Q4, R×P; 24 KR—K1, and if 24 ... P—K5; 25 B×B, K×B; 26 Kt—K3 with advantage to White. Also 21 ... P×P leads to nothing after 22 KKt—Q2, QR—Q1 (22 ... KR—Q1; 23 KKt×P, R×P; 23 Q—B3 is dangerous for Black); 23 P—Q6, Kt(Kt2)×P; 24 Kt×Kt, Kt×Kt; 25 Q×P and the doubled KP will eventually fall.

22 P—Q6

Liquidating the weak QP, but Black still retains the advantage because of his domination of the Queen's file.

22 ...   Kt(Kt2)×P
23 Kt×Kt   R×Kt
24 Q×P   Q—Q2

Threatening to win a piece by 25 ... P—B5. See note to
his 21st move.

25	R—B2	P—B4
26	P—QR4	P—KB5
27	B—Q2	P—KKt4

With the powerful threat of 27 ... P—Kt5 White is
obliged to seek relief in an exchange of Queens.

28	Q—Kt5	Q×Q
29	P×Q	R—Q6
30	R—R1	Kt—Q3
31	R—R6	R—Kt1
32	B—B3	

32 Kt×KtP, B—B3; 33 Kt—B3, Kt×KP is also bad for
White since 34 B—B3 is answered by 34 ... Kt×B; 35
P×Kt, P—K5; 36 Kt—Q2, R—K1 with a winning game.
Alekhine also mentions 32 R—B3, P—B5; 33 R×R,
P×R; 34 R—R3, Kt×KP; 35 R×P, R—R1; and if
36 R—R3, 36 ... R—Q1 and wins.

32	...	Kt×KP
33	B×P	B×B
34	Kt×B	R—Q8 ch
35	K—R2	Kt—Q7

BLACK

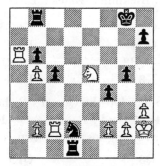

WHITE

A move which lifts the game out of the category of ordinary positional struggles. It is very rare to see a mating attack with such limited forces. White can, of course, avoid the mate by 36 R×Kt, but this is equivalent to resignation.

      36 P—R4

Black is threatening mate in three, beginning 36 ... Kt—B8 ch. If 36 P—Kt3, R—K1; 37 P×P, P×P; 38 Kt—Kt4, Kt—B6 ch; 39 K—Kt2, Kt—K8 ch, etc.

36 ...	R—K1
37 Kt—B3	

Or 37 Kt—Kt4, R(K1)—K8; 38 K—R3, R—R8 ch; 39 Kt—R2, P—R4; 40 P×P, Kt—B8 forcing mate.

37 ...	Kt×Kt ch
38 P×Kt	R(K1)—K8
39 K—R3	P—R4
Resigns	

A remarkable finish.

THE SECOND MATCH

SECOND MATCH GAME

White: Dr. A. Alekhine. Black: E. D. Bogoljubov.

1 P—Q4	Kt—KB3
2 P—QB4	P—B3
3 Kt—QB3	P—Q4
4 P—K3	P—K3

It is not good to develop the Queen's Bishop at this point, i.e. 4 ... B—B4; 5 P×P, P×P; 6 Q—Kt3, and Black's only method of avoiding loss of a pawn is 6 ... B—B1.

5 B—Q3	QKt—Q2
6 Kt—B3	P×P

DR. A. ALEKHINE

7 B×BP	P—QKt4
8 B—Q3	P—QR3

The Meran Defence, one of the most interesting lines of play against the Queen's Gambit.

9 Castles

For the stronger 9 P—K4 see the eighth match game between Bronstein and Botvinnik.

9 ...	P—B4
10 P—QR4	

Best, as it forces Black to a further advance of the QKtP and so furnishes White with a good square for his Knight at QB4.

10 ...	P—Kt5
11 Kt—K4	B—Kt2
12 QKt—Q2	B—K2

Good, here is 12 ... B—Q3; 13 Kt—B4, B—B2, leaving the square K2 vacant for the Queen. In the line chosen the Queen has to develop on the Queen's side where she is exposed to attack.

13 P—R5	Castles
14 Kt—B4	Q—B2
15 Q—K2	Kt—Kt5

This move looks very strong as the threat of 16 ... B×Kt compels White to sacrifice a pawn. Nevertheless, the position of the Black pieces, notably the Queen, becomes uncomfortable, and it may well be that a simpler line such as 15 ... B—K5 is preferable.

16 P—K4

This sacrifice is compulsory as 16 P—KKt3, Q—B3; 17 P—K4, P—B4 would be hopeless for White.

16 ...	P×P
17 P—KR3	

BLACK

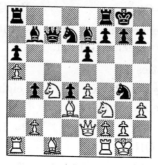

WHITE

| 17 ... | KKt—K4 |

This natural-looking move leads to trouble as it eventually allows the White Knight to settle at QKt6, with disastrous effects. The alternative is 17 ... KKt—B3 against which Alekhine gives the variation 18 B—Kt5, Kt—B4; 19 Kt—Kt6, QR—Q1; 20 QR—B1, Q—Kt1; 21 B×Kt, P×B; 22 R—B4, P—K4; 23 Kt—KR4 with ample compensation for the sacrificial pawn. Black could, of course, play differently on his 18th move, but nothing seems entirely satisfactory. For instance, 18 ... P—K4; 19 QR—B1, Q—Kt1; 20 Kt—R4, R—K1 (if 21 ... P—Kt3; 22 P—B4 with a strong attack); 21 Kt—B5, B—B1; 22 Kt—Kt6, Kt×Kt; 23 P×Kt, with the powerful threats of R—B7 and B×Kt.

18	KKt×Kt	Kt×Kt
19	B—B4	B—Q3
20	B×Kt	B×B
21	Kt—Kt6	R—R2

Shutting the Rook out of play. 21 ... QR—Q1 is slightly better, but after 22 KR—Q1 (better than 22 B×P, B×B; 23 Q×B, Q—B7 followed by P—Q6), the RP must fall and the passed pawn will be tremendously strong.

22 QR—B1	Q—Q3
23 R—B4	P—B4

An attempt at counter-attack which is doomed to failure on account of the unfortunate position of the Queen's Rook. Bogoljubov afterwards suggested that 23 ... B—B5, followed by P—K4 was better, but White can then win the QKtP by Q—K1 and remain with the superior position.

24 P×P	P×P
25 KR—K1	Q—Kt3

The point of his 23rd move. If 25 ... B—B5; 26 Q—K6 ch, with a winning ending. The White Rooks will pick up at least two of the weak Black pawns.

26 P—B3	R—K1

Bogoljubov again decides correctly that, if he moves the Bishop, 27 Q—K6 ch is fatal for him in the long run, and therefore decides to sacrifice a piece for an attack which only fails because Alekhine has a brilliant counter combination.

27 P—B4	Q—Kt6
28 P×B	R×P
29 R—B8 ch	

This is the fly in the ointment. Obviously Black cannot take the Rook and his King is drawn into a mating net.

29 ...	K—B2
30 Q—R5 ch	

30 R—B7 ch, K—Kt1 (if 30 ... K—Kt3; 31 R×P ch, and 32 Q×R ch, or 30 ... K—B1; 31 Kt—Q7 ch); 31 B—B4 ch, K—R1; 32 R—B8 ch, B×R; 33 Q×R also wins.

30 ...	P—Kt3
31 Q×RP ch	K—B3
32 R—B8 ch	K—Kt4

If 32 ... K—K3; 33 Q—Q7 mate.

33 P—R4 ch	K—B5

34	Q—R6 ch	P—Kt4
35	R×P ch	R×R
36	Q—Q6 ch	K—Kt5
37	B×R ch and mates in three moves	

I.e. 37 ... K×B; 38 Q—K6 ch, K—B5; 39 Q—B6 ch, K—Kt5; 40 Q×P mate.

An exciting game with a pretty finish, although, like many of the games of this match, it is rather a "light-weight" for a World Championship encounter.

SEVENTEENTH MATCH GAME

White: E. D. Bogoljubov. Black: Dr. A. Alekhine.

1	P—Q4	P—Q4
2	P—QB4	P×P
3	Kt—KB3	Kt—KB3
4	Kt—B3	P—QR3
5	P—K4	

Having failed to make any impression with sound openings, Bogoljubov decides to try his luck with an unsound one! After this move it is impossible for White to regain the Gambit pawn, which could have been achieved by 5 P—QR4 followed by P—K3.

5	...	P—QKt4
6	P—K5	Kt—Q4
7	Kt—Kt5	P—K3
8	Q—B3	

This short-lived attack is easily repelled by Black.

8	...	Q—Q2
9	Kt×Kt	

This ill-judged exchange, which cuts off the White Knights from the important central square K4, only helps Black. The only possible line was 9 P—QR4, P—R3 (not 9 ... B—Kt2; 10 P×P, P×P; 11 R×R, B×R; 12 Kt×KtP);

10 Kt—K4, B—Kt2; 11 B—K2, but even then White has no adequate compensation for his sacrificed pawn.

        9 ...   P×Kt

        10 P—QR3

And now the threat of B—Kt5 ch forces White to make a defensive move.

        10 ...   Kt—B3

        11 B—K3   Kt—Q1

A clever device which, as will be seen, frees the Queen from her present defensive role.

        12 B—K2   Q—B4

The point of the last move. White cannot capture the QP because of 13 B—Kt2 winning the Queen.

        13 Q—Kt3   P—R3

        14 Kt—R3

If 14 Kt—B3, Q—Kt5 forces the exchange of Queens.

        14 ...   P—QB3

        15 P—B4

If 15 Castles, then, equally, 15 ... Q—B7.

        15 ...   Q—B7

        16 Q—B2

BLACK

WHITE

16 ...   B×P

A highly ingenious surprise combination which completely destroys White's Queen's wing. If White plays 17 R×B (if 17 P×B, Q—B6 ch); 17 ... Q×P; 18 R—R5, Q—Kt5 ch; 19 B—Q2, P—B6.

16 ... Q×P would not be nearly so good, as after 17 Castles, White has distinct chances of counter-attack.

17 Castles   B×P
18 QR—K1   B—B4

Alekhine considers that 18 ... B×Kt; 19 P×B, Kt—K3; 20 P—B5, Kt—Kt4 was a quicker way to win. Of course any reasonable line is good enough.

19 P—Kt4   B—K5
20 P—B5   Kt—Kt2

In order to Castle QR. 20 ... P—QR4 could be met by 21 P—K6, P—B3; 22 Q—B4.

21 Kt—B4   Castles QR
22 Q—Kt3   P—Kt4

Black makes everything absolutely safe before embarking on the winning advance P—QB4.

23 P×P e.p.   P×P
24 B—Q1   Q—B6
25 Kt—K6   QR—K1
26 R—B6   R—K2
27 QR—B1   KR—K1
28 Kt—B4

If 28 Kt—B5, Alekhine points out the nice sacrificial combination 28 ... Kt×Kt; 29 R×P ch, K—Kt2; 30 R×Kt, Q×QP; 31 B×Q, B×B ch; 32 R—B2, R—KB2, etc.

28 ...   Kt—Q1
29 Q—B2

If 29 Kt×KtP; 29 ... B×Kt; 30 R×B, P—B4 or 30 ...

Kt—K3, winning easily. White could have resigned here and the remaining moves require no comment.

29	...	Q—R6
30	B—B3	B×B
31	Q×B	P—Kt4
32	Kt—K2	R—K3
33	R—B5	Q—Q6
34	P—R4	R—Kt3
35	P—R5	R(Kt3)—K3
36	Q—B2	P—B4
37	R—B3	Q—B7
38	Q—K1	Kt—B3
39	R(B1)—B2	Q—K5
40	Kt—Kt3	Q×KtP
41	K—Kt2	B×P
	Resigns	

This game, which was lost by Bogoljubov through his unsound opening, is redeemed from mediocrity by Alekhine's excellent play, particularly on the 16th and 27th moves.

TWENTY-THIRD MATCH GAME

White: E. D. Bogoljubov. Black: Dr. A. Alekhine.

1	P—Q4	P—Q4
2	Kt—KB3	Kt—KB3
3	P—B4	P×P
4	Q—R4 ch	

This method of regaining the Gambit pawn instead of 4 P—K3 has enjoyed a certain amount of popularity in recent years. Its merit is that in some cases White will be able to develop his Queen's Bishop before shutting it in with the King's pawn.

4	...	P—B3

A drawback to White's fourth move is that Black can here

167

force an exchange of Queens by 4 ... Q—Q2; 5 Q×BP, Q—B3. Although White obtains a slight advantage in development after 6 QKt—Q2, Q×Q; 7 Kt×Q, it is very hard to turn it to practical account.

5	Q×BP	B—B4
6	Kt—B3	P—K3
7	P—KKt3	

Transforming the game into a sort of Catalan. A possibility was 7 B—Kt5, B—K2; 8 B×Kt, B×B; 9 P—K4, B—Kt5; 10 Castles QR.

7	...	QKt—Q2
8	B—Kt2	B—B7

A curious move which threatens to win White's Queen by 9 ... Kt—Kt3. Black could hardly have expected White to overlook this and he probably played in this way because he did not like the variation 8 ... B—K2; 9 Kt—KR4 followed by P—K4.

9	P—K3	B—K2
10	Castles	Castles
11	P—QR3	P—QR4
12	Q—K2	B—Kt3
13	P—K4	Q—Kt3
14	P—R3	Q—R3
15	Q—K3	

In this position White's chances lie in direct King's side attack so he naturally avoids the exchange of Queens.

15	...	P—B4
16	P—K5	

A strong threat. Black cannot reply 16 ... P×P because of 17 Q×P, B—QB4; 18 Q—Q1, winning a pawn.

16	...	Kt—Q4
17	Kt×Kt	P×Kt
18	B—Q2	B—K5

19 B—B3

It is necessary to provide further protection to his centre. 19 Kt—K1 would not be good because of 19 ... P×P; 20 Q×P, B—QB4, etc.

19 ...   P—B5

Now Black's only chance lies in the exploitation of his Queen's side majority. From now to the end the game becomes very exciting.

20 Kt—K1	B×B
21 Kt×B	P—QKt4
22 P—B4	Q—R3

Against 22 ... P—B4, White still retains a strong attack by 23 Q—B3, Q—QB3; 24 Kt—K3, Kt—Kt3; 25 P—KKt4, etc.

| 23 Q—B3 | P—Kt5 |
| 24 B—Q2 | Kt—Kt3 |

24 ... Q×P; 25 Q×P, Q—K3; 26 Q—B3 leaves White with an irresistible mass of centre pawns.

| 25 P—Kt4 | Q—QB3 |
| 26 P—B5 | P—B3 |

He must prevent P—B6 but now White's Knight finds a formidable advanced post at K6.

27 Kt—B4	KR—B1
28 KP×P	B×P
29 Kt—K6	P—B6
30 P×BP	Kt—B5

If 30 ... P×BP, White can force home his attack by 31 P—Kt5, P×B; 32 P×B, P×P (other moves seem no better, e.g. 32 ... Q—B6; 33 P—B7 ch, K×P; 34 Q—R5 ch, K—Kt1; 35 P—B6, or 32 ... R—R2; 33 P×P); 33 Q—Kt4 ch, K—B2; 34 Q—Kt7 ch, K—K1; 35 QR—K1, P×R=Q; 36 R×Q and Black cannot escape.

Position after White's 30th move

31 B—B4   Kt×P

This allows White's Bishop to enter the game with fatal
effect.   Rather better was 31 ... P—Kt6; 32 P—Kt5,
P—Kt7; 33 QR—K1, B—Q1; 34 Kt—B5, threatening
R—K6.   White still has the advantage, but Black may be
able to defend himself.

32	P—Kt5	B—Q1
33	B—K5	R—R2
34	Q—R5	Kt—B5

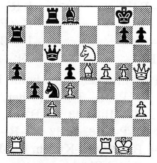

35 P×P

Here White misses his way. He could win at once by 35 P—Kt6, P—R3; 36 B×P, R×B; 37 Q×P (Kt×R would also win), Q—Q2; 38 P—B6, B×P; 39 R×B, etc.

Although the line played also wins, Black has a lot of fight left.

35	...	Kt×B
36	P×Kt	B—Kt3 ch
37	K—R1	P—Q5 dis. ch
38	Q—B3	Q×Q ch
39	R×Q	R—B6

Not 39 ... P×P; 40 R×R, B×R; 41 P—B6 and wins.

40	R(B3)—B1	P—Q6

If 40 ... R×P ch; 41 K—Kt2, R—QB6; 42 P×P, B×P; 43 P—B6 and wins.

41	P—B6	R—B3
42	Kt×P	R×Kt

This is obviously forced.

43	P×R	P×P
44	R—B6	B—Q5

An ingenious try. By the sacrifice of a second Rook Black nearly succeeds in Queening his QP. Anything else is clearly hopeless.

45	R—R8 ch	K×P
46	R×R	P—Q7
47	R—B7 ch	K—Kt3
48	R—Kt8 ch	K—B4
49	R—B8 ch	K—K5

If 49 ... K×P; 50 R—K7 ch, K—Q3; 51 R—Q8 ch, K×R; 52 R×B and wins.

50	R—KB1	B×P
51	R—B4 ch	K—Q6

52	R×P	B—Kt6
53	K—Kt2	

Simpler is 53 R—Kt3 ch, K—K7; 54 R×B, K×R; 55 R—Kt1 ch.

53	...	B—K8
54	R—QKt1	B—R5
55	R—Kt3 ch	K—K7
56	R—Kt5	K—K6
57	R—Q5	K—K7
58	R—B7	Resigns

An interesting and instructive game with many combinative points. In spite of one or two errors towards the end, Bogoljubov deserves great credit for the power with which he drove home his King's side attack. Alekhine should have resigned sooner and the last few moves are merely frivolous.

CHAPTER IV

DR. MAX EUWE

D^{R. MAX EUWE} has the distinction of being the first World Champion to be classified as an amateur. As a boy he showed an aptitude for mathematics which, often, though by no means always, coincides with chess skill, and after he had been awarded the degree of Doctor of Philosophy in 1926, he divided his life between the teaching of science and the practice of chess, a division of labour which, of course, lessened his opportunities for practice at the game. It is questionable, however, whether he would have gone farther had he devoted all his time to chess. As it is, he appears the perfect player, profound in strategy, gifted in combination and possessed of a wide knowledge of theory. His only weakness is a tendency towards comparatively simple blunders, almost inexplicable in so gifted a master.

In the realms of chess theory he stands out on his own. Like Tarrasch, he never retains his theoretical discoveries for his own use. All that he knows he gives to the public, and chess players all over the world owe him a debt of gratitude for his profound yet simply expressed analytical studies.

Dr. Euwe was born in 1901 in Amsterdam where a street is now named after him. He learned chess at the age of five, and at ten played in his first tournament, winning all his games. From then onwards he went steadily forward. In 1921 he won the Championship of his country, a title which he has held ever since, and soon began to make his mark in international events. Owing to his scholastic duties he has not been able to compete in so many big international tournaments as his professional rivals, but in those in which he has taken part he has invariably held a prominent place. Among his best results in such events may be mentioned his 3rd to Bogoljubov and Capablanca at Bad Kissingen in 1928 and his 2nd to Alekhine at Zürich in 1934. He has also gone in a great deal for personal matches which he was able to arrange during college vacations. He always selected the best opponents, as will be seen from the appended records, and though he lost the majority he always put up a stern fight. His victory over Alekhine in 1935 was not so surprising as it seems for, in the previous encounters between them, he had scored five wins against six losses. In this match he certainly showed chess genius of the highest order. That he did not hold the Championship longer was due to his chivalry in immediately agreeing to a return match, an attitude very different from that displayed by Alekhine in regard to Capablanca.

In this second match he showed stern resistance to an Alekhine who was at the very top of his form, and made his opponent fight every inch of the way. Euwe is extremely popular in this country, to which he is a frequent visitor.

Before the war he was a regular competitor in the annual Christmas Congresses organized by the Hastings Chess Club. These proved the scene of two of his brightest successes when he won 1st prize ahead of Capablanca in 1930 and again in 1934 when he tied with Sir George Thomas and Flohr above Capablanca, Botvinnik and Lilienthal. He could, however, never cope with the late Miss Menchik to whom he lost so many games that he was awarded the unenviable title of "President of the Menchik Club," i.e. famous masters who had been defeated by the woman Champion of the World.

During the war Euwe was out of chess. Living in German-occupied territory, he steadfastly refused all offers to take part in German-organized tournaments. On the conclusion of hostilities he was soon in harness again. The World Championship was vacant through the death of Alekhine and Euwe determined to do his best to regain his lost crown, giving up his tutorial duties and devoting all his time to the game. His first efforts were full of promise. At the great tournament at Groningen, in which all possible Championship contenders took part, he finished second, only half a point behind Botvinnik, a long way ahead of the rest of the field. Then, unfortunately, there came a relapse. His tendency to make blunders, with the lack of confidence which it inevitably engenders, increased to an alarming extent, and caused him to put up very poor scores in some comparatively minor events. These results in themselves would not have mattered, all great players have their off days, but their effect on Euwe's trust in his own abilities proved disastrous. In the World Championship Tournament, played in 1948 at The Hague and Moscow, he could only win one game. Others, in which he played superbly up to a point, were frittered away by sheer nervousness.

Golombek, in his excellent book on the World Championship Tournament, suggests that the trouble is the psychological result of the strain of his life under German occupation, and I am inclined to think that he is right. Such events can leave a delayed mark on a sensitive temperament which may take time to show itself. It is very good to see that lately Euwe seems to be regaining some of his old confidence, and there is every hope that this brilliant and cultured master may play a prominent part in the Championship struggles of the future.

As already mentioned, Euwe's appearances in big international tourneys have been few and far between, and his victories in minor events are too numerous to be set out here. The following may be mentioned: Goteborg 1920,

2nd and 3rd; Vienna 1921, 2nd; Bad Kissingen 1928, 3rd; Berne 1932, equal 2nd and 3rd; Zürich 1934, 2nd; Zandvoort 1936, 2nd; Bournemouth 1939, 1st; London, Zaandam, and Maastridt, all 1946, 1st; Groningen 1946, 2nd. In addition he has twice won the Hastings Christmas Congress as well as dividing 1st to 3rd places on the famous occasion when both Botvinnik and Capablanca were outside the prize list. Euwe's match record is longer than that of any other master. The following are the most important results—

1924:	v. E. Colle:	won 5, lost 3, drew 0.
1927:	v. Dr. A. Alekhine:	won 2, lost 3, drew 5.
1928:	v. E. Colle:	won 5, lost 0, drew 1.
1928:	v. E. Bogoljubov:	won 3, lost 5, drew 12.
1931:	v. J. R. Capablanca:	won 0, lost 2, drew 8.
1933:	v. R. Spielmann:	won 2, lost 0, drew 2.
1933:	v. S. Flohr:	won 3, lost 3, drew 10.
1940:	v. P. Keres:	won 5, lost 6, drew 3.

THE FIRST MATCH: EUWE v. ALEKHINE

Like the Alekhine v. Bogoljubov matches, the two contests with Euwe were also played on the perambulatory system, but as Holland is a comparatively small country blessed with first-class arterial roads, there was little hardship to the players. The first match is also memorable as being the first occasion on which the players were given the assistance of "seconds" with whom they were permitted to analyse adjourned games. There is a good deal to be said for this policy in Championship clashes. Chess human nature being what it is, the analysis of adjourned games will always happen and it is probably best to give it a certain amount of recognition. I should, however, be sorry

DR. M. EUWE

to see the principle extended to the ordinary run of tournaments as it offers unfair opportunities to those whose purses are long enough to afford paid assistance. The result of the match caused surprise among the general chess public, but those who had intimate acquaintance with the challenger's real strength always thought that he had a fighting chance.

It is possible that Alekhine had not fully trained for the encounter and that he was rather too appreciative of Dutch hospitality, but nothing can detract from the all-round excellence of Euwe's play.

Final score: Euwe 9; Alekhine 8; Drawn 13.

FIRST MATCH GAME

White: Dr. A. Alekhine. Black: Dr. M. Euwe.

1	P—Q4	P—Q4
2	P—QB4	P—QB3
3	Kt—KB3	Kt—KB3
4	Kt—B3	P×P
5	P—QR4	B—B4
6	Kt—K5	

At the time this match was played this was the most popular move. Now 6 P—K3 is justly regarded as giving White better opportunities.

6 ...   QKt—Q2

Another move which has gone out of fashion. A better line is 6 ... P—K3; 7 P—B3, B—QKt5; 8 B—Kt5 (if 8 P—K4, the sacrifice 8 ... B×KP; 9 P×B, Kt×P is at least good enough for a draw); 8 ... P—KR3, or even 8 ... P—B4, gives Black a game with good counter-chances.

7 Kt×P(B4)   Q—B2

The point of Black's system of defence. He is able to force the advance of P—K4.

8 P—KKt3	P—K4
9 P×P	Kt×P
10 B—B4	KKt—Q2
11 B—Kt2	B—K3

In a game Capablanca v. Vidmar, the continuation 11 ... P—B3; 12 Castles, B—K3; 13 Kt×Kt, P×Kt yielded Black practical equality. The merit of this line is that it disposes permanently of the pin on the Knight at K4. Neglect of this precaution brings Euwe into trouble.

12 Kt×Kt	Kt×Kt
13 Castles	B—K2

13 ... Q—R4, in order to get rid of the pin, seems slightly better. If then 14 Kt—Kt5, R—Q1; 15 Q—B2, P—B3.

14 Q—B2	R—Q1

Now 14 ... Q—R4 is met by 15 Kt—Kt5, P—B3; 16 Kt—Q4, with a splendid game.

15 KR—Q1	Castles
16 Kt—Kt5	R×R ch

This exchange does not help Black, but already his position is very difficult. If 16 ... Q—R4; 17 R×R, R×R; 18 B×Kt, P×Kt; 19 B×QKtP wins a pawn, and if 16 ... Q—Kt3; 17 Kt—Q4, followed by Kt—B5 gives White a splendid game.

17 R×R	Q—R4

Ingenious, as now 18 B×Kt, P×Kt; 19 B×QKtP, P×P would relieve Black of his troubles. The position of the Queen, however, is precarious and Alekhine soon finds a fine combination to drive it back into the pin.

18 Kt—Q4	B—B1

BLACK

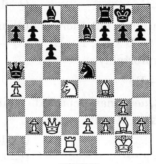

WHITE

19 P—QKt4

This is the combination. The pawn cannot be captured, e.g. 19 ... B×P; 20 Kt—Kt3, Q—B2; 21 Q—K4, B—B6 (if 21 ... B—Q3; 22 Q—Q4 and wins); 22 R—QB1, B—Kt7 (if 22 ... P—KB4; 23 Q—B2, B—Kt5; 24 B×Kt, Q×B; 25 Q—B4 ch, and wins); 23 R—B2, and wins. The Black Queen is therefore driven back to B2 and with his next move White forces an entry for his pieces at Q5.

19 ...	Q—B2
20 P—Kt5	P—QB4
21 Kt—B5	P—B3

The move which should have been made long ago is too late now. Nothing else serves either. If 21 ... B×Kt; 22 Q×B, P—B3 (if 22 ... B—B3; 23 B—K4 and wins); 23 Q—K6 ch, K—R1; 24 B×Kt wins at least a pawn, and if 21 ... B—B3; 22 Kt—Q6, R—Q1; 23 Kt—B4 leaves the Black position hopeless.

22 Kt—K3	B—K3
23 B—Q5	

Even stronger than 23 Kt—Q5. White now secures the domination of the all-important central squares.

| 23 ... | B×B |
| 24 R×B | Q—R4 |

Rather a forlorn hope, but there is nothing to be done. If
24 ... R—Q1; 25 B×Kt, P×B; 26 Q—B5, or 25 Q—B5
at once wins comfortably.

25 Kt—B5

Now that the Queen has departed White proceeds to a
decisive King's side attack.

25 ...	Q—K8 ch
26 K—Kt2	B—Q1
27 B×Kt	P×B
28 R—Q7	B—B3

If 28 ... P—KKt3; 29 Kt—R6 ch, K—R1; 30 R×B, etc.

| 29 Kt—R6 ch | K—R1 |
| 30 Q×P | Resigns |

If 30 ... R—K1; 31 Q—Q5 (threatening the smothered
mate by 32 Q—Kt8 ch, R×Q; 33 Kt—B7 mate); 31 ...
P×Kt; 32 Q—B7 forces mate.

A fine game by Alekhine who took remorseless advantage
of his opponent's small inaccuracies in the opening.

SECOND MATCH GAME

White: Dr. M. Euwe. Black: Dr. A. Alekhine.

1 P—Q4	Kt—KB3
2 P—QB4	P—KKt3
3 Kt—QB3	P—Q4
4 Q—Kt3	

In 1935 this was considered the best move. Now it is
regarded as premature, either 4 P×P, 4 B—B4, or 4 Kt—
B3 being preferred.

| 4 ... | P×P |
| 5 Q×BP | B—K3 |

180

The most energetic reply if properly followed up. White loses a great deal of time with the Queen.

6	Q—Kt5 ch	Kt—B3
7	Kt—B3	R—QKt1

Too defensive. Black should continue 7 ... Kt—Q4; 8 P—K4 (if 8 Q×P, KKt—Kt5; 9 Q—Kt5, Kt—B7 ch; 10 K—Q1, Kt×P with advantage); 8 ... KKt—Kt5; 9 Q—R4, B—Q2; 10 Q—Q1, P—K4; 11 P×P, B—Kt5 with a good game.

8 Kt—K5

Euwe takes immediate advantage of his opponent's last move. He now forces the advantage of two Bishops and his mobile centre becomes very strong.

8	...	B—Q2
9	Kt×B	Q×Kt
10	P—Q5	Kt—Q5
11	Q—Q3	P—K4
12	P—K3	Kt—B4
13	P—K4	Kt—Q3

If the Knight returns to Q5, White can play advantageously 14 B—Kt5, B—Kt2; 15 P—B4, Q—Q3 or K2; 16 Castles, and the position of the Knight at Q5 is uncomfortable.

14	P—B4	Q—K2
15	B—K3	

Very strong. White now threatens 16 P×P followed by 17 B—Q4, and if Black plays 15 ... P×P; 16 B—Q4, B—Kt2; 17 Castles, and the White central advance is irresistible.

15 ...   Kt—Kt5

An ingenious tactical resource. White, it is true, wins a pawn, but Black rids himself of the more dangerous of the two Bishops and obtains counter-chances.

16 B×P	R—R1
17 P—KR3	

The only way to keep the pawn. If 17 B—Kt1, P×P, followed by Kt—K4 is satisfactory for Black, and if 17 B—K3, Kt×B; 18 Q×Kt, B—R3; 19 P—Kt3, P×P; 20 P×P, Q—R5 ch, etc.

17 ...	R×B
18 P×Kt	B—Kt2

Obviously not 18 ... P×P; 19 Q—Q4.

19 Q—K3	R—R4
20 P—B5	B—B3
21 P—R4	B—R5 ch
22 P—Kt3	B—Kt4
23 Q—B3	Castles
24 P—Kt4	QR—R1
25 R—QR2	

Threatening the unusual attack QR—R2.

25 ...	Kt—K1
26 R—QKt2	Kt—B3
27 B—K2	P—B3

This enables White to obtain a passed pawn but it is difficult to find any other line, containing any promise at all. If he confines himself to waiting moves White will Castle and attack the Queen's side at his leisure.

28 QP×P	QKtP×P
29 Castles	QR—Q1
30 K—Kt2	

A necessary preliminary to the advance of the Queen's side pawns on account of the possibilities of check at B4.

30 ...	R—Q5

Some annotators have suggested 30 ... B—Q7 with an awkward attack on White's KP. White, however, could reply 31 P—KKt5, sacrificing a pawn which is of little use to him, and after 31 ... B×P; 32 P—Kt5.

31 P—Kt5	BP×P
32 RP×P	R—Kt1
33 P×P	BP×P

This anti-positional move, rightly condemned by all the annotators, is clear proof that Alekhine was quite out of form in this match. Had he captured with the RP none of the ensuing attacks would have been available and White's road to victory would have been a very hard one.

| 34 P—Kt6 | Q—QKt2 |

BLACK

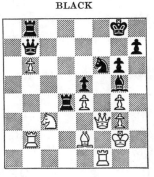

WHITE

35 K—R3

An extremely ingenious method of defending the KP. If Black captures it there follows 35 ... Kt×KP; 36 Kt×Kt, Q×Kt (if 36 ... R×Kt; 37 Q—Kt3 ch followed by B—B3—first instance of the weakness of his 33rd move); 37 Q—B7 ch, K—R1; 38 Q—B7, R(Q5)—Q1; 39 B—Q3 (in order to play R—B7 without being mated at KR8); 39 ... Q—Kt2 (best; if 39 ... Q×B; 40 R—B7 forces mate); 40 R—B7, Q×Q; 41 P×Q, R×R; 42 P×R= Q ch, B×Q; 43 R—B8 ch, K—Kt2; 44 R×B and wins.

183

| 35 ... | R—Q3 |
| 36 Kt—Q5 | |

A clever defence to the QKtP made possible by Black's unfortunate 33rd move. If now 36 ... Kt×Kt; 37 B—B4 wins easily.

| 36 ... | K—Kt2 |
| 37 R—QB2 | |

A temporary sacrifice of the passed pawn which leads to a winning attack. The obvious move 37 R—QR1 is answered by 37 ... Kt×Kt; 38 R—R7, Kt×KtP; 39 R×Q ch, R×R; and it is doubtful whether White can win the ending.

| 37 ... | Kt×Kt |
| 38 P×Kt | R×KtP |

There is nothing better. If 38 ... Q×KtP; 39 Q—B7 ch, followed by R—B7 wins at once and if 38 ... Q×QP; 39 R—B7 ch, K—R3; 40 Q×Q, R×Q; 41 P—Kt7 is decisive.

| 39 R—B6 | R×R |

There is nothing better. If 39 ... R—Kt6; 40 B—Q3 threatening P—Q6.

| 40 P×R | Q—K2 |
| 41 B—B4 | K—R3 |

If 41 ... B—B3; 42 P—Kt5, B×P; 43 Q—B7 ch, Q×Q; 44 R×Q ch, K—R3; 45 P—B7 and wins.

| 42 Q—R1 | |

Threatening the deadly K—Kt2 dis. ch. 42 Q—B7 would not be good on account of 42 ... R—QB1.

| 42 ... | R—Kt7 |

If 42 ... R—KB1; 43 R×R, Q×R; 44 P—B7, Q—B4; 45 Q—Kt7 and wins.

| 43 R—B7 | Q—K1 |

Or 43 ... Q—B4; 44 Q—Q5, threatening mate by 45 R×P ch, and if then 44 ... Q×Q; 45 B×Q and the passed pawn will cost a piece.

44 P—B7   R—QB7

If 44 ... P—K5 to cut off the White Queen. 45 Q—R1 wins a Rook.

45 Q—Kt7   Resigns

For if 45 ... R×B; 46 R×P ch, K×R; 47 P—B8=Q dis. ch.

A splendid game by Euwe.

TWENTY-FIFTH MATCH GAME

White: Dr. A. Alekhine. Black: Dr. M. Euwe.

1	P—Q4	P—Q4
2	P—QB4	P—QB3
3	Kt—KB3	Kt—B3
4	Kt—B3	P—K3
5	B—Kt5	QKt—Q2
6	P—K3	Q—R4
7	P×P	

This is not a good way of meeting the Cambridge Springs Defence as Black gets an extra piece to bear on the pinned Knight at QB3. 7 Kt—Q2 is the correct move.

7 ...   Kt×P

8 Q—Q2

Alekhine had previously won with this move because his opponent failed to find the correct reply. Rather better is 8 Q—Kt3 although even then Black obtains a fine game by 8 ... P—K4 (if 9 P×P, Kt—B4 and R5, or 9 Kt×P, Kt×Kt; 10 P×Kt, B—K3).

8 ...   Kt—Kt3

Stronger than the more obvious 8 ... B—Kt5; 9 R—B1,

185

QKt—B3; 10 B—Q3, threatening P—K4 with a good game.

> 9 B—Q3

It now appears impossible to avoid loss of a pawn. If 9 P—QR3, B—Kt5; 10 R—B1, B×Kt; 11 P×B, Q×RP, although after 12 P—K4, Kt—B3; 13 B—Q3 White's position is rather more promising than he obtained in the game.

9 ...	Kt×Kt
10 P×Kt	Kt—Q4
11 R—QB1	

Or 11 Castles, Q×BP; 12 Q×Q, Kt×Q; 13 KR—B1, Kt—Q4; 14 QR—Kt1. Black's position is cramped but he has a solid pawn to the good and, in the absence of the Queens, has not much to fear.

| 11 ... | Kt×BP |
| 12 Castles | |

Not 12 R×Kt, B—Kt5.

| 12 ... | B—Kt5 |
| 13 P—QR3 | |

This second sacrifice is the only way to make anything out of the position. Black has three distinct threats, viz. 13 ... Kt—K5, 13 ... Kt×RP, and 13 ... Q×RP.

13 ...	Q×P
14 R—R1	Q—Kt6
15 B—B2	Q—Q4
16 P—K4	

And this also is almost forced. If Black is allowed to Castle into safety, White's game is hopeless.

16 ...	Kt×P
17 Q×B	Kt×B
18 Kt—K5	P—QR4
19 Q—R3	P—B3

Best. He has plenty of material to win with already, and further pawn-snatching would be sheer greediness.

BLACK

WHITE

20 B—Kt6 ch

At last Alekhine finds an attacking combination but Euwe has a counter-mine prepared which decides the issue. Anything else would be equally, but less elegantly, fatal.

20 ...	P×B
21 Kt×KtP	Kt—B6 ch

Sounding the death knell of White's hopes. If 22 P×Kt, then, obviously, 22 ... Q—Kt4 ch and 23 ... Q×Kt.

22 Q×Kt	Q×Q
23 P×Q	R—R4

Black, of course, has now an easily won game and the remaining moves are only of interest from the able manner in which Euwe completes his development and exploits his material advantage with the utmost economy of time.

24 Kt—B4	R—KB4
25 Kt—Q3	R×P
26 Kt—B5	P—QKt3
27 K—Kt2	R—B5
28 Kt—Kt3	P—K4

29 P×P	B—K3
30 Kt—B1	Castles

Now that all Black's pieces are in play White could have resigned.

31 P×P	R—Kt5 ch
32 K—B3	

If 32 K—R1, B—B5 wins the exchange.

32 ...	R—B1
33 K—K3	R×P
34 P—B4	P—KKt4
35 Kt—Q3	B—B5
36 P—B5	

If 36 P×P, the simplest is 36 ... R×R; 37 R×R, B×Kt; 38 K×B, R×P.

36 ...	R—R5
37 QR—Q1	R×RP
38 K—K4	R—K7 ch
39 K—B3	R—K1
40 K—Kt4	R—Q1
41 Kt—K5	R×R
42 R×R	B—K7 ch
43 K×P	R×P ch
44 K×R	B×R
45 Kt×P	P—R5
Resigns	

Euwe gave his opponent no chance to recover from his unsound opening tactics.

TWENTY-SIXTH MATCH GAME

White: Dr. M. Euwe. Black: Dr. A. Alekhine.

1 P—Q4	P—K3
2 P—QB4	P—KB4
3 P—KKt3	B—Kt5 ch

188

This move, followed by the retreat of the Bishop, was fashionable at one time as it was considered that White's Queen's Bishop was badly placed on Q2. Now opinion on this point has changed and 3 ... Kt—KB3; 4 B—Kt2, B—K2 is thought to be preferable.

4	B—Q2	B—K2
5	B—Kt2	Kt—KB3
6	Kt—QB3	Castles
7	Kt—B3	Kt—K5

Sounder is 7 ... P—Q4 followed by P—B3 with a stone-wall build up. The line chosen is apt to involve Black in difficulties on the long white diagonal KR1—QR8.

8 Castles

In ultra-close games Knights are usually more effective than Bishops, so White does not mind the possibility of 8 ... Kt×B.

8	...	P—QKt3
9	Q—B2	B—Kt2
10	Kt—K5	Kt×Kt

Quite sound. If White replies 11 B×B, Kt×P ch; 12 K—Kt2, Kt×P; 13 Q—Q3, QKt—B3; 14 Kt×Kt, Kt×Kt; 15 B×R, Q×B, with two good pawns for the exchange.

11	B×Kt	B×B
12	K×B	Q—B1
13	P—Q5	P—Q3
14	Kt—Q3	P—K4
15	K—R1	

A precaution against the possibility of Black playing P—B5.

15	...	P—B3
16	Q—Kt3	

Necessary to prevent P×P followed by Q—B5.

16 …		K—R1
17	P—B4	P—K5
18	Kt—Kt4	P—B4

Otherwise the White Knight will enter at Q5.

19	Kt—B2	Kt—Q2
20	Kt—K3	

BLACK

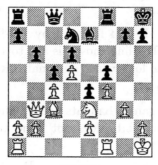

WHITE

20 …		B—B3

This allows White to make a promising sacrifice of a piece for three pawns which, as two of the pawns are passed, is sufficient to give him a strategically won game. No doubt Alekhine saw this continuation, but considered that he had good chances in the tactical complications which ensue. A safer line was 20 … Kt—B3 and possibly 21 … Kt—Kt1 and then B—B3.

21	Kt × P	B × B
22	Kt × QP	Q—Kt1
23	Kt × P	B—B3
24	Kt—Q2	P—KKt4

This is the move on which Alekhine relied when he permitted Euwe's combination. He obtains good attacking chances on the open KKt file.

190

25 P—K4	P×P
26 P×P	B—Q5
27 P—K5	Q—K1
28 P—K6	R—KKt1
29 Kt—B3	

If 29 P×Kt, Q—K7, recovering the piece with an improved position, but the text is not the best either. 30 Q—R3 would make all safe on the King's wing while threatening an irresistible advance of the pawns.

29 ...	Q—Kt3
30 R—KKt1	

This neat counter is the best, for if 30 Kt—Kt5 (30 Kt—R4, Q—Kt5, etc.); 30 ... Kt—K4; 31 QR—Q1 (31 R—KKt1 now is met by 31 ... B×R; 32 R×B, Q—B4); 31 ... P—KR3 and if 32 Q—R3, Kt×P.

30 ...	B×R
31 R×B	

BLACK

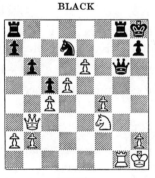

WHITE

31 ...	Q—B3

Better is 31 ... Q—B4 when White has nothing left except 32 P×Kt (if 32 Kt—Kt5, P—KR3); 32 ... R×R ch; 33 K×R, Q×P(Q7) with a probable draw. The text

191

allows White to introduce new complications but should not in itself lose.

32 Kt—Kt5

Finely played. Black cannot now play 32 ... P—KR3 because of 33 Kt—B7 ch, K—R2; 34 Q—Q3 ch, R—Kt3; 35 Kt—K5, Kt×Kt; 36 P×Kt, Q—Kt2; 37 P—Q6, Q—Kt2 ch; 38 Q—Q5, Q×Q ch; 39 P×Q and the mass of White pawns is irresistible. A quaint position.

| 32 ... | R—Kt2 |
| 33 P×Kt | R×P |

He should have played 33 ... Q×BP; 34 Q—QB3 (threatening Q×R ch); 34 ... Q—Q5; 35 Q×Q (there is nothing better. If 35 Q—B3, R×P; 36 Kt—B7 ch, R×Kt; 37 Q×R, Q—K5 ch with perpetual check); 35 ... P×Q; 36 Kt—K6, R×P and Black should draw the ending.

34 Q—K3	R—K2
35 Kt—K6	R—KB1
36 Q—K5	Q×Q

Black must have been very loath to unite White's pawns, but there is no alternative as he is literally without moves.

| 37 P×Q | R—B4 |

If he gives up the exchange his chances in the Rook ending are very small.

| 38 R—K1 | P—KR3 |

This loses quickly. Black's only chance lies in preventing the White Knight from moving by 38 ... K—Kt1, but White can still win by 39 K—Kt2, R—K1 (Black can only mark time. If he allows the Knight to move the pawns cannot be stopped, and pawn moves on the Queen's side are of no account); 40 K—Kt3, P—KR4; 41 P—KR4, R—K2; 42 K—Kt2, R—K1; 43 R—K3, R—K2; 44 R—Kt3 ch, followed by R—Kt5.

39 Kt—Q8	R—B7

Obviously 39 ... R×P loses a Rook.

40 P—K6	R—Q7
41 Kt—B6	R—K1
42 P—K7	P—Kt4
43 Kt—Q8	K—Kt2
44 Kt—Kt7	K—B3
45 R—K6 ch	K—Kt4
46 Kt—Q6	R×KP
47 Kt—K4 ch	Resigns

An interesting and well-fought game, full of rich combinative points.

THE SECOND MATCH: EUWE v. ALEKHINE

I was present at this match and can testify to the grim determination with which Alekhine entered into it. He neither drank nor smoked and had brought himself to the highest pitch of physical fitness. As a result he was, for the last time in his life, in his very best form and his play was, if anything, even better than in his match with Capablanca.

Euwe struggled gallantly and held his own in the early part, but lost ground in the middle and his final rally came too late.

The final score was: Alekhine 10; Euwe 4; Drawn 11.

The match, like the first, was scheduled to consist of thirty games, but when the result was decided, the remaining five ranked as exhibition games. Of these Euwe won two and Alekhine one.

SECOND MATCH GAME

White: Dr. A. Alekhine. Black: Dr. M. Euwe.

1 P—Q4	P—Q4
2 P—QB4	P—QB3

193

3 Kt—KB3	Kt—B3
4 Kt—B3	P×P
5 P—QR4	B—B4
6 Kt—K5	

This match saw the end of this once popular move. It now occurs very rarely in master practice.

| 6 ... | P—K3 |
| 7 B—Kt5 | |

For 7 P—B3 see first game of 1935 match (p. 177).

| 7 ... | B—Kt5 |
| 8 Kt×P(B4) | |

If this is White's best the move 6 Kt—K5 is rightly abandoned. If 8 P—B3, Black can continue either by 8 ... P—KR3; 9 P—K4, P×P; 10 P×B, P—QKt4; 11 P×KP, P×KP; 12 Q—B2, Castles, as in a consultation game played by Alekhine in 1929, or could try 8 ... P—B4; 9 P×P, Q—Q4; with about equal chances in either case.

| 8 ... | Q—Q4 |

This move leads to very interesting play and, for the moment at least, transfers the initiative to Black. The threat is 9 ... Kt—K5 and if White tries 9 Kt—K3, Q—R4; 10 Kt×B, Q×Kt, with a very good game.

| 9 B×Kt | Q×Kt |
| 10 Q—Q2 | |

This uncomfortable-looking move is forced, for if 10 R—B1, P×B; 11 P—K4, Q—R7, winning material.

| 10 ... | P×B |

Alekhine thinks that 10 ... Q—Kt6 was superior. Certainly after 11 B×P, R—KKt1; 12 B—R6, Kt—Q2 the threat of an attack by the Knight via B3 and K5 or Q4 or via Kt3 and R5 is very hard to meet, but White might play 11 B—R4, Kt—Q2; 12 P—B3, with

comparative security. Still there is no doubt that 10 ...
Q—Kt6 retains the initiative whereas the move in the text
leads to equality at the best.

11	P—K4	Q—Kt6
12	P×B	Kt—Q2
13	P×P	P×P
14	B—K2	Castles QR
15	Castles KR	P—K4
16	P×P	Kt×P
17	Q—B1	B×Kt

There is no apparent necessity for this exchange which
opens the QKt file and, incidentally, deprives Black of a
valuable Bishop. 17 ... Kt—Q6, or 17 ... KR—KKt1
seem good enough to secure equality.

18	P×B	KR—Kt1
19	Q—K3	K—Kt1
20	P—Kt3	

A precautionary measure against attacks on the KKt file.

20	...	R—Q2
21	QR—Kt1	Q—B7

BLACK

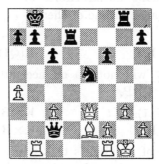

WHITE

22 KR—K1

Alekhine calls this "the most subtle move of the game,"

and it certainly involves profound calculation. The theme of his play is that if he can drive the Black Knight from his post at K4 his Bishop will prove superior to the Knight, particularly if an endgame ensues. At the moment, however, 22 P—KB4 can be effectively met by 22 ... R—Q7; 23 KR—K1, Kt—Q6, and Black wins as 24 B×Kt, R×B; 25 Q—K6 or K7 is met by 25 ... R×P ch.

22 ...	Q—Q7

Now 22 ... Kt—Q6 fails against 23 B×Kt, Q×B (23 ... R×B is worse); 24 Q—B4 ch, Q—Q3; 25 Q×Q ch, R×Q; 26 R—K7, and 22 ... R—Q7 is met by 23 B—R6. The exchange of Queens therefore seems almost forced.

23 Q×Q	R×Q
24 P—KB4	Kt—Kt3
25 B—B4	

White's advantage in this ending consists in the facts: (*A*) That he has a pawn majority on the wing where the Black King is not, and (*B*) that his Bishop is a more effective piece than the Knight on the open board. At the present moment, however, Black's Rooks are formidably placed and White's initial efforts are directed towards forcing the exchange of one of them.

25 ...	KR—Q1
26 R—K6	R(Q1)—Q3

26 ... R—QB7 will not do on account of 27 B—R6, P—Kt3; 28 R×QBP.

27 R(Kt1)—K1	K—B2
28 R×R	R×R

The first part of Alekhine's task is accomplished. The remainder of the game is a splendid example of accurate and incisive endgame play.

29 P—KR4	K—Q2
30 K—B2	Kt—K2

31 K—B3	Kt—Q4

Alekhine points out that against 31 ... P—KB4, he would have played 32 P—KR5 followed by 33 P—Kt4, after which the passed KBP will be tremendously strong. 32 P—Kt4 at once would not have been so good because of 32 ... P×P ch; 33 K×P, R—Kt3 ch, followed by Kt—B4 with counter-chances.

32 B—Q3	P—KR3

If he gives up this pawn White's KRP will decide the issue.

33 B—B5 ch	K—Q1
34 K—Kt4	Kt—K2

If 34 ... Kt×QBP; 35 K—R5, Kt×P; 36 K×P, there is no stopping the KRP.

35 B—Kt1	K—K1
36 K—R5	K—B2
37 B—R2 ch	K—B1
38 K×P	R—Q7
39 B—K6	R—Q6
40 P—Kt4	R×P
41 P—Kt5	Resigns

The two pawns are irresistible. This game is a fine example of Alekhine's play in the second phase of his career. After a slightly inferior opening his strategy is a fine example of that deceptive simplicity which looks so easy but is, in fact, so hard to achieve.

FIFTH MATCH GAME

White: Dr. M. Euwe. Black: Dr. A. Alekhine.

1 P—Q4	P—Q4
2 P—QB4	P×P
3 Kt—KB3	P—QR3
4 P—K3	Kt—KB3

Alekhine usually played here 4 ... B—Kt5; 5 B×P,
P—K3; 6 Q—Kt3, B×Kt. The text move leads to the
normal variation of the opening.

5	B×P	P—K3
6	Castles	P—B4
7	Q—K2	Kt—B3
8	Kt—B3	

Better than 8 R—Q1, if only because of the reply 8 ...
P—QKt4; 9 B—Kt3, P—B5; 10 B—B2, Kt—QKt5,
exchanging White's most dangerous attacking Bishop.

8 ...		P—QKt4

If 8 ... P×P; 9 R—Q1 recovers the pawn with the better
game for White.

9	B—Kt3	B—K2

9 ... B—Kt2 is more usual, but White still retains the
advantage by 10 R—Q1, Q—B2; 11 P—Q5.

10	P×P	B×P

If 10 ... Castles; 11 P—K4, B×P; 12 P—K5, Kt—Q2;
13 P—QR4, P—Kt5; 14 Kt—K4 gives White a dominating
position.

11	P—K4	

Euwe points out that this is superior to 11 R—Q1, Q—B2;
12 P—K4 because of 12 ... Kt—KKt5, with a grip on K4.

11 ...		P—Kt5

11 ... Kt—Q2 is safer but Black's position remains
constrained.

12	P—K5	P×Kt
13	P×Kt	KtP×P

If 13 ... Q×P; 14 Q—B4, P×P (if 14 ... Q—K2; 15
B—K3 wins a piece); 15 B×P, Q×B; 16 Q×B with a
winning position.

| 14 Q—B4 | Q—Kt3 |
| 15 Q×BP | Kt—Q5 |

The only move. 15 ... B—K2; 16 B—K3, Q—Kt2; 17 B—R4, B—Q2; 18 KR—Q1 is hopeless for Black.

| 16 Kt×Kt | B×Kt |
| 17 B—R4 ch | K—K2 |

If 17 ... B—Q2; 18 B×B ch, K×B; 19 R—Q1, P—K4; 20 B—K3, with a speedy win.

| 18 B—K3 | B×Q |

Euwe considers this to be Black's decisive error and points out that the position would still be held by 18 ... R—Q1; 19 QR—Q1, P—K4; 20 B×B, R×B; 21 R×R, P×R (not 21 ... Q×R; 22 Q—B6); 22 Q—B3, R—Kt1, although Black is still saddled with weak scattered pawns.

| 19 B×Q | B—K4 |

Other Bishop moves are worse. If 19 ... B—Kt5; 20 B—B6, R—QKt1; 21 B—B7 wins the exchange, or if 19 ... B×P; 20 B—B5 ch, K—Q1; 21 KR—Q1 ch, K—B2; 22 B—Q6 ch followed by 23 QR—Kt1 and wins.

| 20 QR—Q1 |

BLACK

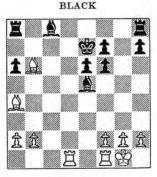

WHITE

| 20 ... | K—B1 |

199

There is no adequate defence now. White threatens 21 B—B5 ch with mate to follow, and if 20 ... B—Q3; 21 R×B, K×R; 22 R—Q1 ch, K—K4; 23 B—B6, QR—Kt1; 24 B—B7 ch and wins; or 20 ... P—B4; 21 B—B5 ch, K—B3; 22 P—B4, B×KtP; 23 R—B2, winning a piece.

21 P—B4		B×KtP
22 R—B3		

Euwe rightly calls this "A move of many threats." There is, in fact, no way by which Black can avert disastrous material loss. The most plausible line 22 ... P—B4 is met by 23 B—B5 ch, K—Kt2; 24 R—QKt3, B—B3; 25 B—B6 and wins.

22 ...		B—Kt2
23 R—KKt3		

Threatening B—B5 mate. If Black plays 23 ... R—B1; 24 R—Q8 ch, K—K2; 25 R—Q7 ch and wins. The best move at this stage would be 23 ... Resigns. Alekhine prefers to carry on a hopeless struggle with a piece to the bad for another eighteen moves.

23 ...	B—R6
24 R×B	R—KKt1
25 R—KKt3	R×R
26 P×R	B—Q4
27 B—Kt3	B×B
28 P×B	K—K1
29 P—QKt4	R—Kt1
30 B—B5	R—B1
31 R—R1	R—B3
32 K—B2	P—B4
33 K—K3	P—B3
34 K—Q4	K—B2
35 K—B4	K—Kt3
36 R—Q1	K—R4

37 R—Q6	R × R
38 B × R	K—Kt5
39 B—K7	K × P
40 B × P	K × BP
41 K—B5	Resigns

A remarkable game in which one or two slightly inferior moves in the opening brought about a surprising disaster. The manner in which Euwe took advantage of his opportunities is highly instructive.

EIGHTH MATCH GAME

White: Dr. A. Alekhine. Black: Dr. M. Euwe.

1 P—Q4	Kt—KB3
2 P—QB4	P—K3
3 Kt—QB3	B—Kt5
4 Q—B2	

Alekhine strongly favoured this move in preference to the more complicated 4 P—K3 or 4 P—QR3. To-day it is considered that Black should equalize without much difficulty.

4 ...	P—Q4
5 P × P	

The simplest continuation. 5 P—QR3, B × Kt ch; 6 Q × B, Kt—K5 leads to complicated variations in which Black seems to hold his own.

5 ...	Q × P

This is generally held to be stronger than 5 ... P × P, to which White can play 6 B—Kt5 with a position akin to the Exchange variation of the normal Queen's Gambit.

6 P—K3	P—B4
7 P—QR3	B × Kt ch
8 P × B	QKt—Q2

It was better to Castle. All Black's subsequent troubles are due to his neglect of this precaution.

> 9 P—B3

A good method of maintaining the initiative. The possibility of P—K4 is a continual menace to Black.

> 9 ...   P×P
> 10 BP×P   Kt—Kt3
> 11 Kt—K2   B—Q2

11 ... Castles, and if 12 Kt—B4 or P—K4, 12 ... Q—Q1 was still possible.

> 12 Kt—B4   Q—Q3

Black seems to underestimate his danger. 12 ... Q—B3 was necessary, although after 13 Q×Q, B×Q; 14 P—K4, White's pair of Bishops and strong centre give him the superior position.

> 13 B—Q2

Now Castling is prevented and Black's King is very unsafe in the centre.

> 13 ...   R—QB1
> 14 Q—Kt2   KKt—Q4
> 15 Kt×Kt   P×Kt
> 16 B—Kt4   Q—K3
> 17 K—B2

White's King is perfectly safe on this square.

> 17 ...   Kt—R5

The commencement of a plan to drive away White's Queen's Bishop with pawns, which turns out badly in consequence of the superiority of White's centre. It seems doubtful whether there is any satisfactory move left. Alekhine suggests as best, 17 ... Kt—B5; 18 B×Kt, R×B; 19 QR—QB1, R×R; 20 R×R, B—B3; but White obtains a powerful attack by 21 P—K4, and if 21 ... P×P; 22 P—Q5.

18 Q—Q2   P—QKt3

Logical but bad. The last hope lay in 18 ... P—B4 to provide an escape for his King.

19 B—R6

Nipping in the bud Black's idea of P—QR4. From now to the end Alekhine plays with tremendous energy.

19 ...   R—QKt1

Hoping to trap the Bishop by P—QKt4. 19 ... R—B2 would also lose after 20 QR—QB1, R×R; 21 R×R, P—QKt4; 22 B—Kt7, threatening both P—K4 and Q—R2.

20 P—K4

BLACK

WHITE

Opening up the centre with decisive effect. If Black tries to make a flight square for his King by 20 ... P—B3, there follows 21 P×P, Q×P; 22 Q—K2 ch, Q—K3 (if 22 ... K—B2; 23 B—B4); 23 Q×Q ch, B×Q; 24 B—Kt5 ch, B—Q2; 25 KR—K1 ch, K—Q1; 26 B—K7 ch, and wins.

20 ...   P—QKt4

Going on with his original plan of winning the Bishop. It is true that after 21 P×P, Q×B; 22 KR—K1 ch, K—Q1, he might be able to withstand the attack.

21 Q—B4

But this intermediate move settled matters.

21 ...   R—Kt3

Or 21 ... R—Q1; 22 P×P, Q×P (or 22 ... Q×B; 23 Q—K5 ch, B—K3; 24 Q×P and wins); 23 KR—K1 ch, B—K3; 24 R—K5, Q×P ch; 25 Q×Q, R×Q; 26 B×P ch, and wins.

22 P×P   Q×P
23 KR—K1 ch   B—K3
24 QR—B1

Threatening immediate destruction by R—B8 ch.

24 ...   P—B3
25 R—B7

Even more decisive than 25 R—B8 ch

25 ...   K—Q1
26 R×RP   Resigns

Mate cannot be averted for more than a few moves. A finely-conducted attack by Alekhine, who must have visualized the combination to the end when he played his 19th move of B—R6.

Twenty-fifth and Deciding Game

White: Dr. M. Euwe. Black: Dr. A. Alekhine.

1 P—Q4   Kt—KB3
2 P—QB4   P—K3
3 Kt—QB3   B—Kt5
4 P—K3   Castles
5 Kt—K2

This move, the trade-mark of Rubinstein, is rather out of place in this particular position. More usual is 5 P—QR3, to make Black commit himself with his Bishop. 5 Kt—B3 or 5 B—Q3 are also, of course, perfectly good.

5 ...	P—Q4
6 P—QR3	B—K2
7 P×P	

Quite logical. White intends to play Kt—Kt3, B—Q3, and Kt—B5.

7 ...	P×P
8 Kt—Kt3	P—B4
9 P×P	

But this exchange is quite wrong and gives Black opportunities for counter play in the centre which completely destroys White's strategic plan. White should continue his development by 9 B—Q3.

| 9 ... | B×P |
| 10 P—QKt4 | |

Apparently overlooking his opponent's reply. 10 B—Q3 was still correct.

| 10 ... | P—Q5 |

A surprising stroke which gives Black the better game in all variations. If White replies 11 Kt—R4, P×P; 12 Q×Q (if 12 Kt×B, P×P ch wins the Queen); 12 ... P×P ch; 13 K—K2, B—Kt5 ch; 14 K—Q3, R×Q ch and wins; or 11 QKt—K4, Kt×Kt; 12 Kt×Kt, B—Kt3; 13 B—Q3, P×P, and White has a broken pawn position.

| 11 P×B | P×Kt |
| 12 Q—B2 | |

12 Q×Q, R×Q; 13 Kt—K2, Kt—K5; 14 P—B3, Kt× QBP; 15 Kt×P, is comparatively better, but it is a melancholy line for White at this early stage. After the text move Black's QBP proves terribly strong while White's opposite number is negligible.

| 12 ... | Q—R4 |
| 13 R—QKt1 | |

He cannot win the pawn by 13 Kt—K2, because of 13 ...
Kt—Q4 threatening Kt—Kt5. 13 B—Q3 is met by 13 ...
Kt—B3, with the same threat, and if 13 B—B4, Q×BP,
and White cannot play 14 Q×P because of 14 ... B—K3.

13 ...	B—Q2

With the powerful threat of B—R5 and P—B7 dis. ch.

BLACK

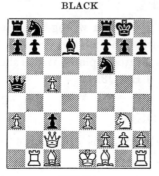

WHITE

14 R—Kt3	

This eventually results in the loss of the exchange, but it
appears to be White's best course. Against 14 B—B4 there
follows 14 ... B—R5; 15 B—Kt3, B—Kt4, threatening
B—Q6; and if 14 R—Kt4, Alekhine gives 14 ... Kt—R3;
15 B×Kt, Q×B; 16 P—K4 (not 16 Q×P, Kt—Q4);
16 ... KR—K1, with a depressing position for White. As
a result of the sacrifice White's game develops unexpected
attacking resources.

14 ...	B—R5
15 Q×P	Q—Q1
16 B—B4	Kt—R3
17 B×Kt	

Or 17 Castles, B×R; 18 B×B, R—B1, and Black should
win comfortably.

17 ...	P×B
18 Castles	B×R
19 Q×B	R—Kt1
20 Q—B2	Q—Q4
21 P—K4	Q—Kt6
22 Q—K2	

After 22 Q×Q, R×Q White must lose one of his Queen's side pawns with a hopeless ending.

22 ...	Q—Kt4
23 Q—B3	

The QBP cannot be saved. White's only hope rests in an attack with Queen and Knight against the Black King.

23 ...	Q×P
24 Kt—B5	R—Kt8

A well-thought-out counter. If now 25 Q—KKt3, Kt—R4; 26 Q—Kt5, K—R1; 27 P—Kt4, P—R3, and White's attack is over.

25 Q—B4	Kt×P
26 P—KR4	

White, of course, can only play for traps, and this is a most ingenious one. If Black plays the apparently powerful 26 ... Kt×P; 27 K—R2 (threatening B—K3), and if 27 ... Kt—Q6; 28 Q—Kt5, Q—K4 ch; 29 B—B4, Kt× B; 30 Kt—R6 ch, winning the Queen.

26 ...	R—K1
27 R—K1	Q—B6
28 R—Q1	

And now he threatens Q×Kt, but Alekhine has a neat reply which produces a much-to-be-desired simplification.

28 ...	Kt—Q7
29 R×Kt	

Forced.

29 ...   R × B ch

Alekhine points out that 29 ... Q × B ch; 30 K—R2,
R—Kt7 would lose because of the neat reply Q—K5.

30 K—R2   Q—B2
31 R—Q6   R—B4

Threatening R × Kt.

32 P—KKt3

A last ingenious trap. 32 ... R × Kt is met by 33 R—K6,
after which Black is forced to give up his Queen and
remains with a doubtful ending.

32 ...   R—KB1

Best. Black still has to exercise a little care against such
possibilities as Kt × P or (in the case of 32 ... R—Q1, or
32 R—QB1), Q—Kt5.

33 P—Kt4

Now he has to guard against the threat of R × Kt.

33 ...   P—B3
34 K—R3

To enable the Queen to move without leaving the Rook in
a pin. If 34 P—R5, to prevent Black's next, 34 ... P—
Kt3; 35 P × P, P × P; 36 Kt—R6 ch, K—Kt2, with the
double threat of R—Q1 and R—KR1.

34 ...   P—KR4

Beginning a decisive counter-onslaught.

35 Q—Q2   P × P ch
36 K × P   Q—B2
37 P—R5   R × Kt

Alekhine describes this Knight as "The most hated
Knight of the match," and it has certainly played a noble
part in the struggle. Now Black obtains a mating attack.

38 K × R   Q × P ch

39 K—B4	Q—R5 ch
40 K—B3	

If 40 K—B5, P—Kt3 ch; 41 K—K6, Q—K5 ch, and mates in two moves.

40 ...	Q—R6 ch
41 K—K4	

If 41 K—K2, R—K1 ch; 42 K—Q1, Q—Kt6 ch wins the Queen, or if 41 K—B4, R—K1, threatening P—Kt4 mate.

41 ...	R—K1 ch
42 K—Q5	Q—Kt6 ch
43 K—Q4	Q×P
Resigns	

A very interesting game which forms a fitting climax to a well-played match. Euwe displayed marvellous ingenuity in a theoretically lost position, and compelled Alekhine also to give of his best.

CHAPTER V

MIKHAIL BOTVINNIK

THE present Champion of the World, Mikhail Botvinnik, was born in 1911* He learned chess at the age of twelve when, as he says himself, "My brain was fresh, it could take in an unlimited amount of the information, the elementary knowledge which is necessary to the perfection of a player's technique and to a master's creative activity at the board." On this task he took four years. In 1927 he was awarded the title of Master of the Soviet Union and, at the age of twenty, he won the title of All-Russian Champion. Since then he has gone from strength to strength, winning the Soviet Championship on five of the seven occasions on which he has competed, gaining the title of Absolute Champion of the Soviet Union in a sex-angular contest, invading the international field with outstanding success, and finally gaining the greatest crown of all, the World Championship.

Botvinnik possesses in a high degree all the qualities which go to make a great chess player: a combination of talent, character, physical health, and the ability to concentrate on preparation. Probably no one prepares for a contest so thoroughly as he does, both on the side of analysis and that of physical fitness. Some of the rules he lays down for himself preparatory to a tournament bear more resemblance to training for a boxing than a chess contest. The thoroughness of his preparation is shown by the fact that finding that he, as a non-smoker, was troubled by the tobacco fumes which impregnate every chess room, he played a match with Ragosin, a continuous smoker, so that he could accustom himself to the atmosphere. Another

*Botvinnik was world champion from 1948-57, 1958-60, and 1961-63.

rare gift which he possesses is that of rigid self-criticism. No matter how finely he seems to have played, or how successful he has been, he tears his own games to pieces, searching out the slightest weaknesses and concentrating on ways and means to eradicate them. Consequently he has made himself equally at home in each department of the game: opening, positional strategy, combinative tactics, and endplay, so that it is impossible to say that he is stronger in one brand of play than another. His best games have the smoothness of an epic poem, rolling on grandly to their appointed end. His determination is enormous. One always feels that success to him is more than a personal triumph; it is something that adds to the glory of his beloved country and consequently, to the natural desire to win, is added a burning patriotic fervour.

In spite of this tremendous will to win he never allows himself to be betrayed into irritability or discourtesy towards his opponents. In fact, he is, if anything, almost over-courteous.

In tournaments it often happens that a player makes his move when his opponent is absent from the board. In such cases there are a few players—happily very few—who press the clock gently and remain with head buried in hands hoping thereby to gain time on the clock. Most relax and look round the room, or themselves rise from the board and have a look at the game next door. At Nottingham, the only tournament in which I have played with him, Botvinnik went much farther than this. He would personally search the tournament room, find the wanderer and escort him back to his place, apparently fearful lest he might be thought to take the slightest unfair advantage. In this tournament I was reporting the games for the *Manchester Guardian* and, consequently, was often at a considerable distance from my board, taking a bird's-eye view of other games, but he never failed to bring me back in spite of the fact that he needed a win to gain first prize outright, and had a very difficult position. With all these qualities combined with great charm of manner, Botvinnik is an ideal World Champion. He might well be described as the perfect chess ambassador. His record to date reads—

1929, won Leningrad Tournament.

1931, Championship of U.S.S.R., 1st—a success repeated in 1933, 1939, 1944, and 1945.

1941, won Sexangular Tournament for title of Absolute U.S.S.R. Champion.

In international tournaments, of which he has taken part in very few, his best performances are: Leningrad 1933, 1st; Moscow 1935, equal 1st with Flohr above Capablanca and Lasker; Moscow 1936, 2nd to Capablanca; Nottingham 1936, equal 1st with Capablanca; A.V.R.O. Tournament (Holland) 1938, 3rd following Keres and Fine; Groningen 1946, 1st; Tchigorin Memorial Tournament, Moscow 1947, 1st.

Since his World Championship match with Bronstein he has given performances which, for him, are poor ones in the Soviet Championship and the Budapest International Tournament (both won by Keres), but these results like those achieved by Bronstein in the same events were probably due to fatigue, following the most strenuous championship match of modern times. He will certainly come back to his old form.

Apart from his fame as a chess player Botvinnik has won distinction as an engineer and was decorated during the war for the invention of an improved trench mortar.

THE WORLD CHAMPIONSHIP TOURNAMENT

The conclusion of the last war saw a revolution in the organization of the World Championship. For a long time chess players had been dissatisfied with a system which allowed the reigning champion, to all intents and purposes, to choose his own opponent. It was finally agreed that the whole matter should be handed over to the International Chess Federation (F.I.D.E.).

The first task of this body was to find a successor to fill the throne vacated by the death of Alekhine, and it was decided that this should be done by means of a tournament of six selected players who should each play four games with all the others. The selected players, undoubtedly the strongest on the most recent form, were M. Botvinnik, P. Keres, and V. Smyslov (U.S.S.R.), R. Fine and S. Reshevsky (U.S.A.), and Dr. Euwe (Holland). Fine was, unfortunately, unable to take part and the number was reduced to five. It was decided that these should play five instead of four games against each other.

The first half of the tournament was played at The Hague, the second in Moscow. I have decided that the best way of presenting a picture of this great event is to give two of the best games played by the winner, Botvinnik, and one specimen from each of the others. For the annotations to these games I am much indebted to the profound and conscientious analysis by H. Golombek in his book, *World Championship Chess* 1948. Short biographies of Keres, Reshevsky, and Smyslov—who have not previously been mentioned in these pages—are appended.

As for the tournament itself Botvinnik went ahead almost from the start and before the first half was completed it was evident that, barring accidents, he was a certain winner. He actually won with three rounds to spare. He lost only two games—to Reshevsky and Keres; the latter after the Championship was already won. His play throughout was superb in all departments and marked him as at least the equal of any of the great champions who have preceded him.

There was a keen fight for second place which eventually went to Smyslov, a great achievement for the youngest and least experienced of the competitors. Reshevsky, one feels, ought to have done better. He was the only player who seriously troubled Botvinnik, winning one game and obtaining a won position in another. His one weakness is that he seems quite unable to keep on terms with his clock. Keres played well against everyone except Botvinnik who seemed to exercise a sort of hypnotic influence over him. Euwe, as already stated, was but a shadow of his true self.

The final score table was—

	Botvinnik	Smyslov	Reshevsky	Keres	Euwe	Total
Botvinnik .	———	½ ½ 1 ½ ½	1 ½ 0 1 1	1 1 1 1 0	1 ½ 1 ½ ½	14
Smyslov .	½ ½ 0 ½ ½	———	½ ½ 1 ½ ½	0 0 ½ 1 ½	1 1 0 1 1	11
Reshevsky .	0 ½ 1 0 0	½ ½ 0 ½ ½	———	1 ½ 0 1 ½	1 ½ ½ 1 1	10½
Keres .	0 0 0 0 1	1 1 ½ 0 ½	0 ½ 1 0 ½	———	1 ½ 1 1 1	10½
Euwe .	0 ½ 0 ½ ½	0 0 1 0 0	0 ½ ½ 0 0	0 ½ 0 0 0	———	4

V. Smyslov

Smyslov, the youngest of the competitors, was born in Moscow in 1921. Like most of the Soviet masters he has played chess practically all his life and tied for the Moscow Championship in 1938. Since then he has always been in the very top flight of Soviet masters, though somehow or other the very highest honours have never come his way. In the Soviet Championship in 1940 he was 3rd and again took that place in the Absolute Championship one year later. In 1944 he improved on this by coming 2nd to Botvinnik and actually tied for the title with Bronstein in 1949, the tie match never being played off. In international tournaments he was placed 3rd at Groningen in 1946, 3rd in the World Championship Candidates Tournament at Budapest in 1950, behind Boleslavsky and Bronstein, and 2nd at Venice 1950. He has been remarkably successful when representing his country in international

matches, winning both his games against Reshevsky in the
Radio Match with U.S.A. and scoring $3\frac{1}{2}$ to $\frac{1}{2}$ in the two
matches U.S.S.R. *v.* Great Britain. In style he is less
aggressive than the majority of Soviet masters, appearing
to model himself on Capablanca rather than on Tchigorin
or Alekhine. Probably his greatest strength is in the endgame which he handles to perfection. Personally, he is a
modest and unaffected young man and is very popular
with all who have met him. Like many chess masters his
hobby is music and he is a pianist of no mean order.

S. RESHEVSKY

Reshevsky, America's greatest player, is a worthy
successor to Morphy, Pillsbury, and Marshall, though in
many ways he is very different from these great masters.
They were all native-born Americans but Reshevsky saw
the light near Lodz, in Poland, and he did not become an
American citizen until he reached the age of maturity. He
learned the moves at the age of five and rapidly became
the most famous of all chess infant prodigies. At the age
of eight he was taken on a chess tour through Europe where
he took on all comers in simultaneous and blindfold
exhibitions.

I remember one exhibition at the Gambit Chess Rooms,
in London, where the sailor-suited boy, whose head hardly
reached the top of the table, smashed up opponent after
opponent with remorseless accuracy and lightning speed.

When he reached America his education was taken in
hand by a Jewish Committee, who saw that he received a
normal training and thus saved him from the usual fate of
infant prodigies. Until his education was completed he
took little part in chess and we first hear of him in a
tournament at Pasadena where he finished 3rd to Alekhine
and Kashdan ahead of a number of leading American

players. Two years later he won a very strong tournament at Syracuse.

He revisited England in 1935 and came 1st in a small but very strong tournament at Margate, where he beat Capablanca. His appearances outside the American continent have, unfortunately, been few and far between, but whenever he has played he has done exceedingly well. He finished equal 3rd to 5th behind Botvinnik and Capablanca at Nottingham in 1936; tied with Flohr and Petrov at Kemeri in 1937 above Alekhine, Keres and Fine; and shared 3rd and 4th prizes with Capablanca at Semmering. In 1939 he was 2nd at Leningrad–Moscow. He also won a strong Hastings Tournament ahead of Keres. Since the war he has finished 2nd to Najdorf at Amsterdam and tied for the Capablanca Memorial Tournament at Havana in 1952.*

In American tournaments he has met with outstanding success. Since 1936 he won the National Championship with unfailing regularity until last year, when he was unexpectedly defeated by Larry Evans—a young man with a bright future ahead of him. All his life Reshevsky's great rival has been his compatriot R. Fine, and the two have fought many stirring battles. In American contests Reshevsky has usually come out on top, but Fine's international record is slightly superior.

Reshevsky's style is a curious one. He seems to rely little on theory and revels in curiously backward positions which always contain hidden resources. Provided he can complicate he is happy. He is a profound analyst, so profound in fact that he loses all consciousness of time and usually finds himself with about fifteen moves to make in two minutes. He is a brilliant lightning player, probably the best in the world, but occasionally, as in his first game

---

* Later in the same year he won a match against M. NAJDORF, who had tied with him at Havana, by 11 points to 7.

with Botvinnik in the series under review, he fails to accomplish his task. This is the principal weakness of his game. If he could manage to co-ordinate his thoughts with the necessities of the time control he might easily be champion of the world.

PAUL KERES

I first met Paul Keres at the Warsaw International Team Tournament in 1935, when he was still a schoolboy, with the face of a cherub and the chess-playing mind of a demon. In this tournament he played first board for Esthonia and, young as he was, proved that he was the equal of the greatest masters. From then onwards his rise was meteoric and his tournament successes too numerous to mention in full.

Especially noteworthy achievements were his tie for 1st place with Alekhine at Bad Nauheim in 1936 and his victory at Vienna, in a strong double-round tournament, with prescribed openings. His greatest success came in 1937 in a double-round tournament played at Semmering-Baden, where he won 1st prize above Fine, Capablanca, and Reshevsky. This great victory at once put him in line for a match for the World Championship but, with a modesty which has never left him, he declared himself too inexperienced to consider such a contest. An even greater triumph than Semmering was to come. In the A.V.R.O. Tournament (double-round), played at Amsterdam in 1938, the competitors were Alekhine, Capablanca, Euwe, Botvinnik, Fine, Reshevsky, Flohr, and Keres, the three living World Champions and all the possible contenders for the title. The result was a tie between Keres and Fine, Keres being awarded 1st prize on the Sonnenborn–Berger system of valuing points. But for the outbreak of war the world title seemed within his grasp.

With the absorption of Esthonia into the U.S.S.R. Keres

became a Soviet citizen and competed in his first championship in 1940 where he finished 4th behind Lilienthal, Smyslov and Bondarevsky. In the Absolute Championship next year he was 2nd to Botvinnik. About this time Keres' style completely changed. All his greatest successes had been won by brilliant combinative play in complicated positions; now he began to rely principally on technique and showed an unwonted readiness to simplify into endgames. His results began to suffer. Although he won the Soviet Championship in 1947 his games were sadly laborious and in the Tchigorin Memorial Tournament the same year, he could only finish 6th.

In the Championship Candidates' Tournament at Budapest, in 1950, he was also disappointing after a good start and ended in 4th place behind Bronstein, Boleslavsky, and Symslov. Many of us thought that he was just another master. Then came a startling change. He has won the last two Soviet Championships in brilliant style, and repeated this success in the very strong International Tournament at Budapest this year when Botvinnik was only 3rd. His play in all these events has been most impressive. He seems to have suddenly recovered all his old brilliance without impairing his technique and if he can keep up this form, it seems very likely that he will be seated opposite Botvinnik in the next Championship match.

He is still well under forty, a slim athletic young man who will lose nothing on the score of physical fitness. He is a lawn-tennis player of some repute and recently reached the final of quite an important tournament.

WORLD CHAMPIONSHIP TOURNAMENT

White: M. Botvinnik. Black: Dr. M. Euwe.

| 1 | P—Q4 | P—Q4 |
| 2 | Kt—KB3 | Kt—KB3 |

3 P—B4	P—K3
4 Kt—B3	P—B3
5 P—K3	QKt—Q2
6 B—Q3	P×P

The Meran Defence, not often seen nowadays, although it is one of the most interesting methods of defending the Queen's Gambit.

7 B×BP	P—QKt4
8 B—Q3	P—QR3
9 P—K4	

Stronger than 9 Castles, after which 9 ... P—B4 gives Black an excellent game.

9 ...	P—B4
10 P—K5	P×P

A line which has been recently tried, 10 ... Kt—Kt5, is effectively met by 11 B—KB4, P×P; 12 Kt—K4.

11 Kt×KtP	P×Kt

Better is 11 ... Kt×P as played in the eighth match game between Bronstein and Botvinnik (see p. 252).

12 P×Kt	Q—Kt3

Comparatively best. 12 ... Q×P is obviously impossible on account of 13 B—Kt5, and 12 ... P×P; 13 Kt×P is very bad for Black.

13 P×P	B×P
14 Castles	

If 14 Q—K2, Black can Castle, and if then 15 Q—K4, P—B4; 16 Q×R, Kt—B4; 17 B—K2, B—Kt2, and White must give up the Queen for two Rooks, after which the Black centre pawns are strong enough to win.

14 ...	Kt—B4

Here 14 ... Castles is not so good as White has completed his development and secures a splendid game by 15 B—

KB4, B—Kt2; 16 R—K1, followed by Kt—K5. Black's trouble in this variation is that his King's position is insecure whether he Castles or keeps in the centre.

15 B—KB4

Botvinnik's handling of this part of the game is a superb example of position judgment. His object is to keep a firm grip on the square K5, thus paralysing the Black centre.

15 ...   B—Kt2

15 ... Castles would be met by the sacrifice 16 B×P ch which had proved successful in two previous games, Kottnauer *v.* Kotov, Groningen 1946, and Kottnauer *v.* Pachmann, Moscow 1947. After 16 ... K×B; 17 Kt—Kt5 ch, K—Kt3 (if 17 ... K—Kt1; 18 Q—R5 wins quickly); 18 Q—Kt4, P—B4; 19 Q—Kt3, Black can never escape with his King to a place of safety.

16 R—K1

Keeping up the pressure on K5.

16 ...   R—Q1

This turns out badly. Rather better was 16 ... Kt×B; 17 Q×Kt, B×Kt (not 17 ... Castles; 18 Kt—Kt5); 18 Q×B, Castles, although White still has many attacking chances.

17 R—QB1   R—Q4

Hoping to find relief in exchanges when White plays B—K5.

18 B—K5	B×B
19 R×B	R×R
20 Kt×R	Kt×B
21 Q×Kt	P—B3

In this position Dr. Euwe says that he considered the following moves: 21 ... R—Kt1; 22 Q×RP, R×P ch; 23 K—B1, and Black has no defence against Q×P ch. 21 ... Castles; 22 Kt—Q7. 21 ... K—K2; 22 Q—R3 ch,

P—Kt5; 23 Q—KKt3, R—KB1; 24 Q—Kt5 ch, P—B3;
25 Q—Kt7 ch and wins; and 21 ... R—KB1; 22 P—
QKt4, P—B3; 23 Q×RP, etc.

Position after White's 21st move

BLACK

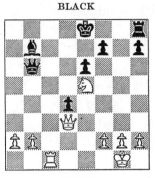

WHITE

22 Q—KKt3

A brilliant move which is not only perfectly sound but is
probably the only method of winning the game. If the
Knight moves, Black would at last have the chance to
Castle with comparative safety.

22 ...   P×Kt

There is nothing better.

23 Q—Kt7   R—KB1
24 R—B7   Q×R

The only way to prolong the game. If 24 ... Q—Q3; 25
R×B, P—Q6; 26 R—R7, Q—Q1; 27 Q×P forces mate.
After the Queen sacrifice the ending contains certain
technical difficulties for White owing to the strength of
Black's QP.

25 Q×Q   B—Q4
26 Q×KP   P—Q6

27 Q—K3	B—B5
28 P—QKt3	R—B2

If he gives up the QP there is no fight left in his game.

29 P—B3

29 P×B, R—Q2; 30 Q×P ch, K—Q1; 31 Q×R ch, K×Q; 32 K—B1 would also win.

29 ...	R—Q2
30 Q—Q2	P—K4
31 P×B	P×P
32 K—B2	K—B2

If 32 ... P—B6; 33 Q×BP, P—Q7; 34 Q—B8 ch, followed by Q×R ch and wins.

33 K—K3	K—K3
34 Q—Kt4	R—QB2
35 K—Q2	R—B3
36 P—QR4	Resigns

A splendid game by Botvinnik whose logical middle-game play and brilliant final attack are equally admirable.

White: V. Smyslov. Black: M. Botvinnik.

1 P—K4	P—QB4
2 Kt—KB3	Kt—QB3
3 P—Q4	P×P
4 Kt×P	Kt—B3
5 Kt—QB3	P—Q3
6 B—KKt5	

The Richter Attack, the object of which is to prevent the King's *fianchetto* development by Black.

6 ...	P—K3
7 B—K2	

This and the next move are rather inconsequential. The only method of making anything of the Richter is 7 Q—Q2, followed by Castles **QR**, with a game full of peril for **both** sides.

7 ...	B—K2
8 Castles	Castles
9 KKt—Kt5	

With the object of breaking up Black's pawn position on the King's wing but the plan does not turn out well. As White has already Castled on the King's side the dislocation of the pawns and the opening of the KKt file prove rather favourable to Black than otherwise. 9 **Q—Q2**, followed by QR—Q1, was better.

9 ...	P—QR3
10 B×Kt	P×B
11 Kt—Q4	K—R1
12 K—R1	R—KKt1
13 P—B4	B—Q2
14 B—B3	R—QB1
15 Kt×Kt	

Black was threatening 15 ... Kt—R4 and Kt—B5, but it is generally agreed that a better way of meeting this is 15 Kt(B3)—K2, Kt—R4; 16 P—QKt3. The text strengthens Black's hold on the central squares.

| 15 ... | P×Kt |

In the Sicilian this is almost invariably better than recapturing with the Bishop.

| 16 Kt—K2 | P—Q4 |
| 17 P—B5 | |

A normal attacking move in the Sicilian, but here it has the effect of increasing the range of Black's King's Bishop. 17 Q—Q3, Q—Kt3; 18 P—Kt3 keeps the position more solid.

| 17 ... | Q—B2 |
| 18 P—B4 | P×QBP |

19 Q—Q4	P—B4
20 Q×P(B4)	B—Q3

Much better than 20 ... B—Kt4; 21 Q—B3. Both Black Bishops now begin to make their influence felt.

21 P—Kt3

The alternative is 21 Q×RP. Against this Black can, of course, play 21 ... B×P, but even stronger seems 21 ... R—QKt1; 22 QR—Q1 (if 22 P—QKt3, B—Kt4, followed by B×P is tremendously strong); 22 ... B—K4 (not 22 ... B×P because of 23 R×B); 23 Q—Q3, B—Kt4; 24 Q—B2, B×RP with a threat of B×Kt and Q—B5 or Q—Kt6.

21 ...	B—Kt4
22 Q—B2	P×P

Opening another diagonal of which Black will be able to make far more use than White.

23 P×P	QR—K1
24 R—B2	R—K6

BLACK

WHITE

25 B—Kt2

The only other plausible continuation is 25 Kt—B3. Then would follow 25 ... B—B3; 26 B—Kt2 (if 26 B×B,

Q×B ch; 27 K—Kt1, B×P and wins, or 26 Kt—Q5, R×B and wins, or 26 Kt—K4, KR—K1; 27 Kt—Q2, B×P; 28 P×B, Q×P; 29 QR—KB1, Q—R6 ch; 30 R—R2, B×B ch, and wins); 26 ... B×P; 27 P×B, R(K6)×P; 28 Kt—K4, R(Kt6)—Kt5; 29 R—K1, R—R5 ch; 30 K—Kt1, Q—R7 ch; 31 K—B1, B—Kt4 ch; 32 QR—K2, Q—R8 ch; 33 B×Q, R×B mate.

| 25 ... | Q—K2 |
| 26 Kt—Kt1 | |

If Knight goes elsewhere, 26 ... R—K8 ch and wins, or if 26 B—B1, KR—K1; 27 Kt—B3, B—B3 ch; 28 K—Kt1, P—B5, followed by B—B4 wins comfortably.

| 26 ... | B—Q6 |
| 27 Q—Q2 | P—B5 |

Threatening 28 ... B—Kt5 and 29 ... R—K8. As Golombek remarks: "The power of the Bishops is almost awe-inspiring."

| 28 R—B3 | R—K1 |
| 29 R—Q1 | |

Smyslov again and again finds the only possible defence. The endgame after 29 R×R, Q×R; 30 Q×Q, R×Q is hopeless for White, who must lose his QKtP, after which Black's QBP will cost a piece.

| 29 ... | B—B4 |
| 30 P—QKt3 | |

Here 30 R×R is slightly better but the game cannot be saved.

| 30 ... | R—K8 |
| 31 P×P | B×QBP |

31 ... B×Kt; 32 Q×B would dissipate his advantage.

| 32 B—B1 | R×R |

33	Q × R	R—Q1

Flohr points out that 33 ... Q—K8 wins even more quickly.

34	Q—B2	B—Q4
35	Q—B3	B—Q5
36	Q—Q3	Q—K6
37	Q × Q	B × Q
38	B—Kt2	B × R
39	B × B	R—Q7
40	Kt—K2	R × P
	Resigns	

One of the many occasions in which Botvinnik has demonstrated the tremendous power of the pair of Bishops. Smyslov put up a stout resistance but for a long time was fighting a forlorn hope.

White: V. Smyslov. Black: S. Reshevsky.

1	P—K4	P—K4
2	Kt—KB3	Kt—QB3
3	B—Kt5	P—QR3
4	B—R4	P—Q3

The Steinitz Defence Deferred which was fairly popular in this tournament. It is a sound method of defence but Black has to put up with a cramped game for some time.

5	P—B3	B—Q2
6	P—Q4	KKt—K2

Steinitz's own move which aims at bringing the Knight to the defence of the KP and so avoiding, for as long as possible, the exchange of this pawn for White's QP. An alternative line is 6 ... P—KKt3; 7 Castles, B—Kt2, and if 8 B—Kt5, P—B3; 9 B—K3, Kt—R3, as played in the twenty-second match game between Alekhine and Bogoljubov, 1929 (see p. 157).

7 B—Kt3

This was also played in the game between Dr. Euwe and Keres (p. 230). It threatens Kt—Kt5 and so compels Black's next.

7	...	P—KR3
8	QKt—Q2	Kt—Kt3
9	Kt—B4	

White's plan is to bring this Knight to a dominant post at Q5.

9	...	B—K2
10	Castles	Castles
11	Kt—K3	B—B3

11 ... Kt—B5 is met by 12 Kt—Q5, after which 12 ... Kt×Kt would cost Black a pawn.

12	Kt—Q5	R—K1

Better is 12 ... P×P, as played by Keres.

13	P×P	

Finely played. Obviously Black cannot recapture with the pawn because of 14 Kt×B ch, and 13 ... QKt×P is met by 14 Kt×Kt, Kt×Kt; 15 P—KB4 with a fine attacking position.

13	...	B×P
14	Kt×B	P×Kt
15	Q—B3	B—K3

Reshevsky is unable to tolerate any longer the objectionable Knight at Q5 and decides, very understandably, to exchange it. The alternative was 15 ... Kt—R4; 16 B—B2, P—QB3.

16	R—Q1	B×Kt
17	R×B	

Best. If 17 P×B, P—K5; 18 Q—Kt4, QKt—K4; 19

Q×P, Kt—R5, with a good counter-attack in return for the sacrificed pawn.

17 ...		Q—K2
18 Q—B5		Kt—B1

If 18 ... QR—Q1; 19 R×R, R×R; 20 B×P (not 20 Q×Kt, R—Q8 ch); 20 ... P×B; 21 Q×Kt ch, etc.

19 B—K3		Kt—K3
20 QR—Q1		KR—Q1

20 ... QR—Q1 seems rather better.

21 P—Kt3

Intending P—KB4, opening lines against the Black King. Black's reply leaves him with a weak pawn but the exchange of even one Rook offers some relief to his cramped position.

21 ...		R—Q3
22 R×R		P×R
23 Q—Kt4		K—R1
24 B—Kt6		

An excellent move which prevents the Rook from supporting the QP.

24 ...   Kt—Kt1

A typical Reshevsky idea. The object is to drive out the White pieces and safeguard the pawn by the manœuvre Kt—Q2, Kt—B3, and Kt—K1. Unfortunately the temporary shutting in of the Rook enables Smyslov to win a pawn by a pretty combination. There is no good move. If 24 ... R—KB1; 25 B×Kt, P×B; 26 R—Q2, Kt—Kt1; 27 Q—Q1, and if 27 ... Kt—Q2; 28 B—B7. If 24 ... R—QB1; 25 R—Q2, Kt—Kt1; 26 Q—Q1, R—B3; 27 B—R7, Kt—Q2; 28 B—Q5, or if 24 ... R—K1; 25 B×Kt, Q×B; 26 Q×Q, R×Q; 27 B—B7, winning a pawn in all cases.

BLACK

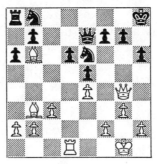

WHITE

25 B × Kt	P × B
26 Q—R4	

A clever move which wins a pawn by force. After the forced exchange of Queens the QP is indefensible.

26 ...	Q—Q2
27 Q—Q8 ch	Q × Q
28 B × Q	Kt—Q2
29 B—B7	Kt—B4
30 R × P	R—QB1

After 30 ... Kt × P; 31 R × P, the second KP is indefensible. With the text Black hopes to smash up White's Queen's side.

31 B—Kt6	Kt—R5
32 R × P	Kt × KtP
33 R × P	Kt—B5

Not 33 ... R × P, because of 34 B—Q4 followed by R—K7.

34 R—K6	Kt × B
35 R × Kt	R × P
36 R × KtP	R—B7
37 P—KR4	R × RP
38 K—Kt2	P—QR4

39	P—R5	P—R5
40	R—R7	K—Kt1

The game was adjourned here, but Black could have resigned.

41	P—Kt4	P—R6
42	K—Kt3	K—B1
43	P—B3	R—R8
44	K—B4	P—R7
45	P—K5	K—Kt1
46	K—B5	R—KB8
47	R×P	R×P ch
48	K—Kt6	K—B1
49	R—R8 ch	K—K2
50	R—R7 ch	Resigns

A very good game by Smyslov who took merciless advantage of one or two slight positional errors and then played the ending with meticulous skill.

White: Dr. M. Euwe. Black: P. Keres

1	P—K4	P—K4
2	Kt—KB3	Kt—QB3
3	B—Kt5	P—QR3
4	B—R4	P—Q3
5	P—B3	B—Q2
6	P—Q4	KKt—K2
7	B—Kt3	P—R3
8	QKt—Q2	Kt—Kt3
9	Kt—B4	B—K2
10	Castles	Castles
11	Kt—K3	B—B3
12	Kt—Q5	

So far identical with Smyslov *v.* Reshevsky (see p. 226 for notes on the opening). Keres' next move is superior to Reshevsky's 12 ... R—K1.

| 12 ... | P×P |
| 13 KKt×P | |

Better than 13 P×P, B—Kt5; 14 B—K3, Kt—R5, with advantage to Black.

| 13 ... | R—K1 |
| 14 Kt×B ch | |

This gains the theoretical advantage of the pair of Bishops, but it greatly frees Black's rather congested position, and it is at least questionable whether White would not have done better to retain the Knight, at any rate in the meantime.

| 14 ... | Q×Kt |
| 15 P—B3 | Kt—B5 |

Threatening 16 ... Kt×Kt; 17 P×Kt, Q×QP ch; 18 Q×Q, Kt—K7 ch, White's reply is almost forced for 16 B—K3 can be met by 16 ... Kt—QR4; 17 B—B2, Kt—B5.

16 Kt×Kt	B×Kt
17 B—K3	QR—Q1
18 Q—Q2	Kt—Kt3
19 B—Q4	Q—K2
20 QR—K1	

BLACK

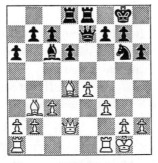

WHITE

231

White has still a very good position but is faced with the dilemma of whether to proceed with the attack on the King's wing or operate on the Queen's side. Golombek inclines to the latter view and suggests 20 P—QB4 to be followed by Q—B3 and KR—K1, while Bronstein, with whom I concur, thinks that the text move, if properly followed up, gives good chances. Incidentally, the latter points out that the violent attack 20 P—KB4 is neatly refuted by 20 ... Q×P; 21 P—B5, Q—K7.

20 ...	Q—Q2
21 P—QB4	

Unfortunately Euwe tries a bit of both the available strategic plans and meets with the usual fate of those who cannot make up their mind. The only logical move was 21 P—KB4, and if 21 ... B×P; 22 B×KtP, K×B; 23 Q—Q4 ch followed by R×B, after which the broken position of Black's King's wing gives White many chances.

21 ...	B—R5

Eliminating the pair of Bishops.

22 B×B	Q×B
23 Q—B3	P—KB3
24 P—B4	

There was probably more chance in the sacrifice 24 B × P, P×B; 25 Q×P, Kt—B1; 26 P—QKt3 (better than 26 P—B4, Q×BP; 27 R—B3, Q—B4 ch; 28 K—R1, R—Q2; 29 Q×RP, R—Kt2); 26 ... Q—Q2; 27 Q×RP, Q—Kt2; 28 Q × Q ch and White's three passed pawns give him fair prospects in the endgame.

The move played, of course, threatens immediate destruction by 25 B×P, but Black has an easy defence.

24 ...	K—R2

Now Black's King's side is safe and he can commence operations against White's Queen's wing.

| 25 P—QKt3 | Q—Q2 |

25 ... Q×RP loses the Queen by 26 R—B2, Q—R6; 27 R—R1.

| 26 Q—B3 |

Black was threatening to win a pawn by P—QB4.

| 26 ... | P—QKt4 |

A fine move which gives Black opportunities for strong action on the Queen's wing. If White, for instance, plays 26 P×P, then 26... P×P and White's QRP is subject to attack while Black has, in addition, the opportunity of obtaining a passed pawn by P—QB4 and P—B5.

| 27 Q—Q3 | P×P |

BLACK

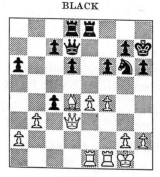

WHITE

| 28 Q×P |

In making this move Euwe obviously overlooked his opponent's brilliant reply which seems to give Black a winning advantage in all variations. It is not often that the tables are turned so completely by a single move.

28 ...	R×P
29 R×R	P—Q4
30 Q×RP	P×R
31 B—K3	Q—Kt5

With the deadly threat of Kt—R5. If White replies 32 P—KR3, Q—Kt6; 33 Q—K2, Kt—R5; 34 K—R1, Kt×P; 35 Q×Kt, Q×B, gives Black a winning game. The move chosen by White gives Keres the opportunity for some truly artistic play.

32 Q—B4	R—Q6
33 B—B1	

If 33 Q×P, Q—K7 wins the Bishop, or if 33 B—B2, Kt×P; 34 Q×P ch, P—B4; 35 Q—B6, Kt—R6 ch, and wins.

33 ...	Kt—R5

Another forcible stroke. If he plays the preliminary 33 ... P—KB4 White might make some sort of defence by 34 P—Kt3, but now this move is met by 34 ... R×P ch.

34 Q×P ch	P—B4
35 Q—Kt7	P—B3

Yet another splendid move, the effect of which is to enable him to reach the seventh rank with his Rook.

36 Q×P	R—QB6
37 Q—Q5	R—B4

The last of a series of Rook moves of great beauty. 37 ... R—B7 could be answered by 38 B—Q2.

38 Q—Q2	R×B

Winning a piece and the game. White could have resigned here.

39 P—KR3	Q—Kt6

Black was desperately short of time here and overlooked the immediate win by 39 ... Kt—B6 ch; 40 K—B2, R×R ch. The remainder is in the nature of anti-climax.

40 Q—K2	Q×BP
41 R×R	Q×R ch
42 K—R2	Q—B5 ch

43	K—Kt1	Kt—Kt3
44	Q—QB2	Kt—K2
45	P—QR4	Q—Q5 ch
46	K—R2	Q—K4 ch
47	K—Kt1	Kt—Q4

Black is gradually preparing a mating attack with his Queen and Knight.

48	Q—Q1	Kt—B6
49	Q—B2	K—Kt3
50	K—R1	

Or 51 Q—B2, Kt—K7 ch; 52 K—B1, Kt—Kt6 ch, followed by P—B5 with play similar to the game.

50	...	Q—K8 ch
51	K—R2	Kt—K7
52	Q—B6 ch	K—R2
53	Q—B5	Kt—Kt6
54	Q—Q6	Kt—B8 ch
55	K—Kt1	P—R4
	Resigns	

White here exceeded the time limit, but, against the only possible move, 56 Q—B4 (which Euwe was in the act of playing when the umpire drew his attention to the fact that he was over time), Black forces mate by 56 ... Kt—K6 ch; 57 K—R2, P—R5.

A fine game by Keres who defended himself cleverly when things were difficult and pressed his counter-offensive with rare brilliancy. It is not seriously marred by the error on the 39th move.

White: M. Botvinnik. Black: S. Reshevsky.

1	P—Q4	Kt—KB3
2	P—QB4	P—K3
3	Kt—QB3	B—Kt5
4	P—K3	P—B4

In an earlier game in the same tournament Reshevsky played 4 ... P—Q4, and after 5 P—QR3, B—K2, secured a fairly even game. The line chosen in this game is one of the most complicated on the chess board.

5	P—QR3	B × Kt ch
6	P × B	Kt—B3
7	B—Q3	Castles
8	Kt—K2	P—QKt3
9	P—K4	Kt—K1

The strategy of the two opponents is already clearly defined. White aims at a quick King's side attack by advancing his massive centre while Black's object is to hold up this attack, and ultimately obtain an advantage through the weakness of White's doubled pawns on the Queen's side. The text move is an important part of Black's plan. He must be ready to play P—KB4 whenever White threatens to advance P—KB5. It is not quite original, as Capablanca tried the same plan in a game against P. Johner at Carlsbad in 1929.

10 B—K3

In a subsequent game, Lilienthal *v.* Najdorf, Saltzjöbaden 1948, White played 10 Castles, P—Q3; 11 P—K5, P × KP; 12 P × KP, B—Kt2; 13 B—B4, P—B4; 14 P × P e.p., and obtained the better game through the power of his two Bishops. In this line, if Black played 10 ... B—R3 instead of 10 ... P—Q3, White could try an interesting pawn sacrifice by 11 Kt—Kt3, P × P; 12 P × P, Kt × P; 13 B—Kt2, with excellent attacking chances.

10	...	P—Q3
11	Castles	Kt—R4
12	Kt—Kt3	B—R3
13	Q—K2	Q—Q2

Another very fine move which threatens to attack the

QBP for the third time by Q—R5 and (much more important) enables him to play P—KB4.

14 P—B4

The normal attacking move in this variation, but against the defensive plan which Black has prepared, it proves ineffective. Better, as Golombek points out, is 14 P—K5, after which the pawn winning line 14 ... QP×P; 15 P×KP, Q—R5 is too dangerous on account of 16 Q—R5, P—B4 (if 16 ... P—KKt3; 17 Q—R6, with a winning attack); 17 P×P e.p., Kt×P; 18 Q—R4, B×P; 19 Kt—K4. However Black defends himself White's Bishops will exercise more influence than in the game.

BLACK

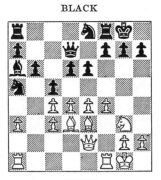

WHITE

14 ...   P—B4

The key to the defence. Reshevsky shows that 14 ... Q—R5 would result in favour of White, i.e. 14 ... Q—R5; 15 P—B5, B×P (if 15 ... KP×P; 16 KP×P, B×P; 17 P—B6); 16 BP×P, B×B (if 16 ... B×P; 17 B—QKt5, Q—Kt6; 18 P—Q5, B—B1; 19 B—Q2, and Black's Queen is entangled, or 16 ... P×KP; 17 R×R ch, K×R; 18 R—B1 ch, K—Kt1; 19 Q—B3, Kt—B3; 20 B×B, Q×B; 21 P—K5 and wins); 17 P×P ch, with much the better game.

15 QR—K1

This proves to be loss of time. Better was 15 QR—Q1 or
15 KP×P. 15 P—Q5 is met by 15 ... P—Kt3, and if then
16 QP×P, Q×P wins the QBP in safety.

15 ...	P—Kt3
16 R—Q1	Q—KB2

It is still unsafe to play for the immediate attack on the
QBP. If 16 ... Q—R5; 17 P—Q5, B×P; 18 QP×P,
B×P (if 18 ... P×P; 19 P—K7, R—B2; 20 Kt×P,
R×P; 21 Q—B3, with a strong attack); 19 P×P, B×P
(if 19 ... P×P; 20 B×P); 20 Kt×B, P×Kt; 21 R—B3,
and the Black King is terribly exposed.

17 P—K5

17 P—Q5 holds out more possibilities although Black is
quite safe after 17 ... Kt—Kt2.

17 ...	R—B1
18 KR—K1	

Hoping for the reply 18 ... BP×P; 19 B×P, B×P;
20 P×P, Kt×P; 21 Q—K5; or if, in this 19 ... Kt×P;
20 P×P, KKt×P; 21 Q×P, etc.

18 ...	QP×P
19 QP×P	Kt—Kt2

Now Black is perfectly safe on the King's wing and has
only to counter White's pressure on the Queen's file and
attack the weak pawns. A win, however, is still far off.

20 Kt—B1	KR—Q1
21 B—KB2	

Intending 22 B—R4, which Black promptly prevents.

21 ...	Kt—R4
22 B—Kt3	Q—K1
23 Kt—K3	Q—R5
24 Q—R2	

A sad necessity, but he cannot afford to give up pawns on the Queen's side.

| 24 ... | Kt×B |
| 25 P×Kt | P—R4 |

To hold back the KKtP which, even now, might provide White with an attack.

26 B—K2	K—B2
27 K—B2	Q—Kt6
28 Q×Q	Kt×Q
29 B—Q3	

Black was threatening 29 ... Kt—Q7, followed by 30 ... Kt—K5 ch.

29 ...	K—K2
30 K—K2	Kt—R4
31 R—Q2	

White has a choice of unattractive moves and can only wait for his opponent's plans to develop.

| 31 ... | R—B2 |
| 32 P—Kt4 | |

A good try. If Black answers 32 ... RP×P; 33 R—KR1, R—KB1; 34 R—R6, or 32 ... BP×P; 33 B×P, Kt×P; 34 Kt×Kt, B×Kt ch; 35 K—K3, and White is completely out of his troubles.

32 ...	R(B2)—Q2
33 P×BP	KtP×P
34 R(K1)—Q1	

After this White is lost, being soon reduced to complete immobility. The only chance lay in 31 R(Q2)—Q1, and if then 31 ... Kt—Kt6, as suggested by Golombek, 32 R—KR1, K—B2; 33 B—B2 (not 33 R×P, R×B; 34 R×R, Kt—B8 ch); 33 ... R×R (what else?); 34 R×R, R×R; 35 K×R, Kt—R4; 36 B—Q3, P—R5; 37 K—K1 appears to draw. Black, of course, could play 31 ... K—B2, instead of **31 ... Kt—Kt6**, but after **32 P—Kt3**, Black's win, if possible, will be very difficult.

BLACK

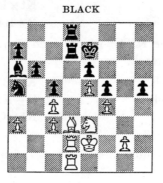

WHITE

34 ...		**P—R5**

The final stroke. White is in complete "zugzwang." If either Rook moves, **35 Kt × P** is decisive.

35	K—K1	Kt—Kt6
36	Kt—Q5 ch	

This desperate sacrifice is as good as anything else. If **36 K—K2, Kt × R; 37 R × Kt, R—KKt1** wins simply.

36	...	P × Kt
37	B × P	Kt × R
38	R × Kt	P × P

Simplest. If the Rook moves **39 P × P** still leaves White with remote chances.

39	B × R	R × B
40	R—KB2	K—K3
41	R—B3	R—Q6
	Resigns	

A very fine effort by Reshevsky, of great importance to the theory of the openings. Reshevsky is the great master of cramped yet essentially sound systems of defence.

White: Dr. M. Euwe. Black: V. Smyslov.

1 P—Q4	Kt—KB3
2 P—QB4	P—KKt3
3 Kt—QB3	P—Q4
4 Kt—B3	

Invariably played in this tournament. It is, of course, sound and good, but 4 P×P, Kt×P; 5 P—K4 is, at the moment, considered stronger. See Second Match game, Bronstein *v.* Botvinnik (p. 248).

4 ...	B—Kt2
5 Q—Kt3	P×P
6 Q×BP	Castles
7 P—K4	B—Kt5

Smyslov's speciality. The object is to retire the King's Knight to Q2, followed by bringing the piece to QKt3, where it exercises pressure on the white squares on the Queen's side. It seems rather artificial but made quite good results in the tournament under review. The alternative is 7 ... P—B3.

8 B—K3	KKt—Q2
9 Q—Kt3	

Although this attack is successful in the present instance it is doubtful whether it is as good as 9 Kt—Q2, Kt—Kt3; 10 Q—Q3, P—QB3; 11 P—B3, B—K3; 12 R—Q1, with a fine position in the centre (Botvinnik *v.* Smyslov), or 9 B—K2, Kt—Kt3; 10 Q—Q3, B×Kt; 11 P×B, P—K3; 12 P—KR4, followed by Castles QR as played by Kotov against Smyslov, Parnu 1947.

9 ...	Kt—Kt3
10 P—QR4	P—QR4

He must prevent the further advance of the RP. 10 ... B×Kt; 11 P×B, B×P, loses a piece after 12 B×B, Q×B; 13 P—R5, KKt—Q2; 14 Q×P.

11 P—Q5	Kt—R3

Better is 11 ... B×Kt; 12 P×B, Q—Q3, followed by Q—Kt5 as played by Smyslov in a later game against the same opponent.

12 B—K2	P—K3
13 P—R3	B×Kt
14 B×B	P×P
15 P×P	Q—R5

After this curious sally Black has a bad game. Better was 15 ... Q—Q3, aiming at Q—Kt5.

16 Kt—K4

A very strong reply which cuts the Black Queen off from the Queen's side and threatens to win her by 17 B—Kt5.

16 ...	QR—K1
17 P—Kt3	Q—Q1

An inglorious retreat. 17 ... Q—K2 is met by 18 P—Q6, Q—K4 (if 18 ... Q—K3; 19 Q×Q, R×Q; 20 P×P); 19 Castles KR, Q×KtP; 20 Q×Q, B×Q; 21 QR—Kt1, with advantage to White for 21 ... Kt×P is answered by 22 R×B, Kt×R; 23 Kt—B6 ch, K—Kt2; 24 Kt×R ch, R×Kt; 25 B×P, etc.

18 P—Q6	Kt—B1

18 ... Kt—Kt5 would have been rather better though White still has a big advantage in space.

19 P×P	Q×P
20 Castles	R—K3

And here 20 ... R—K2 guarding the QKtP was preferable.

21 QR—B1	Q—K4

21 ... R—B3 or 21 ... Q—K2 are met by 22 Kt—Kt5, winning at least the QKtP.

22 Q×P

Finely played. Black cannot reply 22 ... Q×P because of the brilliancy 23 Q×KKt, R×Q; 24 R×R ch, B—B1; 25 B—R6 and wins.

22 ...	Kt—K2
23 Kt—Kt5	

White now wins the exchange by force.

23 ...	R—KB3
24 B—B4	R×B
25 P×R	Q×P

25 ... Q—B3 would avoid further loss but the game is hopeless.

26 Q×Kt(K7)	B—B3

BLACK

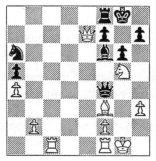

WHITE

    27 Q—K3

Good enough to win but it is a pity that Dr. Euwe missed the brilliant continuation 27 Q×P ch, R×Q; 28 R—B8 ch, B—Q1 (if 28 ... R—B1; 29 R×R ch, K×R; 30 Kt—K6 ch, or 28 ... K—Kt2; 29 Kt—K6 ch); 29 R×B ch, R—B1; 30 Kt—K6, Q×B; 31 R×R ch, Q×R; 32 Kt×Q, K×Kt; 33 R—B1, and Black must resign.

27 ...	Q×Q
28 P×Q	B×Kt

29	R—B3	P—B4
30	R—Q1	Kt—B4
31	P—Kt3	R—K1

If 31 ... R—Kt1; 32 K—Kt2, Kt×P; 33 R×Kt, R×R; 34 B—Q5 ch.

32	R—Q5	B×P ch
33	K—Kt2	Kt—R3
34	R—Q7	B—B5
35	R—R7	Kt—Kt5
36	R×QRP	K—Kt2
37	R—Kt5	B—Q7
38	R—B7 ch	K—B3
39	R—Q7	B—K8
40	R—Kt6 ch	K—Kt4
41	P—R4 ch	K—B5

If 41 ... K—R3; 42 R(Kt6)—Kt7, R—KR1; 43 P—QR5, and Black will have to give up a piece for the RP.

42	R×Kt ch	Resigns

Euwe found his true form in this game and took energetic advantage of his opponent's slight positional errors.

THE MATCH WITH BRONSTEIN
D. BRONSTEIN

David Bronstein, Botvinnik's first challenger under the F.I.D.E. system of qualifying tournaments, certainly earned his right the hard way. First of all he had to qualify for the Inter-zonal Tournament, which he did by securing 3rd place in the U.S.S.R. Championship. Then in the tournament itself, which included all the best players of the world with the exception of those who had taken part in the World Championship Tournament, he won 1st prize without losing a game. Next he tied with Boleslavsky in the Candidates' Tournament, and finally secured the coveted honour by winning against the latter by three games to two with nine draws in a magnificently-fought match.

Bronstein is only twenty-eight, the youngest of all the present-day Grand Masters. He received his chess education at the House of Young Pioneers in Kiev where he came under the tuition of the famous master, Konstantinopolsky, later to be his second in the Championship match. His record is naturally a short one but is none the less very impressive. In his first appearance in the Soviet Championship he finished in the lower half of the table, but showed his prowess by beating Botvinnik in their individual game. In 1946 he won the Moscow Championship ahead of such famous players as Bondarevsky, Kotov, Lilienthal, and Smyslov, and followed this up by taking 3rd prize in the All-Union Championship. In the next two Championships he did even better, finishing equal 1st with Kotov and Smyslov respectively. Owing to the pressure of the international programme these ties were never played off.

Apart from the two Championship Qualifying Tournaments he has never taken part in congresses outside the Soviet Union, but he visited London with the Soviet touring team and earned golden opinions by his genial manners and his keen sense of humour. No one laughed more than he when he was excluded from the match room by an official who mistook him for an intrusive spectator.

In his approach to the game Bronstein exemplifies the experimental attitude of the new Soviet school of chess masters. This is particularly evident in his treatment of the openings, where he is the complete chess iconoclast. He has revived the long obsolete King's Gambit with great success and is constantly experimenting with other forgotten and discredited lines. One of his greatest assets is his enormous courage. He is never afraid to take prodigious risks when the situation demands such a course.

His desperate tie match with Boleslavsky was a case in

point. It had been arranged that it should consist of twelve games but when these had been completed the scores were equal. F.I.D.E. then ruled that the match should continue until a win was scored. The thirteenth game was drawn but then Bronstein, with that flash of psychological genius which is so reminiscent of Lasker, played a move in the French Defence which has been condemned by all the analysts. Boleslavsky, taken by surprise, failed to find the right reply and Bronstein emerged triumphant.

His style in general is hard to define as it does not yet appear to be fully developed. His motto seems to be to complicate at all costs, and in such tactical complexities he has probably no living equal. Even in the most hopeless-looking positions he is always apt to turn the tables by a surprise blow which transforms an apparently dead position into one full of life and fire. In the present match even so great a strategist as Botvinnik occasionally found himself taken by surprise when he seemed to be on the brink of an easy victory. This dynamic quality of Bronstein's chess, useful though it is, does contain its own weakness. Once in a way he fails to realize that the conditions of a position render tactical combinations an impossibility and in such cases he loses games by seeking for counter-attacks when dour defensive play would probably secure a draw.

As a strategist he is, not unnaturally, still inferior to Botvinnik and although he is a very fine player of end-games, the more rigorous critics insist that there is still room for improvement in that department of his game. The Botvinnik match, which we can be sure he will review in the spirit of self-criticism so much encouraged in the Soviet Union, should be of inestimable benefit to him, and there can be little doubt that he is destined, at no distant date, to win the crown which, at his first attempt, so narrowly eluded him.

THE MATCH

This encounter was unique in the history of World Championship matches in many ways. It was the first to be played under the new system by which the International Federation selects the challenger and, apart from the short match between Lasker and Schlechter, it is the only one to end in a tie. The games, too, were of a character never before seen in a world championship. Usually the openings used are confined to a few of the most orthodox variations; here the first six games all opened differently and some of the variations were completely new. These led to a type of game of a very different character from the careful positional struggles customarily seen in world championships. From start to finish both players scorned simplification and seemed determined to avoid draws if they could possibly help it. In such circumstances, of course, there were inevitably mistakes but, taken all in all, the games are superb examples of all that is best in modern chess.

From start to finish it was a ding-dong struggle with never more than a point between the two antagonists. With two games to go Bronstein led by five to four, but in the twenty-third game Botvinnik made a supreme effort and outplayed his young opponent in the ending. In the last game Bronstein staked all on a sacrificial attack in the opening but failed to drive it home against the champion's deadly accurate defence, and with a pawn down and no attack had to agree to a draw.

The match was played at Moscow in the spring of 1951, in the presence of a large crowd of international celebrities as well as thousands of local enthusiasts.

The final score was: Botvinnik 5; Bronstein 5; Drawn 14. The notes are based on those in *The World Chess Championship*, 1951, by W. Winter and R. G. Wade.

SECOND MATCH GAME

White: D. Bronstein. Black: M. Botvinnik.

1	P—Q4	Kt—KB3
2	P—QB4	P—KKt3
3	Kt—QB3	P—Q4
4	P×P	Kt×P
5	P—K4	Kt×Kt
6	P×Kt	P—QB4
7	B—QB4	B—Kt2
8	Kt—K2	Castles
9	Castles	Kt—Q2

Boleslavsky, in his match against Bronstein in 1950, played here 9 ... P×P; 10 P×P, Kt—B3; 11 B—K3, B—Kt5; 12 P—B3, Kt—R4; 13 B—Q3, B—K3; intending to occupy QB5, but after 14 P—Q5 White obtained a tremendous attack in return for the sacrifice of the exchange. The move played is not altogether satisfactory either.

10 B—KKt5

Well played. The irritating threat to his KP almost compels Black to weaken his King's side by P—KR3.

10	...	P—KR3
11	B—K3	Q—B2
12	R—B1	P—R3
13	Q—Q2	K—R2
14	B—Q3	P—QKt4
15	Kt—B4	

White is planning to take advantage of his opponent's King's side weakness by P—K5, P—KR4, and P—R5.

15 ...   P—K4

This move thwarts the intended attack but allows White a powerful post for his Knight at Q5. Rather better seems

15 ... B—Kt2, and if 16 P—K5, Kt—Kt3; or if 16 P—KR4, P—K4; 17 Kt—Q5, B×Kt.

16 Kt—Q5	Q—Q3
17 P×BP	Kt×P
18 P—QB4	Kt×B
19 Q×Kt	R—Q1

After 19 ... P×P; 20 Q×P, White has far too many threats for effective defence. Black is therefore forced to allow his opponent a strong passed pawn.

20 P—B5

Stronger is 20 B—Kt6. The Rook has no good square and if 20 ... P×P; 21 R×P, R—Q2 (or 21 ... R—KKt1; 22 R—B7 with an overwhelming position); 22 Q—B3, B—Kt2; 23 B—B5, followed by Kt—Kt6, winning the exchange.

20 ...	Q—QB3
21 KR—Q1	B—K3
22 R—Q2	R—Q2
23 QR—Q1	P—QR4
24 P—QR3	QR—Q1
25 Q—Kt3	R—QKt1
26 P—B3	R(Q2)—Kt2
27 Q—Kt2	P—Kt5

In this pawn lies Black's only chance of successful resistance.

28 Kt—Kt6	B—KB1
29 P×P	P×P
30 R—QB1	

If 30 Q×KP, B—Kt2; 31 Q—Q6, Q×Q; 32 P×Q (or 32 R×Q, P—Kt6, with counter chances); 32 ... P—Kt6; 33 P—Q7, R—Q1, and Black has a lot of fight left.

| 30 ... | P—Kt6 |

31 Kt—Q5	B—Kt2
32 R—Q3	R—Kt4
33 P—R4	

33 R(B1)—B3 at once would not do because of 33 ...
B—B1 winning the QBP, but the text creates a weakness
which, later on, allows Black to save himself by an ingenious
combination. The best move was 33 P—R3, followed by
K—R2 and R(B1)—B3 as in the game, after which Black's
passed pawn seems doomed to destruction.

33 ...	R(Kt1)—Kt2
34 K—R2	P—B4
35 R(B1)—B3	P×P
36 P×P	R—Kt5

BLACK

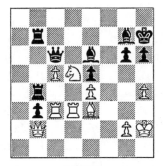

WHITE

A brilliant move, obviously prepared some moves in
advance, which changes the aspect of the game. If White
wishes to play for a win he must accept the sacrifice as
37 R×P is met by 37 ... R×R; 38 R×R, B×Kt; 39
P×B, Q—R5; 40 R×R, Q×P ch and draws by perpetual
check. The weakness of White's 33rd move is now clearly
seen.

| 37 Kt×R | R×Kt |

38 R—Q6	Q×KP
39 B—B2	

Not 39 R×B, Q×RP ch, and mates in two.

39 ...	Q—B5 ch
40 B—Kt3	Q—B4
41 R—B3	Q—Kt5

The correct move. If 41 ... Q—B7; 42 R—B2, Q×Q; 43 R×Q, P—K5; 44 R—Kt1, B—B4; 45 R—Kt6, R×R; 46 P×R, P—Kt7; 47 P—Kt7 and wins, or if 41 ... P—K5; 42 R×Q, B×Q; 43 R—B2, B—B6; 44 R×B, P—Kt7; 45 R×QKtP, B×R; 46 P—B6 and wins.

42 P—B6	P—Kt4

42 ... P—K5 would be a mistake on account of 43 R—Q7, B×R; 44 R—B7 and wins.

43 P—B7

Not 43 P×P, P—K5; and the combination in the last note is not possible because of Black's check at KR4.

43 ...   R—QB5

The saving clause. 43 ... P—K5 would again be wrong on account of 44 R—Q7, B×R; 45 R—B7, P×P; 46 B—K5, etc.

44 R×P	P—K5
45 Q—KB2	P×P
46 B—B4	R×P

An attempt to win by 46 ... R—B7 fails against 47 Q×R, Q×B ch; 48 K—Kt1, Q×R; 49 Q×P ch, etc.

47 R×B	Q×R
48 B×R	Q×R
49 Q—B5 ch	

Drawn

A game extremely rich in combinative points.

EIGHTH MATCH GAME

White: D. Bronstein. Black: M. Botvinnik.

1 P—Q4	P—Q4
2 P—QB4	P—QB3
3 Kt—QB3	Kt—B3
4 Kt—B3	P—K3
5 P—K3	QKt—Q2
6 B—Q3	P×P

The Meran Defence, once all the rage, has now gone out of fashion for no apparent reason. It is one of the most interesting and difficult methods of play against the Queen's pawn and gives plenty of chances to both players.

7 B×BP	P—QKt4
8 B—Q3	P—QR3
9 P—K4	P—B4
10 P—K5	P×P
11 Kt×KtP	Kt×KP

This, the oldest form of the variation, is also the best.
11 ... P×Kt; 12 P×Kt, Q—Kt3 has been tried but turned out unsatisfactorily in two games won by Kottnauer (White) against Kotov and Pachmann, and also in the World Championship game, Botvinnik *v.* Euwe (see p. 218).

12 Kt×Kt	P×Kt
13 Q—B3	

This is now considered White's strongest continuation.
After 13 B×P ch, B—Q2; 14 B×B ch (if 14 Kt×B, Q—R4 ch; 15 B—Q2, Q×B); 14 ... Kt×B; 15 Kt×Kt, Q×Kt, Black's strong centre is fully equivalent to White's Queen's wing which takes a long time to get into motion.

13 ...	B—Kt5 ch
14 K—K2	R—QKt1

BLACK

WHITE

15 Kt—B6

15 Q—Kt3, Q—Q3 best; 16 Kt—B3 (if 16 Kt—B6, Q×Kt; 17 Q×R, Castles, with a strong attack); 16 ... Q×Q; 17 RP×Q, B—Q3 is recommended by the theorists but only leads to equality.

15 ...   B—Kt2
16 B—KB4

Inferior is 16 B×P, Q—Kt3; 17 Kt×R dis. ch, Q×B ch; 18 Q—Q3, Q—K4 ch.

16 ...   B—Q3
17 Kt×Q   B×Q ch
18 K×B   R×Kt

Not 18 ... B×B because of 19 Kt—B6.

19 B×P ch   K—K2

A typical position in this defence which always leads to interesting and critical play. The exchange of Queens has increased the effectiveness of White's passed pawns but Black's strong centre is still able to hold the balance.

20 B—Q2   R—QKt1
21 P—QR4   Kt—Q4

Threatening to win a pawn by Kt—B2.

22 P—QKt3	P—B4
23 KR—QB1	P—K4
24 K—K2	

Best. If 24 R—B6, P—Q6, threatening P—K5 mate.

24 ...	P—K5
25 R—B6	KR—QB1
26 QR—B1	R × R
27 R × R	R—Kt3
28 R × R	Kt × R
29 P—R5	Kt—Q4
30 P—R6	

A rather more complicated line is 30 P—QKt4. If Black then plays 30 ... Kt × P; 31 P—R6 will win a piece, but he can draw by 30 ... Kt—B6 ch; 31 B × Kt, P × B; 32 P—R6, B—Kt1.

30 ...	B—B4
31 P—QKt4	B—R2
32 B—B6	K—Q3
33 B—Kt7	P—R3
34 P—R4	P—Kt4

A well-timed advance which ensures the draw.

| 35 P × P | P × P |
| 36 B × P | |

The alternative 36 B × Kt is no better, i.e. 36 ... K × B; 37 B × P, K—B5; 38 B—K7, K—Kt4 (not 38 ... P—B5; 39 B—B5 and wins); 39 P—B3, P × P ch (if 39 ... P—K6; 40 P—Kt4 and wins); 40 P × P, K × P; 41 K—Q3, K—Kt4 with a clear draw.

36 ...	Kt × P
37 B—B8	K—K4
38 B—Q2	Kt—Q4
39 B—Kt7	Kt—B6 ch

40 B×Kt	P×B
41 P—Kt3	

Drawn

A very fine game in which it is almost impossible to suggest any improvement on the lines of play actually chosen by the two contenders.

EIGHTEENTH MATCH GAME

White: D. Bronstein. Black: M. Botvinnik.

1 P—Q4	P—Q4
2 P—QB4	P—QB3
3 Kt—QB3	Kt—B3
4 Kt—B3	P—K3
5 P—K3	P—QR3

5 ... QKt—Q2; 6 B—Q3, P×P leads to the Meran Defence as played in the eighth game. The text is safe enough but rather cramping.

| 6 B—Q3 | |

6 P—B5 is also good. After 6 ... QKt—Q2; 7 P—QKt4, P—QR4; 8 P—Kt5, P—K4, Black has liberated his position in the centre but White has many chances on the Queen's wing. The text would lead into a Queen's Gambit Accepted if Black played 6 ... P×P.

6 ...	P—QKt4
7 P—QKt3	QKt—Q2
8 Castles	B—Kt2
9 P—B5	B—K2

9 ... P—K4 would not be good because of 10 P×P, Kt—Kt5; 11 P—K6, P×P; 12 Kt—Q4.

10 P—QR3	P—QR4
11 B—Kt2	Castles
12 Q—B2	P—Kt3

13	P—QKt4	P×P
14	P×P	Q—B2
15	QR—K1	

Hoping for an effective advance of P—K4. Black was threatening to reduce White's chances of success to a minimum by 15 ... R×R; 16 R×R, R—R1.

15 ...		KR—K1
16	Kt—K2	B—KB1
17	P—R3	

Not 17 Kt—K5 because of 17 ... Kt×Kt; 18 P×Kt, Kt—Kt5.

17 ...		B—Kt2
18	Kt—K5	Kt—B1

18 ... Kt×Kt; 19 P×Kt, Kt—Q2; 20 P—B4, P—B3; 21 P×P, Kt×P; 22 Kt—Q4, or if 21 ... B×P; 22 P—K4, seems rather in favour of White.

19 P—B3

Intending 20 P—K4, an idea which Black nips in the bud.

19...		KKt—Q2
20	P—B4	

If 20 Kt×Kt, Q×Kt; 21 P—K4, P×P; 22 P×P, P—K4, Black has an excellent game. White therefore decides to abandon the idea of P—K4 and close up the centre.

20 ...		P—B3
21	Kt—KB3	R—K2

Black, in his turn, is trying to open the centre by P—K4. If he plays the move at once the Soviet analysts give the following fine continuation: 21 ... P—K4; 22 BP×P, P×P; 23 Kt—Kt5; and if 23 ... P—K5; 24 B×P, R×B (if 24 ... P×B; 25 Q—Kt3 ch with a mating attack); 25 Kt×R, P×Kt; 26 Q—Kt3 ch, K—R1; 27 R—B7 with a splendid position.

| 22 Kt—B3 | P—B4 |

Closing the centre in his turn. 22 ... P—K4; 23 P—K4 is very good for White. Play now switches to the Queen's wing.

23 R—R1	R(K2)—K1
24 Kt—K5	R × R
25 R × R	R—R1
26 Q—Kt1	

BLACK

WHITE

| 26 ... | Q—B1 |

This enables White to make a fine sacrifice of a piece for two pawns which gives him many winning chances. Had Black played 26 ... Q—Kt1, the sacrifice would not have been so good, i.e. 26 ... Q—Kt1; 27 B × KtP, Kt × Kt; 28 BP × Kt, P × B; 29 Kt × KtP, B—QR3, and White's pawns are blockaded.

| 27 B × KtP | Kt × Kt |
| 28 BP × Kt | B—KR3 |

28 ... P × B; 29 Kt × KtP, B—QR3 is not possible now because of 30 Kt—Q6, Q—Kt1; 31 P—Kt5. The text move is much better than 28 ... P × B as will be seen from the next note.

| 29 B—QB1 | P × B |

30 Kt×KtP	Kt—Q2
31 Kt—Q6	R×R
32 Q×R	Q—R1
33 Q—B3	

If 33 Q×Q, B×Q; 34 P—Kt5, Kt—Kt1, Black will always be able to maintain a blockade of the Queen's side pawns, or give up a piece for two pawns, with a clear draw in either case. White's only winning chance lies in 35 Kt—B8, K—B2; 36 Kt—R7, which is met by 36 ... B—Kt4, and if 37 P—B6, B—Q1. With White's Bishop on QKt2 and Black's on KKt2 this variation would win for White, a striking example of the far-sightedness of Black's 28th move.

| 33 ... | B—KB1 |
| 34 P—Kt5 | B×Kt |

It was absolutely necessary to rid himself of the dominant Knight, even at the cost of allowing White another passed pawn.

| 35 KP×B | Q—R5 |
| 36 Q—Kt2 | |

Here 36 P—B6 is better. After 36 ... Q×KtP; 37 P×B, Q×P; 38 Q—R5, it is very difficult to find a saving line for Black.

| 36 ... | K—B2 |
| 37 K—R2 | P—R3 |

Intending to advance his King's side, but the move creates a weakness which allows White to obtain fresh winning chances by a brilliant stroke. The best move seems to be 37 ... Kt—B3, followed by Kt—K5.

38 P—K4

Very finely played. If Black replies 38 ... BP×P; 39 B×P, threatening Q—B2 ch leaves his King badly exposed, and after 38 ... QP×P; 39 B×P, threatens the deadly

P—Q5. Possible continuations then are 39 ... B—Q4;
40 P—B6, B×P; 41 P—Q5 and wins, or 39 ... Kt—B3;
40 P—Q5, B×P; 41 P—Q7, Kt×P (if 41 ... Q—R4 or
41 ... Q—R1; 42 P—B6 wins easily); 42 Q—Kt7 ch,
K—K1; 43 Q—Kt8 ch and wins.

> 38 ...   P—B5

The only reply. If White now plays 39 B×P, P—Kt4;
40 B—K3, P×P, holds the position together.

> 39 P—K5   P—Kt4
> 40 Q—K2   K—Kt2

If 40 ... Q×P; 41 P—B6, B×P (if 41 ... Kt×P; 42
P×B, Kt—Q2; 43 B—Kt2, followed by Q—R5 ch and
wins); 42 P×B, Kt×P; 43 P—B7 and wins.

> 41 Q—Q3

A possibility suggested by some analysts is 41 P—B6,
B×P; 42 P×B, Q×BP; 43 B×P, P×B; 44 Q—Kt4 ch,
followed by Q×BP with possibilities of winning either the
KP or KRP. This may be stronger than the text move
but a win for White is by no means clear.

> 41 ...   Kt—Kt1
> 42 P—R4   Q—B5
> 43 Q—KR3

BLACK

WHITE

259

43 ...   Q×KtP

Simplest and best. White's last move represents an ingenious attempt to win by sacrificing a second piece in order to shatter Black's pawn position. The idea is 43 ... Q×B; 44 P×P, P×P; 45 Q×KP, etc., but Black seems able to draw by playing after 44 P×P, 44 ... Q—K6; 45 Q×P ch, K—Kt1; 46 Q×P ch, K—Kt2; 47 Q—R6 ch, K—Kt1; 48 Q—R4, K—Kt2, and if 49 Q—Kt4, B—B1. Nevertheless, the position is dangerous and Black is wise to choose a simpler path.

44	P×P	P×P
45	Q×P	Q—Q6
46	Q—B6 ch	K—R2
47	Q—B7 ch	

If 47 Q×P, Q—Kt6 ch; 48 Q×Q, P×Q ch; 49 K×P, B—B1; 50 K—B4, K—Kt3 and White cannot win.

47 ...   K—R1

If 47 ... K—R3; 48 B×P, P×B; 49 Q×P ch, White will be able to win one of the Black pieces and at the same time evade the perpetual check.

48	Q—B6 ch	K—R2
49	B×P	

A last unavailing effort to win. 49 Q×KtP is met by 49 ... Q—Kt6 ch as in previous note.

49	...	P×B
50	Q—B7 ch	K—R1
51	Q—K8 ch	K—Kt2
52	Q—K7 ch	K—R1
53	Q—K8 ch	K—Kt2
54	Q—K7 ch	K—R1
55	Q—B8 ch	K—R2
56	Q—B7 ch	K—R1
57	Q×B	

White submits to the inevitable. If 57 Q×P, Q—R2 ch will draw easily.

57 ...	Q—Kt6 ch
58 K—Kt1	Q—K8 ch

Drawn by perpetual check

This is the finest game of the match and one of the most exciting ever seen in a world championship contest.

Twenty-first Match Game

White: M. Botvinnik. Black: D. Bronstein.

1 P—Q4	Kt—KB3
2 P—QB4	P—Q3
3 Kt—QB3	P—K4
4 Kt—B3	

White gains no advantage from 4 P×P, P×P; 5 Q×Q ch.

4 ...	QKt—Q2
5 P—KKt3	P—KKt3
6 B—Kt2	B—Kt2
7 Castles	Castles
8 P—K4	P—B3
9 P—KR3	Kt—R4

Formerly Bronstein was fond of 9 ... P×P; 10 Kt×P, Kt—Kt3; 11 P—Kt3, P—Q4, but the complications after 12 KP×P, P×P; 13 P—B5 tend in favour of White. There is much to be said for the text move which maintains the centre and prepares for P—KB4 should White move his Queen off the diagonal Q1—KR5.

10 B—K3	Q—K2
11 Kt—R2	

If 11 Q—Q2, P—KB4 would be good. The text threatens Kt—Kt4 and Kt—R6 ch, but Black has a simple reply and the Knight at R2 remains out of play for some time. 11 R—K1 was probably best.

| 11 ... | K—R1 |
| 12 R—K1 | |

12 Kt—Kt4 can be answered by 12 ... P—KB4.

| 12 ... | P—QR3 |

Preparing to advance on the Queen's wing.

13 P—QR3

This move is the cause of much subsequent trouble. It is only explainable on the assumption that when he made it, White intended to continue with P—QKt4. As he afterwards abandons this idea the only result is to create a weakness on QKt3 of which Black takes admirable advantage later on. Quite good would have been 13 P—QR4, holding up Black's Queen's side advance for the time. Konstantinopolsky suggests 13 P—QKt3.

13 ...	QR—Kt1
14 B—KB1	KKt—B3
15 Q—Q2	P—QKt4
16 BP×P	RP×P
17 QR—Q1	Kt—Kt3

BLACK

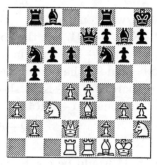

WHITE

18 B—R6

This does not turn out well. White has no chances of

attack on the King's wing and, in the present position, his Bishop is more active than his opponent's. The natural line is 18 P×P, P×P; 19 P—QKt4, Q—Kt2 (if 19 ... KKt—Q2; 20 Q—Q6); 20 Kt—B3.

18 ...	B×B
19 Q×B	B—K3
20 Kt—B3	

If 20 P×P, P×P; 21 Q—Kt5, then 21 ... B—Kt6 is quite satisfactory.

20 ...	B—Kt6
21 R—Q2	KKt—Q2
22 Q—K3	B—B5

Black has now secured a clear advantage on the Queen's wing. He dominates the squares QB5 and QKt6 and can force the advance of P—Kt5, bringing his battery of Rooks into action as soon as he is ready. White, in the meantime, can only await events.

23 B—Kt2	P—B3
24 R—B2	B—Kt6
25 QR—K2	Kt—B5
26 Q—Q3	Kt—R4

Not 26 ... Kt(Q2)—Kt3 because of 27 Kt—Q5. Black's manœuvres with his Knights are very clever.

27 R—Q2	Kt—Kt3
28 Q—Kt1	

28 P×P, QP×P; 29 Q—Q6 would lose a pawn after 29 ... Q×Q; 30 R×Q, Kt(Kt3)—B5.

28 ...	Kt(Kt3)—B5
29 R(Q2)—K2	P—Kt5

The decisive advance. Black now completes the conquest of the Queen's side.

30 RP×P	R×P

31 P—R4	Kt—Kt3
32 Kt—QR2	

This results in the speedy loss of the QKtP, but there seems to be no good continuation.

32 ...	B×Kt
33 Q×B	Kt(Kt3)—B5
34 P—R5	KR—QKt1
35 RP×P	RP×P
36 Q—Kt1	

If he protects the QKtP further by 36 R—Kt1, then 36 ... Q—Kt2, threatening R—R1 and Kt—Kt6.

36 ...	K—Kt2
37 P×P	BP×P
38 Q—B1	Kt×P
39 Q—B3	Kt—R5
40 Q—B1	R—B5
41 Q—Kt5	

The exchange of Queens seems to offer the best chance, although a very slight one. If 41 R—B2, R(B5)—Kt5, followed by Kt—Kt6, Kt—Q5, and an advance of the QBP will soon prove decisive.

41 ...	Q×Q
42 Kt×Q	Kt—Kt6
43 P—B4	Kt—Q5
44 R—R2	R—Kt7

Thwarting any hopes of counter-attack by 45 R(K1)—R1 or 45 B—B1 followed by R—KR2.

45 R×R	Kt×R
46 K—R2	

46 R—R1 leads to a lost ending after 46 ... R—B8 ch; 47 R×R, Kt—K7 ch; 48 K—B2, Kt×R.

46 ...	Kt—Q6

47 R—K3	R—B6
48 B—B1	R—B7 ch
49 K—R3	

If 49 K—Kt1, there is no answer to Kt—B8.

49 ...	Kt—B7 ch
50 K—R4	R—B8
51 B—Kt2	R—KKt8
52 B—R3	R—KR8

Good enough, but Konstantinopolsky points out that 52 R—QR8 threatening R—R1 and R—R1 ch is even more decisive.

53 P×P	P×P
54 R—R3	K—B3

BLACK

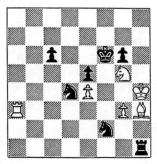

WHITE

55 Kt—R7 ch

Of course not 55 R—R7 on account of 55 ... R×B ch; 56 Kt×R, Kt—B6 mate.

55 ...	K—K2
56 Kt—Kt5	K—Q3

56 ... Kt—K3 would win a piece, but the game is over now.

57 Kt—B7 ch	K—K2
58 K—Kt5	

If 58 Kt—Kt5 no doubt Bronstein would have played
58 ... Kt—K3.

58 ...	K×Kt
59 R—R7 ch	K—K1
60 B—Q7 ch	K—Q1
61 K×P	Kt×P
62 P—Kt4	R—KB8
63 B—B5	Kt×B
64 P×Kt	K—K1
Resigns	

A very fine example of a Queen's side attack with some
neat technical points in the concluding stages.

Twenty-third Match Game

White: M. Botvinnik. Black: D. Bronstein.

1 P—Q4	Kt—KB3
2 P—QB4	P—KKt3
3 P—KKt3	P—B3

In the nineteenth game Bronstein played 3 ... B—Kt2;
4 B—Kt2, P—Q4, which leads to sharper play than the
line in the text.

4 B—Kt2	P—Q4
5 P×P	P×P
6 Kt—QB3	B—Kt2
7 Kt—R3	B×Kt

This is apparently best. After 7 ... Castles; 8 Kt—B4,
P—K3, Black's game is very cramped.

8 B×B	Kt—B3
9 B—Kt2	P—K3
10 P—K3	Castles
11 B—Q2	R—B1
12 Castles	Kt—Q2

| 13 Kt—K2 | Q—Kt3 |
| 14 B—QB3 | KR—Q1 |

A good move which threatens to force the exchange of one of White's Bishops by B—KB1 and Kt5, as it would be bad for White to advance P—QR3 on account of the weakening of the white squares QKt3 and QB4.

15 Kt—B4

To meet 15 ... B—B1, by 16 Kt—Q3.

| 15 ... | Kt—B3 |
| 16 Q—Kt3 | |

Best. Black is again threatening to force off one of the Bishops by 16 ... Kt—K5, and 16 Kt—Q3 is met by 16 ... Kt—K5; 17 B—K1, P—K4, with a good game for Black.

16 ...	Kt—K5
17 Q×Q	P×Q
18 B—K1	Kt—R4
19 Kt—Q3	B—B1

If 19 ... R—B7; 20 Kt—Kt4, and Black cannot take the QKtP because of 21 B×Kt, P×B; 22 B—B3, R—K7; 23 KR—B1, and the Rook is trapped.

20 P—B3	Kt—Q3
21 B—B2	B—R3
22 QR—B1	Kt(R4)—B5
23 KR—K1	Kt—R4

If 23 ... Kt—B4, White is not obliged to move 24 P—B4, which would leave a fine post for Black's Knight at K5, but could continue 24 P—KKt4, Kt(B4)×KP; 25 B—R3, Kt×KKtP (there is nothing better in view of the threat of P—QKt3); 26 P×Kt, B×R; 27 R×B, with two Bishops against Rook and two pawns.

Position after White's 23rd move

BLACK

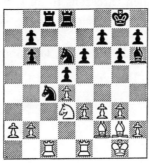

WHITE

24	K—B1	B—Kt2
25	P—KKt4	Kt—B3
26	P—Kt3	Kt—Kt4
27	K—K2	B—B1

Threatening to drive the Rook off the QB file by B—R6.

28	P—QR4	Kt—B2
29	B—Kt3	Kt—R3
30	B—B1	P—B3

A necessary preliminary to 30 ... Kt—R4 which could now be answered by 31 B—R4, R—K1; 32 R×R, R×R; 33 R—B1, R×R; 34 Kt×R, B—R6; 35 K—Q1, B×Kt; 36 K×B, Kt×P ch; 37 K—B2, Kt—R4; 38 B—Q8, recovering the pawn with a splendid position.

31 KR—Q1

This results in the loss of a pawn, but the Black Knights are awkwardly placed and White always seems to hold a slight advantage. 31 K—Q2 would be inferior to the text as after 31 ... Kt—R4; 32 R—B3, R×R; 33 K×R, R—B1 ch; 34 K—Kt2, Kt—Kt5, Black clearly stands better.

31 ...	Kt—R4
32 R×R	R×R
33 R—B1	R×R
34 Kt×R	B—R6
35 K—Q1	B×Kt

He could delay the capture by 35 ... K—B2, to which White's best answer seems 36 P—K4, probably transposing into the game.

36 K×B	Kt×P ch
37 K—B2	Kt—R4
38 K—B3	K—B2
39 P—K4	P—B4

This opens up the position and increases the power of White's Bishop. Better was 39 ... Kt—B3, and if possible the other Knight to Kt1 and Q2.

40 KtP×P	KtP×P
41 B—Q3	K—Kt3
42 B—Q6	

Stronger was 42 B—Kt1, threatening P×QP, and B—R2, to which Black has no satisfactory reply. If 42 ... BP×P; 43 P×P, P×P; 44 B×P ch, K—Kt2, there is a beautiful variation pointed out by both Dr. Euwe and Flohr: 45 B×KtP, Kt×B; 46 K—B4, and Black must lose a Knight as well as his QKtP. Other lines are no better. If 42 ... Kt—B3; 43 P×P, P×P; 44 B—R2, Kt—K2; 45 B—R4.

42 ...	Kt—B3
43 B—Kt1	K—B3

Here Black should have played 43 ... Kt—R2; 44 P×QP, P×P; 45 B—R2, P—Kt4, with good chances of saving the game.

44 B—Kt3	

With this fine move White restores the winning position. If Black replies 44 ... Kt(R3)—Kt5; 45 B—K5 ch (a nice *finesse*); 45 ... K—Kt3; 46 B—Q6, Kt—R3; 47 P×QP, P×P; 48 B—R2 and wins.

44 ...	BP×P
45 P×P	P—R3
46 B—B4	P—R4
47 P×P	P×P
48 P—R4	Kt(R3)—Kt1
49 B—Kt5 ch	K—B2
50 B—B5	Kt—R2

If 50 ... Kt—K2, White can win a pawn by 51 B×Kt, K×B; 52 B—Kt6, but even stronger may be 51 B—R3, followed by B—Kt2.

51 B—B4	Kt(Kt1)—B3
52 B—Q3	Kt—B1
53 B—K2	K—Kt3
54 B—Q3 ch	K—B3
55 B—K2	K—Kt3
56 B—B3	Kt(B3)—K2

If 56 ... Kt(B1)—K2; 57 B—B7 wins a pawn.

57 B—Kt5	Resigns

BLACK

WHITE

Black is in "zugzwang" and must lose the Queen's pawn,

but he seems not to have realized that he could still put up a stout resistance by playing his Knights on QB3 and Q3.

White can still win but the play is quite difficult. The principal variation after 57 ... Kt—B3; 58 B×QP, Kt—Q3; 59 B—B3, is 59 ... P—Kt4; 60 B—B4 (not 60 B×Kt, P×B; 61 P—R5, Kt—K5 ch and draws); 60 ... Kt—B4; 61 B×Kt, P×B; 62 P—R5, Kt—K2; 63 P—R6, Kt—Q4 ch (if 63 ... Kt—B1; 64 K—Kt4, K—B4; 65 B—Q2 wins easily); 64 K—Kt3, K—B4; 65 P—R7, Kt—Kt3; 66 P—Q5, best, P×P; 67 B—K3, Kt—R1; 68 K—Kt4, K—K5 (or 68 ... K—K3; 69 K×P, K—Q2; 70 K—B5, K—B1; 71 K×P, and wins as the Black Knight can be prevented from capturing White's KRP); 69 B—Q2, P—Q5; 70 K×P, K—Q4; 71 B—R5, P—Q6; 72 B—Kt4 and wins.

On the 59th move, if Black plays 59 ... K—B4; 60 P—Q5, Kt—K4; 61 B×P, or Smyslov's suggestion, 60 B—B1, P—Kt4; 61 B×Kt, both win easily; or if 59 ... Kt—B4; 60 P—Q5, Kt—K4; 61 B—K4 leaves Black helpless.

Bronstein's resignation caused general surprise but the win for White, although lengthy, is quite clear.

The game, particularly the ending, is a fine example of Botvinnik's deep strategic skill.

A CATALOGUE OF SELECTED DOVER BOOKS
IN ALL FIELDS OF INTEREST

A CATALOGUE OF SELECTED DOVER BOOKS
IN ALL FIELDS OF INTEREST

AMERICA'S OLD MASTERS, James T. Flexner. Four men emerged unexpectedly from provincial 18th century America to leadership in European art: Benjamin West, J. S. Copley, C. R. Peale, Gilbert Stuart. Brilliant coverage of lives and contributions. Revised, 1967 edition. 69 plates. 365pp. of text.
21806-6 Paperbound $3.00

FIRST FLOWERS OF OUR WILDERNESS: AMERICAN PAINTING, THE COLONIAL PERIOD, James T. Flexner. Painters, and regional painting traditions from earliest Colonial times up to the emergence of Copley, West and Peale Sr., Foster, Gustavus Hesselius, Feke, John Smibert and many anonymous painters in the primitive manner. Engaging presentation, with 162 illustrations. xxii + 368pp.
22180-6 Paperbound $3.50

THE LIGHT OF DISTANT SKIES: AMERICAN PAINTING, 1760-1835, James T. Flexner. The great generation of early American painters goes to Europe to learn and to teach: West, Copley, Gilbert Stuart and others. Allston, Trumbull, Morse; also contemporary American painters—primitives, derivatives, academics—who remained in America. 102 illustrations. xiii + 306pp. 22179-2 Paperbound $3.00

A HISTORY OF THE RISE AND PROGRESS OF THE ARTS OF DESIGN IN THE UNITED STATES, William Dunlap. Much the richest mine of information on early American painters, sculptors, architects, engravers, miniaturists, etc. The only source of information for scores of artists, the major primary source for many others. Unabridged reprint of rare original 1834 edition, with new introduction by James T. Flexner, and 394 new illustrations. Edited by Rita Weiss. 6⅝ x 9⅝.
21695-0, 21696-9, 21697-7 Three volumes, Paperbound $13.50

EPOCHS OF CHINESE AND JAPANESE ART, Ernest F. Fenollosa. From primitive Chinese art to the 20th century, thorough history, explanation of every important art period and form, including Japanese woodcuts; main stress on China and Japan, but Tibet, Korea also included. Still unexcelled for its detailed, rich coverage of cultural background, aesthetic elements, diffusion studies, particularly of the historical period. 2nd, 1913 edition. 242 illustrations. lii + 439pp. of text.
20364-6, 20365-4 Two volumes, Paperbound $6.00

THE GENTLE ART OF MAKING ENEMIES, James A. M. Whistler. Greatest wit of his day deflates Oscar Wilde, Ruskin, Swinburne; strikes back at inane critics, exhibitions, art journalism; aesthetics of impressionist revolution in most striking form. Highly readable classic by great painter. Reproduction of edition designed by Whistler. Introduction by Alfred Werner. xxxvi + 334pp.
21875-9 Paperbound $2.50

JOHANN SEBASTIAN BACH, Philipp Spitta. One of the great classics of musicology, this definitive analysis of Bach's music (and life) has never been surpassed. Lucid, nontechnical analyses of hundreds of pieces (30 pages devoted to St. Matthew Passion, 26 to B Minor Mass). Also includes major analysis of 18th-century music. 450 musical examples. 40-page musical supplement. Total of xx + 1799pp.

(EUK) 22278-0, 22279-9 Two volumes, Clothbound $15.00

MOZART AND HIS PIANO CONCERTOS, Cuthbert Girdlestone. The only full-length study of an important area of Mozart's creativity. Provides detailed analyses of all 23 concertos, traces inspirational sources. 417 musical examples. Second edition. 509pp. (USO) 21271-8 Paperbound $3.50

THE PERFECT WAGNERITE: A COMMENTARY ON THE NIBLUNG'S RING, George Bernard Shaw. Brilliant and still relevant criticism in remarkable essays on Wagner's Ring cycle, Shaw's ideas on political and social ideology behind the plots, role of Leitmotifs, vocal requisites, etc. Prefaces. xxi + 136pp.

21707-8 Paperbound $1.50

DON GIOVANNI, W. A. Mozart. Complete libretto, modern English translation; biographies of composer and librettist; accounts of early performances and critical reaction. Lavishly illustrated. All the material you need to understand and appreciate this great work. Dover Opera Guide and Libretto Series; translated and introduced by Ellen Bleiler. 92 illustrations. 209pp.

21134-7 Paperbound $1.50

HIGH FIDELITY SYSTEMS: A LAYMAN'S GUIDE, Roy F. Allison. All the basic information you need for setting up your own audio system: high fidelity and stereo record players, tape records, F.M. Connections, adjusting tone arm, cartridge, checking needle alignment, positioning speakers, phasing speakers, adjusting hums, trouble-shooting, maintenance, and similar topics. Enlarged 1965 edition. More than 50 charts, diagrams, photos. iv + 91pp. 21514-8 Paperbound $1.25

REPRODUCTION OF SOUND, Edgar Villchur. Thorough coverage for laymen of high fidelity systems, reproducing systems in general, needles, amplifiers, preamps, loudspeakers, feedback, explaining physical background. "A rare talent for making technicalities vividly comprehensible," R. Darrell, *High Fidelity*. 69 figures. iv + 92pp. 21515-6 Paperbound $1.25

HEAR ME TALKIN' TO YA: THE STORY OF JAZZ AS TOLD BY THE MEN WHO MADE IT, Nat Shapiro and Nat Hentoff. Louis Armstrong, Fats Waller, Jo Jones, Clarence Williams, Billy Holiday, Duke Ellington, Jelly Roll Morton and dozens of other jazz greats tell how it was in Chicago's South Side, New Orleans, depression Harlem and the modern West Coast as jazz was born and grew. xvi + 429pp.

21726-4 Paperbound $2.50

FABLES OF AESOP, translated by Sir Roger L'Estrange. A reproduction of the very rare 1931 Paris edition; a selection of the most interesting fables, together with 50 imaginative drawings by Alexander Calder. v + 128pp. 6½x9¼.

21780-9 Paperbound $1.50

AGAINST THE GRAIN (A REBOURS), Joris K. Huysmans. Filled with weird images, evidences of a bizarre imagination, exotic experiments with hallucinatory drugs, rich tastes and smells and the diversions of its sybarite hero Duc Jean des Esseintes, this classic novel pushed 19th-century literary decadence to its limits. Full unabridged edition. Do not confuse this with abridged editions generally sold. Introduction by Havelock Ellis. xlix + 206pp. 22190-3 Paperbound $2.00

VARIORUM SHAKESPEARE: HAMLET. Edited by Horace H. Furness; a landmark of American scholarship. Exhaustive footnotes and appendices treat all doubtful words and phrases, as well as suggested critical emendations throughout the play's history. First volume contains editor's own text, collated with all Quartos and Folios. Second volume contains full first Quarto, translations of Shakespeare's sources (Belleforest, and Saxo Grammaticus), Der Bestrafte Brudermord, and many essays on critical and historical points of interest by major authorities of past and present. Includes details of staging and costuming over the years. By far the best edition available for serious students of Shakespeare. Total of xx + 905pp. 21004-9, 21005-7, 2 volumes, Paperbound $7.00

A LIFE OF WILLIAM SHAKESPEARE, Sir Sidney Lee. This is the standard life of Shakespeare, summarizing everything known about Shakespeare and his plays. Incredibly rich in material, broad in coverage, clear and judicious, it has served thousands as the best introduction to Shakespeare. 1931 edition. 9 plates. xxix + 792pp. (USO) 21967-4 Paperbound $3.75

MASTERS OF THE DRAMA, John Gassner. Most comprehensive history of the drama in print, covering every tradition from Greeks to modern Europe and America, including India, Far East, etc. Covers more than 800 dramatists, 2000 plays, with biographical material, plot summaries, theatre history, criticism, etc. "Best of its kind in English," *New Republic*. 77 illustrations. xxii + 890pp. 20100-7 Clothbound $8.50

THE EVOLUTION OF THE ENGLISH LANGUAGE, George McKnight. The growth of English, from the 14th century to the present. Unusual, non-technical account presents basic information in very interesting form: sound shifts, change in grammar and syntax, vocabulary growth, similar topics. Abundantly illustrated with quotations. Formerly *Modern English in the Making*. xii + 590pp. 21932-1 Paperbound $3.50

AN ETYMOLOGICAL DICTIONARY OF MODERN ENGLISH, Ernest Weekley. Fullest, richest work of its sort, by foremost British lexicographer. Detailed word histories, including many colloquial and archaic words; extensive quotations. Do not confuse this with the Concise Etymological Dictionary, which is much abridged. Total of xxvii + 830pp. 6½ x 9¼. 21873-2, 21874-0 Two volumes, Paperbound $6.00

FLATLAND: A ROMANCE OF MANY DIMENSIONS, E. A. Abbott. Classic of science-fiction explores ramifications of life in a two-dimensional world, and what happens when a three-dimensional being intrudes. Amusing reading, but also useful as introduction to thought about hyperspace. Introduction by Banesh Hoffmann. 16 illustrations. xx + 103pp. 20001-9 Paperbound $1.00

EAST O' THE SUN AND WEST O' THE MOON, George W. Dasent. Considered the best of all translations of these Norwegian folk tales, this collection has been enjoyed by generations of children (and folklorists too). Includes True and Untrue, Why the Sea is Salt, East O' the Sun and West O' the Moon, Why the Bear is Stumpy-Tailed, Boots and the Troll, The Cock and the Hen, Rich Peter the Pedlar, and 52 more. The only edition with all 59 tales. 77 illustrations by Erik Werenskiold and Theodor Kittelsen. xv + 418pp. 22521-6 Paperbound $3.00

GOOPS AND HOW TO BE THEM, Gelett Burgess. Classic of tongue-in-cheek humor, masquerading as etiquette book. 87 verses, twice as many cartoons, show mischievous Goops as they demonstrate to children virtues of table manners, neatness, courtesy, etc. Favorite for generations. viii + 88pp. 6½ x 9¼.
22233-0 Paperbound $1.25

ALICE'S ADVENTURES UNDER GROUND, Lewis Carroll. The first version, quite different from the final *Alice in Wonderland,* printed out by Carroll himself with his own illustrations. Complete facsimile of the "million dollar" manuscript Carroll gave to Alice Liddell in 1864. Introduction by Martin Gardner. viii + 96pp. Title and dedication pages in color. 21482-6 Paperbound $1.25

THE BROWNIES, THEIR BOOK, Palmer Cox. Small as mice, cunning as foxes, exuberant and full of mischief, the Brownies go to the zoo, toy shop, seashore, circus, etc., in 24 verse adventures and 266 illustrations. Long a favorite, since their first appearance in St. Nicholas Magazine. xi + 144pp. 6⅝ x 9¼.
21265-3 Paperbound $1.75

SONGS OF CHILDHOOD, Walter De La Mare. Published (under the pseudonym Walter Ramal) when De La Mare was only 29, this charming collection has long been a favorite children's book. A facsimile of the first edition in paper, the 47 poems capture the simplicity of the nursery rhyme and the ballad, including such lyrics as I Met Eve, Tartary, The Silver Penny. vii + 106pp. 21972-0 Paperbound $1.25

THE COMPLETE NONSENSE OF EDWARD LEAR, Edward Lear. The finest 19th-century humorist-cartoonist in full: all nonsense limericks, zany alphabets, Owl and Pussycat, songs, nonsense botany, and more than 500 illustrations by Lear himself. Edited by Holbrook Jackson. xxix + 287pp. (USO) 20167-8 Paperbound $2.00

BILLY WHISKERS: THE AUTOBIOGRAPHY OF A GOAT, Frances Trego Montgomery. A favorite of children since the early 20th century, here are the escapades of that rambunctious, irresistible and mischievous goat—Billy Whiskers. Much in the spirit of *Peck's Bad Boy,* this is a book that children never tire of reading or hearing. All the original familiar illustrations by W. H. Fry are included: 6 color plates, 18 black and white drawings. 159pp. 22345-0 Paperbound $2.00

MOTHER GOOSE MELODIES. Faithful republication of the fabulously rare Munroe and Francis "copyright 1833" Boston edition—the most important Mother Goose collection, usually referred to as the "original." Familiar rhymes plus many rare ones, with wonderful old woodcut illustrations. Edited by E. F. Bleiler. 128pp. 4½ x 6⅜. 22577-1 Paperbound $1.25

VISUAL ILLUSIONS: THEIR CAUSES, CHARACTERISTICS, AND APPLICATIONS, Matthew Luckiesh. Thorough description and discussion of optical illusion, geometric and perspective, particularly; size and shape distortions, illusions of color, of motion; natural illusions; use of illusion in art and magic, industry, etc. Most useful today with op art, also for classical art. Scores of effects illustrated. Introduction by William H. Ittleson. 100 illustrations. xxi + 252pp.

21530-X Paperbound $2.00

A HANDBOOK OF ANATOMY FOR ART STUDENTS, Arthur Thomson. Thorough, virtually exhaustive coverage of skeletal structure, musculature, etc. Full text, supplemented by anatomical diagrams and drawings and by photographs of undraped figures. Unique in its comparison of male and female forms, pointing out differences of contour, texture, form. 211 figures, 40 drawings, 86 photographs. xx + 459pp. 5⅜ x 8⅜.

21163-0 Paperbound $3.50

150 MASTERPIECES OF DRAWING, Selected by Anthony Toney. Full page reproductions of drawings from the early 16th to the end of the 18th century, all beautifully reproduced: Rembrandt, Michelangelo, Dürer, Fragonard, Urs, Graf, Wouwerman, many others. First-rate browsing book, model book for artists. xviii + 150pp. 8⅜ x 11¼.

21032-4 Paperbound $2.50

THE LATER WORK OF AUBREY BEARDSLEY, Aubrey Beardsley. Exotic, erotic, ironic masterpieces in full maturity: Comedy Ballet, Venus and Tannhauser, Pierrot. Lysistrata, Rape of the Lock, Savoy material, Ali Baba, Volpone, etc. This material revolutionized the art world, and is still powerful, fresh, brilliant. With *The Early Work,* all Beardsley's finest work. 174 plates, 2 in color. xiv + 176pp. 8⅛ x 11.

21817-1 Paperbound $3.00

DRAWINGS OF REMBRANDT, Rembrandt van Rijn. Complete reproduction of fabulously rare edition by Lippmann and Hofstede de Groot, completely reedited, updated, improved by Prof. Seymour Slive, Fogg Museum. Portraits, Biblical sketches, landscapes, Oriental types, nudes, episodes from classical mythology—All Rembrandt's fertile genius. Also selection of drawings by his pupils and followers. "Stunning volumes," *Saturday Review*. 550 illustrations. lxxviii + 552pp. 9⅛ x 12¼.

21485-0, 21486-9 Two volumes, Paperbound $7.00

THE DISASTERS OF WAR, Francisco Goya. One of the masterpieces of Western civilization—83 etchings that record Goya's shattering, bitter reaction to the Napoleonic war that swept through Spain after the insurrection of 1808 and to war in general. Reprint of the first edition, with three additional plates from Boston's Museum of Fine Arts. All plates facsimile size. Introduction by Philip Hofer, Fogg Museum. v + 97pp. 9⅜ x 8¼.

21872-4 Paperbound $2.00

GRAPHIC WORKS OF ODILON REDON. Largest collection of Redon's graphic works ever assembled: 172 lithographs, 28 etchings and engravings, 9 drawings. These include some of his most famous works. All the plates from *Odilon Redon: oeuvre graphique complet,* plus additional plates. New introduction and caption translations by Alfred Werner. 209 illustrations. xxvii + 209pp. 9⅛ x 12¼.

21966-8 Paperbound $4.00

MATHEMATICAL PUZZLES FOR BEGINNERS AND ENTHUSIASTS, Geoffrey Mott-Smith. 189 puzzles from easy to difficult—involving arithmetic, logic, algebra, properties of digits, probability, etc.—for enjoyment and mental stimulus. Explanation of mathematical principles behind the puzzles. 135 illustrations. viii + 248pp.

20198-8 Paperbound $1.25

PAPER FOLDING FOR BEGINNERS, William D. Murray and Francis J. Rigney. Easiest book on the market, clearest instructions on making interesting, beautiful origami. Sail boats, cups, roosters, frogs that move legs, bonbon boxes, standing birds, etc. 40 projects; more than 275 diagrams and photographs. 94pp.

20713-7 Paperbound $1.00

TRICKS AND GAMES ON THE POOL TABLE, Fred Herrmann. 79 tricks and games—some solitaires, some for two or more players, some competitive games—to entertain you between formal games. Mystifying shots and throws, unusual caroms, tricks involving such props as cork, coins, a hat, etc. Formerly *Fun on the Pool Table*. 77 figures. 95pp.

21814-7 Paperbound $1.00

HAND SHADOWS TO BE THROWN UPON THE WALL: A SERIES OF NOVEL AND AMUSING FIGURES FORMED BY THE HAND, Henry Bursill. Delightful picturebook from great-grandfather's day shows how to make 18 different hand shadows: a bird that flies, duck that quacks, dog that wags his tail, camel, goose, deer, boy, turtle, etc. Only book of its sort. vi + 33pp. 6½ x 9¼.   21779-5 Paperbound $1.00

WHITTLING AND WOODCARVING, E. J. Tangerman. 18th printing of best book on market. "If you can cut a potato you can carve" toys and puzzles, chains, chessmen, caricatures, masks, frames, woodcut blocks, surface patterns, much more. Information on tools, woods, techniques. Also goes into serious wood sculpture from Middle Ages to present, East and West. 464 photos, figures. x + 293pp.

20965-2 Paperbound $2.00

HISTORY OF PHILOSOPHY, Julián Marias. Possibly the clearest, most easily followed, best planned, most useful one-volume history of philosophy on the market; neither skimpy nor overfull. Full details on system of every major philosopher and dozens of less important thinkers from pre-Socratics up to Existentialism and later. Strong on many European figures usually omitted. Has gone through dozens of editions in Europe. 1966 edition, translated by Stanley Appelbaum and Clarence Strowbridge. xviii + 505pp.

21739-6 Paperbound $3.00

YOGA: A SCIENTIFIC EVALUATION, Kovoor T. Behanan. Scientific but non-technical study of physiological results of yoga exercises; done under auspices of Yale U. Relations to Indian thought, to psychoanalysis, etc. 16 photos. xxiii + 270pp.

20505-3 Paperbound $2.50

Prices subject to change without notice.

Available at your book dealer or write for free catalogue to Dept. GI, Dover Publications, Inc., 180 Varick St., N. Y., N. Y. 10014. Dover publishes more than 150 books each year on science, elementary and advanced mathematics, biology, music, art, literary history, social sciences and other areas.